CAPTURING THE DIGITAL ECONOMY
A PROPOSED MEASUREMENT FRAMEWORK
AND ITS APPLICATIONS

*A Special Supplement to Key Indicators for Asia
and the Pacific 2021*

AUGUST 2021

ADB

ASIAN DEVELOPMENT BANK

Contents

Tables, Figures, and Boxes

Boxes

Foreword

Digital technologies are transforming the way businesses operate and how societies interact. Their widespread impacts can be seen in the ease with which enterprises can access markets and exploit new ways of delivering products. Governments, private institutions, the media, and academia started to take notice when global firms began to be led by digital companies. Since about 2010, trade in digital products has risen steeply along global value chains. Demands for jobs and skills are also changing, radically so, with emerging technologies such as artificial intelligence predicted to be ubiquitous in the near term. As the COVID-19 pandemic has intensified society's reliance on technology platforms, the so-called digital revolution is no longer a matter for future generations: it is already upon us.

History suggests that previous industrial revolutions often came with short-term dislocations as the economy adjusted to new ways of doing things. In this current period of technological change, appropriate policies are needed to manage any unintended consequences and realize the full economic and social benefits of digitalization. Navigating shifts in labor demand; bridging access to technologies, especially among small and medium-sized enterprises; strengthening the integrity of the tax system; and ensuring productivity gains in the long run—these are just some of the pivotal issues that require policy attention. Importantly, as policymakers turn to official statistics for evidence on which to base meaningful strategies and programs, meeting the demand for data will be even more challenging than it is today.

In that spirit, I welcome this special supplement to *Key Indicators for Asia and the Pacific 2021*. Highly relevant to current global issues, this timely report provides comprehensive statistical perspectives on the digital economy, especially for developing economies. It addresses the lack of consensus in defining the digital economy, by proposing a thorough measurement approach based on existing macroeconomic frameworks as well as standard industry and product classifications. The study draws a perimeter around the core digital economy by identifying pertinent digital sectors, while anchoring the data requirements within the capacities of statistics offices. The real and nominal contributions of core digital industries to the broader economy are quantified, including an assessment of how digitally dependent traditional industries have transformed themselves over time. The report concludes with thematic applications of the proposed measurement framework. Here, the authors explore the structural changes in jobs in the digital economy, participation in global value chains, impacts during the COVID-19 pandemic, and the future trajectory of emerging digital technologies.

This supplement is the culmination of rigorous study, analysis, and meaningful inputs from experts, researchers, and statistical partners. The publication team was led by Mahinthan Joseph Mariasingham, under the overall direction of Elaine Tan. The core research team included John Arvin Bernabe, Ma. Charmaine Crisostomo, Jahm Mae Guinto, Angeli Grace Juani, Angelo Jose Lumba, Mahinthan Joseph Mariasingham, and Clara Torelli. This report also benefitted from significant contributions by Julian Thomas Alvarez, Gienneen Antonio, Nikko Angelo Antonio, Michael John Barsabal, Donald Jay Bertulfo, Renz Marion Catapang, Samantha Joy Cinco, Geraldine Guarin, Julieta Magallanes, Kenneth Anthony Luigi Reyes, Ana Francesca Rosales, Albert San Juan, and Eric Suan. Valuable insights and feedback from Nadim Ahmad, Pramila Crivelli, Sanjiv Mahajan, and Mathilde Pak helped refine the study, as did comments from participants of the Asian Impact Webinar on Measuring the Digital Economy conducted by the Asian Development Bank. Krizia Anne Garay provided expert insights and industry perspectives that aided the conceptualization of this report. The study team also acknowledges the support of our data partners, official statistics agencies, and economies participating in the bank's statistical and analytical capacity-building initiatives. Eric Suan provided administrative and operational support throughout the course of the study and publication process. The cover of the supplement was designed by Jahm Mae Guinto and the accompanying infographics were designed by Mike Cortes. Paul Dent edited the manuscript, while Joe Mark Ganaban led the layout, page design, and typesetting process.

I hope this report will be a valuable resource for statistical compilation, research, and analysis of the digital economy, acting as a driver for evidence-based policymaking and program implementation. It is also hoped that the insights from this report serve to further stimulate research and collaboration on this relevant topic.

Yasuyuki Sawada
Chief Economist and Director General
Economic Research and Regional Cooperation Department
Asian Development Bank

Abbreviations

ADB	Asian Development Bank
ADC	analog-to-digital converters
AEG	Advisory Expert Group on National Accounts
ASEAN	Association of Southeast Asian Nations
BEC	Broad Economic Classification
CAD	computer-aided design
CAGR	compound annual growth rate
CAPEX	capital expenditure
CHM	Computer History Museum
COVID	coronavirus disease
CPA	Classification of Products by Activity
CPC	Central Product Classification
ENIAC	Electronic Numerical Integrator and Computer
FCE	final consumption expenditure
FBS	Fiji Bureau of Statistics
GDP	gross domestic product
GFC	global financial crisis
GFCF	gross fixed capital formation
GIA	Global Industry Analysts
GVA	gross value-added
GVC	global value chain
IaaS	infrastructure as a service
IBM	International Business Machines Corporation
ICT	information and communication technology
IDB	Inter-American Development Bank
IFR	International Federation of Robotics
ILO	International Labour Organization
IMF	International Monetary Fund
IOT	input-output table
IoT	internet of things
ISIC	International Standard Industrial Classification of All Economic Activities
ISP	internet service provider
ISWGNA	Inter-Secretariat Working Group on National Accounts
IT	information technology
ITU	International Telecommunication Union
LCU	local currency unit
MAD	mean absolute deviation
MOSPI	Ministry of Statistics and Programme Implementation (India)

MRIO	multiregional input-output
MRIOT	multiregional input-output table
NAICS	North American Industry Classification System
NIOT	national input-output table
NSO	national statistics office
OECD	Organisation for Economic Co-operation and Development
PBX	public branch exchange
PPI	producer price index
PRC	People's Republic of China
PREDICT	Prospective Insights on Research and Development and Information and Communications Technology
PSTN	public switched telephone network
ROK	Republic of Korea
SAM	social accounting matrix
SDA	structural decomposition analysis
SIC	Standard Industrial Classification
SNA	System of National Accounts
SUT	supply and use table
UN	United Nations
UNCTAD	United Nations Conference on Trade and Development
US	United States
USBEA	United States Bureau of Economic Analysis
VoIP	voice over internet protocol
WEF	World Economic Forum
WIOD	World Input-Output Database

Highlights

- **There is a lack of consensus on an established framework to estimate the digital economy.** Amid the growing trend of digitalization of socioeconomic activities, a variety of proposed definitions and measurement methods related to the digital economy have arisen. As a result, organizations and economies use different measures, which are challenging to compare.

- **The authors of this study seek to progress the discourse by proposing a simple and practical measurement framework rooted in input-output analysis.** Using readily available national accounts data, an input-output analytical framework is used to measure the gross domestic product (GDP) attributable to the digital economy. This is composed of the value-added of an established set of digital industries and that of the nondigital industries enabling their production.

- **A concrete definition of the digital economy and the identification of the core digital products and industries are essential.** Based on criteria that describe purely digital products, the authors recognize five main product groupings as digital. Digitally enabling and digitally enabled products, while excluded from this list, are captured in the digital GDP via sector linkages.

- **Backward and forward linkages may respectively represent the extent of digitally enabling and digitally enabled industries' contribution to GDP.** Using Leontief coefficients and matrices extracted from an input-output table, the linkages of the digital industries with industries from which they require inputs and to which they provide output can be measured. A core digital GDP equation (Equation 10) is formulated to capture these elements, including the production requirements of digitally enabling nondigital capital.

- **Input-output tables or supply and use tables are the foremost requirements to execute the framework.** Data adjustments, such as the disaggregation of industries that partially include digital industries and harmonization for uniformity across tables, may be necessary. The authors obtained tables mainly from national statistics offices for domestic estimates and disaggregated the Asian Development Bank (ADB) Multiregional Input-Output Tables for regional and/or global analyses.

- **A few framework limitations exist.** Apart from the need to ensure the accuracy and consistency of data, it must be noted that the framework hinges on the narrowest definition of digital products, excludes the contributions of imports, and assumes that industry's production recipes are fixed in a year. Supplementary analyses concerning the digitally dependent economy address some of these points.

- **Domestic digital economy estimates are made for 16 economies across several regions, and result in approximately 2% to 9% of economy-wide GDP.** The current price estimates per economy across two time periods reveal overall declining growth rates of the digital economy as a percentage of GDP, but positive growth rates are observed in level terms. The structure of the digital economy by type of linkage and by subsector contribution varies in each economy. Some economies act more as suppliers of value-added to nondigital sectors, while others act more as users of nondigital sectors' value-added.

- **The digitally dependent economy, calculated based on one set of digitally disrupted sectors and the identified digital sectors, ranges from 17% to 35% of GDP across economies.** Using three methods of analyzing the forward contributions of digital sectors to nondigital sectors, the most digitalized sectors vary greatly. It can, however, be observed that service-oriented economies tend to have deeper forward linkages with the core digital economy and that digitalization in services is increasing.

- **"Free" digital content indirectly generates the multibillion-dollar advertising revenues of the largest online platforms through data-related investments.** Experimental sum-of-cost approaches to estimate the magnitude of data assets used by developed economies were replicated for India, resulting in significant shares of total assets albeit at a lower level than that of advanced economies. The content's inclusion in GDP and possible measurement approaches are still a topic of debate within the statistics community.

- **Comparison between multipliers of digital sectors and nondigital sectors reveals large positive digital–nondigital gaps for some economies, indicating the stronger interlinkages of digital sectors to other economy-sectors.** Multipliers relative to the global economy are generally higher than those relative to the domestic economy, as the former accounts for interregional spillovers. Domestically, many economies exhibited lower output multipliers for latter time periods, whereas value-added multipliers are more stable over time.

- **Percentage estimates of selected economies' digital GDP grew across time periods when using constant price tables, compared to their decline using current price tables.** This points to decreasing prices coupled with increasing productivity of core digital products. In general, the set of key industries with strong backward and forward linkages to digital sector are preserved, regardless if one is using current price or constant price NIOTs, hinting that prices only marginally affect digital economy linkages.

- **Improvements in sector technology generally contribute negatively to labor demand across selected economies' digital and digitally enabled sectors.** However, this effect is generally offset by other factors, such as increased consumption of digital products, increased overall consumption, and increased labor requirements in digital sectors.

- **Global value chain participation of digital sectors grew faster than that of nondigital sectors from 2009 to 2019.** Results indicate more rapid trading in services than in goods within the digital economy from 2014 to 2019. The slowing of goods trading, replaced by rapid exchange in digital services and cross-border data flows, is considered the new "face" of globalization.

- **The digital economy as a share of GDP declined for most economies from 2019 to 2020, likely due to the effects of COVID-19 on economic activity.** However, increases in the demand for digital orders suggest that the pandemic has sped up the pace of e-commerce adoption in 2020. Moreover, Industry 4.0 is expected to grow in the next decade, with higher growth rate estimations and forecasts post-2019 than in previous years.

- **The measurement framework proposed in this study is demonstrably feasible for any economy, given that data requirements are met, and allows for various associated analyses.** Moving forward, further digital economy analyses related to policymaking and taxation, COVID-19 ramifications, the effect of global value chains on jobs, and the evolution of digitally dependent sectors, among others, will be conducted.

Introduction

Quantum leaps in scientific and technical progress usually result from what historians call a general-purpose technology. Impacts of such technologies cut across sectors and disrupt industrial productivity. Throughout history, only three technologies made such an impact: the steam engine, the electricity generator, and the printing press (Mühleisen 2018). The steam engine provided a reliable energy source and therefore enabled cheaper and more efficient production; electricity generation paved the way for modern production lines; the printing press introduced the rapid dissemination of ideas, allowing experimentation with new tools and processes.

With the rise of computers in the 20th century came a widespread notion that this technology ushered in a fourth industrial revolution. In 1943, the first digital programmable computer called the Colossus was built by the United Kingdom in an effort to break German cipher during World War II. Further computing breakthroughs were conceived in the United States, such as with the room-sized Electronic Numerical Integrator and Computer (ENIAC) and Harvard Mark 1 (CHM n.d.). In 1956, International Business Machines (IBM) announced the first magnetic disk storage system and random access to data for data-processing machines, which were used by businesses to electronically record real-time transactions (IBM 1956). While production of these IBM computers ceased in 1961, the disk drive remains an important component in computing systems.

In 1965, Gordon Moore predicted that computer performance would double every 2 years, which guided the information technology industry for the next 50 years (Shalf 2020).[1] In the same decade, Charles Bachman spearheaded the standardization of the database management system, establishing the fundamentals of data manipulation and network data models (Haigh n.d.). In 1970, Edgar Codd put forward his theories behind the relational database model, considered one of the greatest strides in the database field, and its commercial use began to rise by the end of the decade (Date n.d.).[2] During this time, Intel introduced the first commercial microprocessors, which led to the production of the first commercial and personal computers. Entering the 1980s, computers evolved and proliferated, with companies such as Apple, IBM, and Commodore becoming household names (CHM n.d.). Within 5 years, the compact disc began commercial production and overtook the sale of vinyl records (BBC 2007).

---

[1] The trend, commonly known as Moore's Law, is expected to flatten by 2025 due to the physical limitations in the miniaturization of circuits (Shalf 2020).

[2] One such product is the ATM, which was popularized in the 1970s through substantial investments by Citibank (History 2018).

In the early 1990s, digital signaling was introduced in television systems and in cellular networks, and the first web page went live, followed by the first web-published images, publications, and advertisements. Digital technologies increasingly revolutionized a number of industries, such as camera systems and photo storage, computer-generated imagery in movie production, and the establishment of digital libraries, among many others (Press 2015). Soon after the turn of the 21st century, the majority of information storage worldwide was already digital (Hilbert and Lopez 2011). The emergence of new digital audio and video devices, social media, and online platforms was no doubt tied to the growing user base of the internet, which was close to 2 billion by 2010 (ITU 2021a). Since then, such products have become ubiquitous and conventional. Automation, robotics, digital currencies, and three-dimensional (3D) printing are just some at the forefront of innovation. Today, fully functioning operating systems are accessible in small devices such as watches.

Over the years, digital technologies have developed at an incessant pace, resulting in components that are far smaller, more efficient, and cheaper to manufacture and operate than their analog counterparts. Nondigital products will continue to exist and be the norm in many industries, from food to furniture and heavy mechanics to power distribution, to name a few. However, digital technologies in the form of miniaturized computing, communications, and storage devices now play a prominent role in modern life. In response to this, development, academic, government, and even private institutions have started developing methods to measure digitalization, making use of actual information on private and public transactions related to digital goods and services. The collective value of such products and the resulting interplay concerning them have been loosely referred to as "the digital economy."

This report presents a simple and practical measurement framework for the digital economy, fundamentally rooted in input-output analysis (Leontief 1936), that makes use of readily available national accounts data. The framework is applied to 16 economies across Asia, Europe, North America, and the Pacific, including Australia, to generate estimates of the digital economy. The estimates are further examined according to relevant issues and key phenomena, including the "digitally dependent economy," temporal changes, jobs, global value chains, COVID-19 impacts, and Industry 4.0 technologies. The report concludes with a presentation of some further applications of the framework (beyond the scope of this report), as well as the areas of future research within the digital economy (for which the framework can be extended).

The Core of the Digital Economy: A Proposed Framework

The term "digital economy" is believed to have been coined by Don Tapscott in the 1996 publication *The Digital Economy: Promise and Peril in the Age of Networked Intelligence*. Since then, proposed definitions of the digital economy have evolved and grown in number, and these have varied in concreteness and differed in classification systems (Bukht and Heeks 2017). Pinning down the definition of the digital economy is an essential first step preceding the development of a measurement method that consistently and strictly isolates the digital economy from all other economic transactions that do not meet the definition. The proposed framework in this report is comprised of both the definition of the core of the digital economy and the measurement method that is rooted in a value-added-based calculation (Figure 1).

Figure 1: Proposed Framework in Developing an Estimate of the Digital Economy

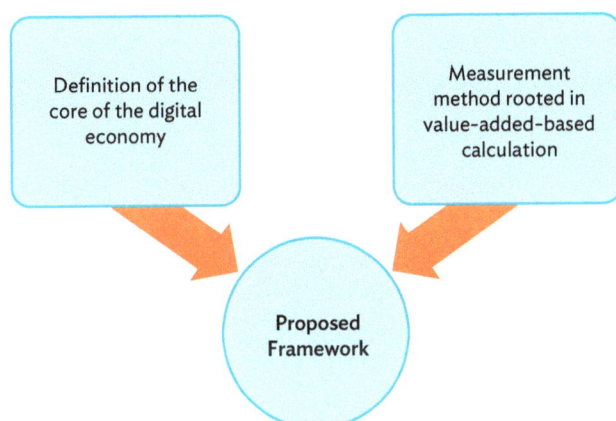

Source: Graphics generated by the Digital Economy Measurement Framework study team.

While the digital economy may be considered a recent phenomenon, traditional national accounts and statistics actually offer a rich source of data to capture and quantify the concept. The measurement method in the framework makes use of national accounts and couches the digital economy within the context of gross domestic product (GDP). Although it is generally agreed that GDP does not provide a comprehensive measure of welfare and economic well-being, it is indisputable that it provides information that is closely related to welfare (Dynan and Sheiner 2018). Therefore, measuring the digital economy in terms of its value-added contribution to economy-wide GDP provides a suitable lower boundary in assessing its welfare effects on the wider economy. In general, the measurement is accomplished by using input-output analysis, which shows that the **value-added contribution of the digital economy is given by the entire GDP of the digital industry plus the portion of the nondigital industry's GDP that enables production in the digital industry**.

The definition and measurement of the digital economy are two concepts that, while highly intertwined in the framework for estimating the digital economy, are independently discussed in this report. This discussion approach makes the framework extremely flexible, as users may independently derive results suitable to their desired level of analysis. For example, users may use the measurement method to test alternative definitions of the core of the digital economy. Such was the approach adopted in defining the "digitally dependent economy," covered in a later section.

The Organisation for Economic Co-operation and Development (OECD) and the United States Bureau of Economic Analysis (USBEA) similarly proposed a measurement method based on national accounts (Mitchell 2018; Barefoot 2018). In particular, both the OECD and the USBEA propose a method that utilizes the supply and use framework. To contrast the two, the former includes the entire value of transactions involving digital platforms as well as the value of the platforms themselves, while the latter counts only the margins and broker fees on such transactions. Another measurement framework is by Brynjolfsson et al. (2019), which supplements national accounts statistics by proposing a welfare-based measurement, called GDP-B. Meanwhile, Huawei and Oxford Economics (2017) utilized digital spillover effects to estimate the global digital economy, which they estimate at $11.5 trillion.

Table A4.1 (Appendix 4) compares the framework in this report with other published estimation methods in more detail. While some economies already follow frameworks proposed by such institutions,[3] others such as the People's Republic of China (PRC) have devised their own.[4]

Defining the Core of the Digital Economy

There exists a plethora of working definitions for the digital economy encompassing varying inclusions of economic activities. This forms part of the reason why organizations arrive at different results when analyzing the digital economy's development and influence on the wider economy. However, several terms related to the concept have been generally agreed upon by experts in the field and may be used as a premise to define the digital economy.

To understand how to classify products and industries as digital, one can begin by distinguishing the two main types of data encoding: analog and digital. The term "analog" refers to information expressed using a "continuously variable physical quantity." A simple example of this continuously variable physical quantity is the human voice, which reaches a listener's ear via differences in air pressure. Another

---

[3] Canada's digital economy estimates are based on the OECD framework (Statistics Canada 2021).

[4] China Academy of Information and Communication Technology (CAICT) includes value-added of the information industry and contribution to digitized traditional industries using a growth accounting model (CAICT 2020).

example is the high-frequency electromagnetic wave transmitted into the ether, which is the propagation medium for amplitude modulation used on certain radio devices.

In contrast, the term "digital" refers to the use of discrete encoding (e.g., 0 and 1), instead of a continuously variable physical quantity, that is used to generate, process, and store information. In modern cellular phones and radio networks, voice and audio signals are encoded in a stream of discrete values and converted into an analog form only when interacting with the physical medium or a human recipient. As there is a clear delineation between analog and digital technologies, the digital economy would naturally encompass those products that are related to digital encoding ("digital products").

The term "digital economy" is often associated with terms such as internet economy, cloud economy, sharing economy, and on-demand economy. While each pertains to a set of business activities, what is common among them is the use of digital technologies, including software applications, internet infrastructure, and advanced computers, to greatly enhance existing business processes or create new and innovative ones.

Digital products involved in a typical digital transformation are at the core of any definition of a digital economy.[5] Hence, in this report, **the digital economy is ultimately defined as the contribution of any economic transaction involving both digital products and digital industries to GDP**. The centerpiece to this definition is the identification of specific digital products and industries.

The proposed framework defines digital products to be goods and services with the main function of generating, processing, and/or storing digitized data.[6] The primary producers of such products (i.e., industries that supply these products more so than any other industry in the economy) are considered as the digital industries. The framework identifies core digital products that can be summarized into five main product groupings: (i) hardware, (ii) software publishing, (iii) web publishing, (iv) telecommunications services, and (v) specialized and support services.[7] The corresponding activity codes from the United Nations Statistical Commission's Central Product Classification (CPC) Version 2 are identified in Table 1. The equivalent industry groups and codes in International Standard Industrial Classification of

---

[5] The changes brought about by digital products (referred to interchangeably as "digital technologies") can generally be categorized in three ways representing different degrees of integration: digitization, digitalization, and digital transformation. First, digitization refers to the process of converting data into a digital format, and second, digitalization refers to the incorporation of digitized data into established production processes to achieve higher efficiency (Burkett 2017). The third is digital transformation, which is similar to digitalization except that it refers to a more extensive integration of digital products, such as a large enterprise involving hundreds of employees and tools in its strategic use of digital technologies.

[6] Information and communications technology in national accounts usually refers to anything related to the equipment and techniques in handling and processing information, which do not necessarily encompass exclusively digital products.

[7] In consequence, digital industries are the main producers of the core digital products identified by the framework.

Table 1: Main Digital Product Groups, Central Product Classification Version 2

Main Activity Group	Code	Product
Hardware	452	Computing machinery and parts and accessories thereof
	475	Disks, tapes, solid-state nonvolatile storage devices, and other media, not recorded
Software publishing	38582	Software cartridges for video game consoles
	478	Packaged software
	83143	Software originals
	8434	Software downloads
	84391	Online games
	84392	Online software
Web publishing	83633	Sale of internet advertising space (except on commission)
	843	Online content[a]
Telecommunications services	841	Telephony and other telecommunications services
	842	Internet telecommunications services
Specialized and support services	8313	IT consulting and support services
	83141	IT design and development services for applications
	83142	IT design and development services for networks and systems
	8315	Hosting and IT infrastructure provisioning services
	8316	IT infrastructure and network management services

IT = information technology.
[a] Excluding items under Central Product Classification Version 2, 843 already counted under Software Publishing – 8434, 84391, 84392.
Source: Methodology of the Digital Economy Measurement Framework study team, using United Nations' Central Product Classification: Version 2 (2008).

All Economic Activities (ISIC) Revision 4 are included in Table A4.2 (Appendix 4). The reason this framework excludes certain products that other frameworks may include as digital or digitalized is discussed in Box 1.

Box 1: Digitally Enabling and Digitally Enabled Products

Components and accessories supporting digital goods and services, although necessary in the production of digital products, are not considered part of the core digital products. Without the assembly process, such products cannot generate, process, and store data by themselves. For example, semiconductors used for electrical conductivity are integral components of computer manufacturing but, by themselves, do not have a direct function in relation to digitized data. In this study, these products are referred to as "digitally enabling products." While not considered within core digital products, digitally enabling products are still captured in the framework's core digital economy equation through its backward linkages with core digital products, as will be discussed under the measurement framework.

For the same reason, products that use digital products as components or accessories are also not considered core digital products. While digital technologies may play a significant role in the production process of a certain product, its primary function does not change relative to its original function using only analog products. For example, car manufacturing companies are increasingly adding digital components into their vehicles, which includes connected in-car entertainment experiences, vehicle systems management, and self-driving capabilities, among others. Despite these novel features, highly digitalized cars are still considered to be transportation equipment, not digital hardware. In this study, these products are referred to as "digitally enabled products." Like digitally enabling products, digitally enabled products are also captured in the framework's core digital economy equation through its forward linkages with core digital products.

Source: Methodology of the Digital Economy Measurement Framework study team.

By narrowing down a core set of digital products, the framework avoids inaccuracies resulting from attempts to measure the portions of mixed product groupings relating to digital products (e.g., digital microphones among total microphones) and from having to make judgment calls on how "digital" certain products are (e.g., what percentage of a "smart" appliance is digital). Nonetheless, disaggregation and adjustments among products may still be necessary depending on the data granularity of the economy in question, but measurement error is minimized compared to more general and relatively arbitrary classification schemes. The following provides a detailed discussion of the product groupings identified in Table 1.

Hardware

Digital hardware refers to the physical component of digital computing technologies. Basing the digital economy on the products of the entire information and communications technology (ICT) sector would likely overestimate what is actually digital, as ICT products include both analog and digital technologies. Instead, only hardware that relates to primary digital technology is considered. This includes two main components: computers, computer parts, and peripheral equipment (CPC Version 2; Code 452) and unrecorded digital media (CPC Version 2; Code 475).

Computers, computer parts, and peripheral equipment

Computers and computer parts include the entire assembled physical infrastructure of a data-processing machine itself (e.g., laptops, personal digital assistants, mainframe computers) and all parts necessary for it to operate (e.g., central processing unit, volatile memory). The hardware itself only allows basic functions to run (e.g., to turn on), and system software is always required to allow a computer to process digitized information (Mullins 2011). Therefore, computers are generally classified as hardware, with preinstalled system software assumed to be embedded.

Unrecorded digital media

Unrecorded digital media pertains to blank physical devices that store data coming from computers and other devices with computing abilities.[8] The most common examples of unrecorded digital media include magnetic storage (e.g., hard discs, floppy discs), optical storage (e.g., compact discs, DVDs), and flash memory (e.g., memory sticks, solid-state drives). Similar to computers, these also come with system software required to store data (Mullins 2011).

---

8   Note that memory built in or essential for the use of computers would fall under computers and computer parts.

Another type of hardware that should theoretically be classified as a digital product are analog-to-digital converters (ADCs). These are electronic integrated circuits that convert analog signals to digital output. These function independently from a computer, are used by many types of digital sensors, and may be produced in-house for use in different types of equipment such as cellular phones. However, ADCs are not easily identifiable in most detailed levels of product classification systems, such as in CPC Version 2,[9] and thus may not be captured within the digital economy estimates of the framework.[10]

Software Publishing

While hardware refers to the physical parts of a computer, software generally refers to a programming code, which is a set of instructions by which a computer operates. Software publishing pertains to software that is made publicly available as ready-to-use software for consumers.[11] There are three main modes for the distribution of software: (i) via physical media (e.g., boxed software sold on shelves); (ii) via online distribution direct to consumer (e.g., online stores that sell licenses to download the software); and (iii) via application marketplaces (e.g., first-party mechanisms like App Store and Google Play). Two main types of software publishing are considered: system software (portions of CPC Version 2; Codes 478 and 83143) and application software (CPC Version 2; Codes 38582, 478, 83143, 8434, 84391, and 84392).

System software

System software is essential in the most fundamental functions of a computer system. For this reason, it is also referred to as "low-level software." The operating system that comes with a computer, or any device that runs on digital computing technology, is the most well-known type of system software and allows users to interact with the hardware. Popular examples of operating systems include Microsoft Windows, Mac OS or Apple iOS, Android, and Linux. Other kinds of system software include (i) device drivers, which allow input and output devices to function with an operating system (e.g., drivers required to use keyboards, printers); (ii) firmware, which is embedded in nonvolatile digital media (e.g., in read-only memory and flash chips); (iii) programming translators, which convert source code (e.g., C++, Java, Python) to machine code; and (iv) utility software, which aids in the overall function of a computer system (e.g., antiviruses, compression tools, disk cleanup) as described in Amuno (2021).

---

9   Following the Standard Industrial Classification (SIC) system, ADCs may fall under electronic integrated circuits (CPC Version 2; Code 47160). In the SIC system, ADCs are specified under SIC Code 38250201 (instruments to measure electricity).

10   In addition, ADCs may not constitute significant components of digital hardware products. In the United States, latest data from the Orbis database, which provides extensive information on private companies worldwide, show that there are only 35 companies that specialize in the manufacture of ADCs out of 1,852 total businesses engaged in instruments to measure electricity (Bureau van Dijk 2018).

11   Custom design and development of software for consumer-specific needs are not under software publishing, and are instead considered as IT design and development services.

Application software

Application software, or apps, help end-users perform specific tasks, such as presentation and analysis of data, online communication, and graphics design. In contrast to system software, apps are not considered essential for the fundamental functions of a computer system, and their installation is left as an option for the user. Specific types of apps include word processors (e.g., Microsoft Word), spreadsheet software (e.g., Microsoft Excel), database software (e.g., Oracle, MySQL), multimedia software (e.g., QuickTime, VLC), communication software (e.g., Zoom, Skype), and web browsers (e.g., Google Chrome, Internet Explorer), to name a few (Franklin 2019).

Web Publishing

Web publishing refers to information generated and published in exclusively digital forms. Firms and institutions publish various kinds of data online. These are contained in files.[12] Some examples of web publishing activities include the video files that Netflix provides as a streaming service, copyrighted stock photos sold by Shutterstock as licenses to use, and online articles published by The New York Times. The products considered to be published digitized data are included in online content (CPC Version 2; Code 843).

Online content, however, excludes software publishing and advertising space on the internet (CPC Version 2; Code 83633). Software publishing has already been discussed as part of the core digital products. Advertising space on the internet is essentially published web content, but it is reflected under another classification because of the substance of the product.[13] Therefore, the authors of this study augment this specific product as part of web publishing. A prime example of an institution offering this product is Facebook Inc., which sells advertising space on its multiple social media platforms (e.g., Facebook, Messenger, Instagram) from where the vast majority of its revenues are generated—98.5% in 2019 (Facebook 2020).

Telecommunications Services

Telecommunications (telecom) refers to the exchange of information (e.g., voice, text, sound, video) through a transmitting medium between two or more stations. When multiple transmitting and receiving stations exchange data among themselves, this is termed a network (Chai and Lazar n.d.). Product and industry

---

12   A file refers to a named and ordered sequence of bytes. Bytes are comprised of a group of eight bits, the smallest unit of digital information (PREMIS 2015). Some of the most common file types include PDF for immutable documents, JPEG for images, and HTML for web page creation (Shannon 2012).

13   Advertising space on the internet specifies online "space" as the main commodity. This means that a portion of a company's web page or an HTML document is purchased or rented by another company to publish their own content.

classification systems classify telecom either by types of medium or by types of networks.[14] The CPC classifies telecom by the latter. In CPC Version 2, telecom is divided between two major networks: telephony and other telecommunications services (CPC Version 2; Code 841), and internet services (CPC Version 2; Code 842). Both networks utilize a variety of wired and wireless equipment.

Telephony and other telecommunication services

Telephony relates to the primary services provided by telephone carriers and service providers (e.g., calls and short messaging services through mobile phone systems). At its foundation are public switched telephone networks (PSTNs), which refer to the collection of interconnected voice-oriented public telephone networks around the globe, providing landline phone services. Telephony's original forms were purely analog, but over time worked with digital signals and internet connectivity. While PSTNs continue to evolve, entirely new telephony technologies have also been developed and designed specifically for digital data transmission, such as the integrated services digital network (ISDN), which is considered a more efficient alternative to PSTNs (Mitchell 2019).

Internet services

The internet pertains to the largest global interconnection of computers consisting of private, public, academic, business, and government networks. These networks are linked together by data routes employing a broad array of electronic, wireless, and optical networking technologies. The principal and largest data routes comprise the internet backbone, providing networks to smaller distributors or directly to internet service providers (Christensson 2015).

The internet has evolved over the years in terms of the mediums or systems used, resulting in great improvements to data transfer speeds and overall user convenience. These include dial-up through a PSTN, digital subscriber lines, cable television lines, and fiber optic cables.[15] Nowadays, the boundary between telephony and internet networks is becoming increasingly vague, with newer technologies integrating both into one system. One example is the development of the voice over internet protocol (VoIP), also known as IP telephony or internet telephony, which allows the transmission of voice communication through the internet (Mitchell 2019).

---

[14] There are two main modes of transmission: wired and wireless. "Wired" refers to the transmission of data using a physical medium, e.g., fiber optic cable, electrical or copper cable, while "wireless" refers to the transmission of data over electromagnetic waves, without the use of a physical medium, e.g., cellular phone services, wi-fi, bluetooth, satellite transmission (Chai and Lazar n.d.). The North American Industry Classification System (NAICS) 2012 and International Standard Industrial Classification (ISIC) Revision 4 apply this categorization, with wireless further divided into wireless excluding satellite and satellite.

[15] Data transmission across large networks (such as the internet) involves transmission of data across many nodes, ideally in the most efficient path. As such, transmission between different nodes may have several segments that are wireless, while the rest are wired transmissions.

In neither "by medium" nor "by network" system of classifying telecom, do granular products categories encapsulate purely digital telecom. Similar to computers, telecom depends on analog components in order to function interactively with humans. While cables and relayed data signals may be analog, they could very well be converted both from transmitting and for receiving digital terminals. Even the most traditional phone systems still in operation, such as private branch exchange (PBX) systems employed by hotels using standard copper wiring and analog telephone sets, are often integrated or supplemented with digital technologies to improve telecom functionality. Examples include the incorporation of digital PSTNs and VoIP to enable landline calls from PBX systems to public networks. Given that digitalization is so pervasive in telecommunications infrastructure, the analog components are so well integrated in the dynamics of telecom systems that both have become necessary for service delivery and too interrelated to be viably differentiated. Thus, the framework does not differentiate these under "telecom services."

Specialized and Support Services

Specialized and support services is a broad term referring to customized and technical services related to the core digital products (i.e., digital hardware, software, digitized data, and telecom). These services usually provide solutions to entities that don't have the internal human or physical capital for their specific information technology (IT) needs. The correspondence of CPC with the North American Industry Classification System 2012 succinctly describes these products as: custom computer programming services (CPC Version 2; Code 8313), computer systems design services (CPC Version 2; Codes 83141 and 83142), data processing, hosting and related activities (CPC Version 2; Code 8315), and computer facilities management services (CPC Version 2; Code 8316). While these activities appear similar to each other and are often interrelated, key characteristics differentiate them.

Custom computer programming

> Custom computer programming refers to software and web page design, development, modification, analysis, testing, and support services that are tailored to fit the needs of a customer (NAICS 2018). For example, an electricity company might outsource a software developer to create a mobile application that would allow customers to track their electricity usage, provide online billing and payment options, and obtain real-time user reports about power outages.

Computer systems design

> Computer systems design pertains to the integration of digital products (such as hardware, software, and communication technologies) to achieve client-specific solutions. This may entail choosing the optimal and most compatible products, as well as system analysis, design, development, implementation, and maintenance,

among others (NAICS 2018). A simple example is the configuration of an office's local area network with a modem, a router, and all servers and devices (e.g., office-owned computers, personal laptops, wireless printers), including the installation of system software such as a firewall to monitor network traffic.

Data processing, hosting, and related services

Data processing, hosting, and related services pertains to information services that support the publishing of digital products. "Data processing" refers to the modification and organization of data using software to produce purposeful information, in a readable and readily usable form for the client (e.g., charts, reports). For example, the Global Data-Processing and Forecasting System is one of the major components of the World Weather Watch System, in order to produce meteorological analyses, numerical weather predictions, and weather forecasts and warnings (Lee 2020). "Hosting" is a general term that means the provision of infrastructure for websites and software to function. Hosting is implemented depending on particular requirements and can range from simple leasing of server capacity of a predefined quantity to highly configurable infrastructure as a service (IaaS) platforms.[16] Amazon, Microsoft, and Google are some of the most popular providers of this type of service.

Computer facilities management

Computer facilities management is the on-site management, operation, and support services to a client's computer systems and/or data processing facilities (NAICS 2018). As opposed to other services outlined in this section, which provide new digital capabilities and components to companies, establishments engaging in computer facilities management deliver maintenance and improvement to existing computer facilities. For example, IBM has an Integrated Workplace Management System that incorporates Internet of Things (IoT) data, analytics, and artificial intelligence technologies to optimize productivity for facility managers (IBM 2021).

---

[16] IaaS platforms are for time-critical and demanding applications and high-traffic websites that can be billed according to resources used per hour or minute.

Evolution of Digital Products and Industries through Time

Timing is an important consideration in choosing the elements of the core digital products. Before the onset of the digital era, only analog existed, largely in the form of analog computers and telecom. Gradually, enterprises manufacturing analog commodities started to integrate digital computing technologies into their products. In some cases, analog products were rendered obsolete and were completely replaced with digital versions. As a result, new products and enterprises came into existence. An example is the phasing out of cassette tapes, an analog magnetic medium, with compact discs becoming the most widespread form of audio recording. After a few years, compact discs became less common (but not yet obsolete), with the rise of more advanced digital products such as digital audio formats and streaming platforms.

Given that a core digital product is defined as one that generates, processes, and/or stores digitized data or is itself digitized data, product groups may only be considered "purely" digital by the time their analog counterparts have become entirely obsolete or so minuscule in the market as to be irrelevant. The length of transition of a product group before becoming purely digital would vary depending on the conception and life cycle of the product. It may also differ by location, given that markets adopt advancements at different speeds, depending on factors such as the degree of trade liberalization, capacity to participate in required stages of production, and consumer demand. This assessment is unnecessary for products that are explicitly distinguished as digital (e.g., online audio content) and products that exist only because of their digital nature (e.g., software).

From the identified main digital activities using CPC classifications, only hardware and telecom services require an assessment of timing. Within these product groups, products such as computers (and parts), unrecorded media, and telecom services had analog versions under the same terminology. While it would be difficult to pinpoint the exact moment in time when practically all units in a product group supplied in a given economy became digital, a conservative approximation based on published studies may be the most convenient option. Using the example of cassette tapes, research suggests that music companies in the United States (US) ceased production of these by 2002 (Fung 2017). Therefore, when measuring the digital economy of the US, one can extrapolate by saying that the definition of core digital products (including blank magnetic media) is applicable to data from 2003 onward. While this timeline may mirror that of similar economies, such as Canada, the same cannot be safely assumed for less-similar economies.

In such instances, where the digital economy must be measured for a period of time in which the identified core digital activities may still include analog units, it is necessary to disaggregate the group to attain the most reasonable allocation of digital and nondigital components (this is covered in greater detail under "Methodological Requirements" on page 23).

Measurement Framework

The models involved in the proposed measurement framework are rooted in input-output analysis, mainly using Leontief coefficients (Leontief 1936), as well as forward and backward linkages to directly measure the sector interdependencies in terms of value-added contributions.

In this section, a step-by-step derivation of the digital GDP equation is shown.[17] The components of the digital economy measurement framework are summarized in Figure 2. Given that each term pertains to a specific measure, users applying this framework may choose to calculate only certain terms for their purposes (e.g., only term 2 is needed to obtain the forward linkages of digital industries). Moreover, adjustments or extensions to the framework may be made to suit specific analyses, such as the measurement of specific global value chain (GVC) indicators, which is also covered in a later section.

Figure 2: Proposed Digital Economy Measurement Framework

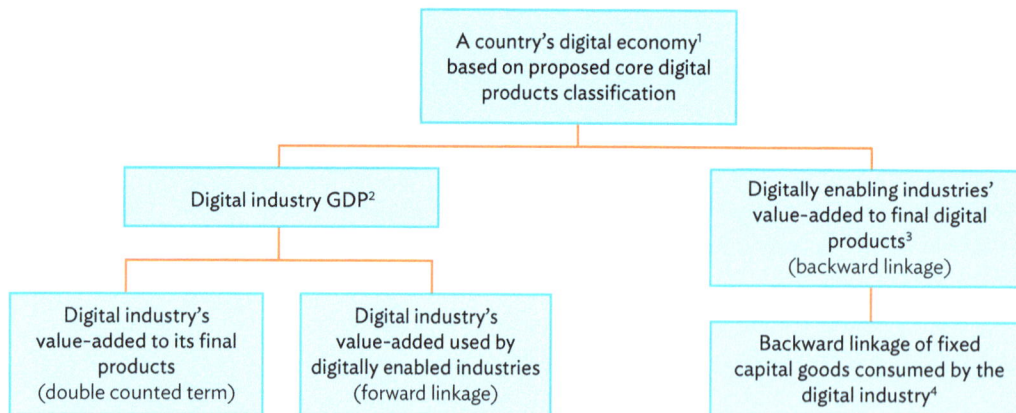

GDP = gross domestic product.
[1] Given by the $GDP_{digital}$ equation, $i^T \hat{V}B\hat{Y}\boldsymbol{\varepsilon}_1 + i^T (\hat{V}B\hat{Y})^T \boldsymbol{\varepsilon}_1 - [diag(\hat{V}B\hat{Y})]^T \boldsymbol{\varepsilon}_1 + (i - \boldsymbol{\varepsilon}_1)^T \hat{V}B\hat{Y}\hat{r}\boldsymbol{\varepsilon}_2$.
[2] Given by the second term of the $GDP_{digital}$ equation.
[3] Given by the first term of the $GDP_{digital}$ equation.
[4] Given by the fourth term of the $GDP_{digital}$ equation.
Source: Methodology of the Digital Economy Measurement Framework study team, using Leontief (1936) coefficients.

---

[17] Throughout this report, digital GDP (or $GDP_{digital}$) refers to the gross value-added (GVA) of the digital sector. In a strict sense, digital GDP and digital GVA are similar, except that digital GDP includes net taxes on digital products. Despite the difference, digital GDP and digital GVA are expected to follow the same trends when only shares of digital GVA to total GVA are being examined, as was done in this report.

Deriving Gross Domestic Product in Terms of Leontief Inverse Coefficients

In Appendix 1, it is shown through Equations 1 to 3, that gross outputs $\mathbf{x}$ in a standard input-output table (IOT) can be concisely represented as a function of the Leontief Inverse, $(\mathbf{I} - \mathbf{A})^{-1}$, and final demand, $\mathbf{y}$. Equation 4 describes this relationship.

$$\mathbf{x} = (\mathbf{I} - \mathbf{A})^{-1}\mathbf{y} \tag{4}$$

Further mathematical manipulations would also allow derivation of a similar equation for economy-wide GDP. For brevity, let the Leontief inverse, $(\mathbf{I} - \mathbf{A})^{-1} \equiv \mathbf{B}$. A direct value-added coefficient vector is defined as

$$\mathbf{v} = (v_1 \ v_2 \ ... \ v_n) = \left(\frac{gva_1}{x_1} \ \frac{gva_2}{x_2} \ ... \ \frac{gva_n}{x_n} \right) \tag{5}$$

where, gva_j, $j = 1, 2, ..., n$, refers to the gross value-added (GVA) generated by industry j and x_j refers to the gross output of the same industry j. Thus, each entry in $\mathbf{v}$ is the ratio of industry j's GVA to its own output. It is shown below that pre-multiplying $\mathbf{v}$ from Equation 5 to $\mathbf{x}$ from Equation 4 would yield an expression that calculates economy-wide GDP via the production approach (Equation 6).[18] Knowing how to derive economy-wide GDP using the $\mathbf{vBy}$ formulation in Equation 6 is the first step in understanding how a more disaggregated digital GDP is quantified.

$$\mathbf{vx} = \mathbf{vBy}^{[19]}$$
$$\rightarrow gva_1 + gva_2 + ... + gva_n = \sum_{i=1}^{n} \sum_{j=1}^{n} v_i \, b_{ij} \, y_j \tag{6}$$
$$= \text{economy-wide GDP}$$

---

18   GDP via the production approach is calculated by summing value-added generated by all economic sectors.

19   In expanded matrix form, $\mathbf{vx} = \mathbf{vBy}$

$$\rightarrow (v_1 \ v_2 \ ... \ v_n)\begin{pmatrix} x_1 \\ x_2 \\ \vdots \\ x_n \end{pmatrix} = (v_1 \ v_2 \ ... \ v_n)\begin{bmatrix} b_{11} & b_{12} & ... & b_{1n} \\ b_{21} & b_{22} & ... & b_{2n} \\ \vdots & \vdots & \ddots & \vdots \\ b_{n1} & b_{n2} & ... & b_{nn} \end{bmatrix}\begin{pmatrix} y_1 \\ y_2 \\ \vdots \\ y_n \end{pmatrix}$$

$$\rightarrow \left(\frac{gva_1}{x_1} \ \frac{gva_2}{x_2} \ ... \ \frac{gva_n}{x_n} \right)\begin{pmatrix} x_1 \\ x_2 \\ \vdots \\ x_n \end{pmatrix} = (v_1 \ v_2 \ ... \ v_n)\begin{bmatrix} b_{11} & b_{12} & ... & b_{1n} \\ b_{21} & b_{22} & ... & b_{2n} \\ \vdots & \vdots & \ddots & \vdots \\ b_{n1} & b_{n2} & ... & b_{nn} \end{bmatrix}\begin{pmatrix} y_1 \\ y_2 \\ \vdots \\ y_n \end{pmatrix}$$

Disaggregating Gross Domestic Product across Users and Suppliers of Value-Added

The economy-wide GDP that is calculated using Equation 6 can be further disaggregated to an $n \times n$ matrix where an industry's backward and forward linkages can be derived. In particular, this matrix will show an industry's sources (backward linkages) and destination (forward linkages) of value-added. In the context of the digital economy, these sources and destinations respectively refer to industries on which digital sectors are dependent (digitally enabling industries), and industries that are enabled by digital sectors (digitally enabled industries).

Simple matrix operations involving the $\mathbf{v}$, $\mathbf{B}$, and $\mathbf{y}$ matrices are performed to get an industry's backward and forward linkages. Diagonalizing the direct value-added coefficient vector from Equation (5) and the final demand vector results in matrices $\hat{\mathbf{v}}$ and $\hat{\mathbf{y}}$ below.

$$\hat{\mathbf{v}} = \begin{bmatrix} v_1 & 0 & \cdots & 0 \\ 0 & v_2 & \cdots & 0 \\ \vdots & \vdots & \ddots & \vdots \\ 0 & 0 & \cdots & v_n \end{bmatrix}; \quad \hat{\mathbf{y}} = \begin{bmatrix} y_1 & 0 & \cdots & 0 \\ 0 & y_2 & \cdots & 0 \\ \vdots & \vdots & \ddots & \vdots \\ 0 & 0 & \cdots & y_n \end{bmatrix}$$

Pre-multiplying $\hat{\mathbf{v}}$ to $\mathbf{B}$ and then post-multiplying the matrix product to $\hat{\mathbf{y}}$ gives the $\hat{\mathbf{v}}\mathbf{B}\hat{\mathbf{y}}$ matrix in Equation 7, which is an $n \times n$ matrix that disaggregates the scalar economy-wide GDP across all industries that use and supply value-added.

$$\hat{\mathbf{v}}\mathbf{B}\hat{\mathbf{y}} = \begin{bmatrix} v_1 & 0 & \cdots & 0 \\ 0 & v_2 & \cdots & 0 \\ \vdots & \vdots & \ddots & \vdots \\ 0 & 0 & \cdots & v_n \end{bmatrix} \begin{bmatrix} b_{11} & b_{12} & \cdots & b_{1n} \\ b_{21} & b_{22} & \cdots & b_{2n} \\ \vdots & \vdots & \ddots & \vdots \\ b_{n1} & b_{n2} & \cdots & b_{nn} \end{bmatrix} \begin{bmatrix} y_1 & 0 & \cdots & 0 \\ 0 & y_2 & \cdots & 0 \\ \vdots & \vdots & \ddots & \vdots \\ 0 & 0 & \cdots & y_n \end{bmatrix}$$

$$\hat{\mathbf{v}}\mathbf{B}\hat{\mathbf{y}} = \begin{bmatrix} v_1 b_{11} y_1 & v_1 b_{12} y_2 & \cdots & v_1 b_{1n} y_n \\ v_2 b_{21} y_1 & v_2 b_{22} y_2 & \cdots & v_2 b_{2n} y_n \\ \vdots & \vdots & \ddots & \vdots \\ v_n b_{n1} y_1 & v_n b_{n2} y_2 & \cdots & v_n b_{nn} y_n \end{bmatrix} \tag{7}$$

On the one hand, the rows of the $\hat{\mathbf{v}}\mathbf{B}\hat{\mathbf{y}}$ matrix correspond to the distribution of the use of the value-added created from a particular industry across all industries in the economy. Therefore, adding all row entries gives an industry's GDP. Analogously, tracing the $\hat{\mathbf{v}}\mathbf{B}\hat{\mathbf{y}}$ matrix row-wise corresponds to the forward linkages of the industry. The columns, on the other hand, correspond to the breakdown of value-added contributions of all industries in an economy to final goods and services production of a particular industry. Thus, summing all entries in a column result in the value of an industry's final products. In parallel, tracing the $\hat{\mathbf{v}}\mathbf{B}\hat{\mathbf{y}}$ matrix column-wise shows the backward linkages of the industry.

Quantifying the Digital Economy in a Two-Industry Economy

For simplicity, it can first be assumed that there are two industries in a given economy, with Industry 1 being the digital industry. This will result in the 2 × 2 $\hat{v}B\hat{y}$ matrix below.

$$\hat{v}B\hat{y} = \begin{bmatrix} v_1 b_{11} y_1 & v_1 b_{12} y_2 \\ v_2 b_{21} y_1 & v_2 b_{22} y_2 \end{bmatrix}$$

As mentioned, the sums of the first and second rows are equal to the GDP totals of the digital and nondigital industries, respectively.

$$\hat{v}B\hat{y} = \begin{bmatrix} \boxed{v_1 b_{11} y_1 \quad v_1 b_{12} y_2} \\ v_2 b_{21} y_1 \quad v_2 b_{22} y_2 \end{bmatrix} \text{ GDP of digital industry}$$

$$\hat{v}B\hat{y} = \begin{bmatrix} v_1 b_{11} y_1 \quad v_1 b_{12} y_2 \\ \boxed{v_2 b_{21} y_1 \quad v_2 b_{22} y_2} \end{bmatrix} \text{ GDP of nondigital industry}$$

In measuring the digital economy, the entirety of the digital industry's GDP must be obtained. The term $v_1 b_{11} y_1$ accounts for the digital industry's value-added contribution to its own final products. The second term, $v_1 b_{12} y_2$, is the value-added originating from the digital industry that is required by the nondigital industry. This also happens to be the contribution of the digital industry to the value of the nondigital industry's final products. Assuming that $v_1 b_{12} y_2$ is not zero, even if the second industry does not produce digital goods and services, its production is enabled by the digital industry.[20] In this sense, Industry 2 is digitally enabled through forward linkage.

However, it is apparent in the first column that the value of the digital industry's final goods and services may be comprised not only of contributions from itself ($v_1 b_{11} y_1$) but also from the nondigital industry ($v_2 b_{21} y_1$). Assuming that $v_2 b_{21} y_1$ is not zero, it is evident that the nondigital industry enables the production of the digital industry. In this sense, Industry 2 is digitally enabling through backward linkage. For this reason, $v_2 b_{21} y_1$ will also be counted as part of the digital economy. The term $v_2 b_{22} y_2$, on the other hand, pertains to value-added that originated from, and is used by, the nondigital industry. Since this does not involve transactions with the digital industry, it will not be counted as part of the digital economy.

Thus, the **GDP attributable to the digital economy is given by the entire GDP of the digital industry plus the portion of the nondigital industry's GDP that enables production in the digital industry**:

$$GDP_{digital} = GDP_1 + GDP_2 - v_2 b_{22} y_2$$

$$GDP_{digital} = v_1 b_{11} y_1 + v_1 b_{12} y_2 + v_2 b_{21} y_1$$

---

20 One can say that a portion of the digital industry's value-added goes to the nondigital industry.

This can be directly calculated using the equation below:

$$\text{GDP}_{\text{digital}} = \mathbf{i}^T\hat{\mathbf{v}}\mathbf{B}\hat{\mathbf{y}}\boldsymbol{\varepsilon}_1 + \mathbf{i}^T(\hat{\mathbf{v}}\mathbf{B}\hat{\mathbf{y}})^T\boldsymbol{\varepsilon}_1 - [\text{diag}(\hat{\mathbf{v}}\mathbf{B}\hat{\mathbf{y}})]^T\boldsymbol{\varepsilon}_1 \tag{8}$$

$$= (1 \quad 1)\begin{bmatrix} v_1b_{11}y_1 & v_1b_{12}y_2 \\ v_2b_{21}y_1 & v_2b_{22}y_2 \end{bmatrix}\begin{pmatrix}1\\0\end{pmatrix} + (1 \quad 1)\begin{bmatrix} v_1b_{11}y_1 & v_2b_{21}y_1 \\ v_1b_{12}y_2 & v_2b_{22}y_2 \end{bmatrix}\begin{pmatrix}1\\0\end{pmatrix}$$

$$- \begin{pmatrix} v_1b_{11}y_1 \\ v_2b_{22}y_2 \end{pmatrix}^T \begin{pmatrix}1\\0\end{pmatrix}$$

$$= (v_1b_{11}y_1 + v_2b_{21}y_1 \quad v_1b_{12}y_2 + v_2b_{22}y_2)\begin{pmatrix}1\\0\end{pmatrix}$$

$$+ (v_1b_{11}y_1 + v_1b_{12}y_2 \quad v_2b_{21}y_1 + v_2b_{22}y_2)\begin{pmatrix}1\\0\end{pmatrix}$$

$$- (v_1b_{11}y_1 \quad v_2b_{22}y_2)\begin{pmatrix}1\\0\end{pmatrix}$$

$$= v_1b_{11}y_1 + v_2b_{21}y_1 + v_1b_{11}y_1 + v_1b_{12}y_2 - v_1b_{11}y_1$$

$$= v_1b_{11}y_1 + v_1b_{12}y_2 + v_2b_{21}y_1$$

The first term, $\mathbf{i}^T\hat{\mathbf{v}}\mathbf{B}\hat{\mathbf{y}}\boldsymbol{\varepsilon}_1$, of Equation 8 directly calculates the backward linkage related to the digital industry while the second term, $\mathbf{i}^T(\hat{\mathbf{v}}\mathbf{B}\hat{\mathbf{y}})^T\boldsymbol{\varepsilon}_1$, gives the forward linkage. To account for the double-counted term, the diagonal entry in the $\hat{\mathbf{v}}\mathbf{B}\hat{\mathbf{y}}$ matrix that corresponds to the digital industry is removed, which is why $[\text{diag}(\hat{\mathbf{v}}\mathbf{B}\hat{\mathbf{y}})]^T\boldsymbol{\varepsilon}_1$ is subtracted in $\text{GDP}_{\text{digital}}$. An "eliminator vector" $\boldsymbol{\varepsilon}_1$ is used to mathematically eliminate entries that should not be included in calculations. Such eliminator vectors will be used throughout the framework.

Quantifying the Digital Economy in a Simple Three-Industry Economy without Capital Formation

Implementing the method in the example above results in double counting if there are two or more digital industries that interact with each other. To demonstrate, let there be three industries in an economy, represented by the $\hat{\mathbf{v}}\mathbf{B}\hat{\mathbf{y}}$ matrix below.

$$\hat{\mathbf{v}}\mathbf{B}\hat{\mathbf{y}} = \begin{bmatrix} v_1b_{11}y_1 & v_1b_{12}y_2 & v_1b_{13}y_3 \\ v_2b_{21}y_1 & v_2b_{22}y_2 & v_2b_{23}y_3 \\ v_3b_{31}y_1 & v_3b_{32}y_2 & v_3b_{33}y_3 \end{bmatrix}$$

Assume that Industry 1 and Industry 2 are digital. Applying Equation (8), $\text{GDP}_{\text{digital}}$ is expanded as a linear equation below.

$$\text{GDP}_{\text{digital}} = \mathbf{i}^T\hat{\mathbf{v}}\mathbf{B}\hat{\mathbf{y}}\boldsymbol{\varepsilon} + \mathbf{i}^T(\hat{\mathbf{v}}\mathbf{B}\hat{\mathbf{y}})^T\boldsymbol{\varepsilon} - [\text{diag}(\hat{\mathbf{v}}\mathbf{B}\hat{\mathbf{y}})]^T\boldsymbol{\varepsilon}$$

$$\text{GDP}_{\text{digital}} = v_1b_{11}y_1 + v_2b_{21}y_1 + v_3b_{31}y_1 + v_1b_{12}y_2 + v_2b_{22}y_2 + v_3b_{32}y_2 + v_1b_{12}y_2 + v_1b_{13}y_3 + v_2b_{21}y_1 \\ + v_2b_{23}y_3$$

As seen above, the terms, $v_2b_{21}y_1$ and $v_2b_{12}y_2$ are double counted since all value-added use of and value-added contribution to all digital industries in the economy are recorded. For example, $v_2b_{21}y_1$ is the value-added generated by Industry 2, which is used by Industry 1 and is therefore counted from a forward perspective. However, this also happens to be a source of value-added for Industry 1's final products and is then counted from a backward perspective.

From here, further adjustments are made in the framework to account for the interdependence of digital industries. A neat and simple solution is by aggregating similarly classified industries and treating them as a single sector, i.e., "the digital sector," since the two-industry case reveals that the $GDP_{digital}$ equation precludes any double counting when there is only a single digital industry.

In the framework, carrying out aggregations for the **Z**, **x**, **f**, and **gva** matrices makes use of "aggregator matrices." The full demonstration of how these matrices work can be found in Appendix 2. Therefore, after aggregating digital subsectors into one digital sector, the procedure in the two-industry case is still preserved, except that aggregator matrices are integrated into the framework. Thus, only some notational changes are necessary given by the following:

$$\mathbf{x}_{agg} = \mathbf{Z}_{agg}\mathbf{i} + \mathbf{y}_{agg}$$

$$\mathbf{x}_{agg} = \left(\mathbf{I} - \mathbf{A}_{agg}\right)^{-1}\mathbf{y}_{agg}$$

$$\left(\mathbf{I} - \mathbf{A}_{agg}\right)^{-1} \equiv \mathbf{B}_{agg}$$

$$\mathbf{v}_{agg} = \begin{pmatrix} v_1 & v_2 & \cdots & v_{n-q-1} \end{pmatrix}$$

Integrating these notational changes with Equation 8 results in the revised $GDP_{digital}$ equation in Equation 9.

$$GDP_i = v_ib_{i1}y_1 + v_ib_{i2}y_2 + \cdots + v_ib_{i,n-q-1}y_{n-q-1}, \quad i = 1,2,\ldots n-q-1$$

$$\hat{\mathbf{v}}_{agg}\mathbf{B}_{agg}\hat{\mathbf{y}}_{agg} = \begin{bmatrix} v_1b_{11}y_1 & v_1b_{12}y_2 & \cdots & v_1b_{1,n-q-1}y_{n-q-1} \\ v_2b_{21}y_1 & v_2b_{22}y_2 & \cdots & v_2b_{2,n-q-1}y_{n-q-1} \\ \vdots & \vdots & \ddots & \vdots \\ v_{n-q-1}b_{n-q-1,1}y_1 & v_{n-q-1}b_{n-q-1,2}y_2 & \cdots & v_{n-q-1}b_{n-q-1,n-q-1}y_{n-q-1} \end{bmatrix}$$

$$GDP_{digital} = \mathbf{i}^T\hat{\mathbf{v}}_{agg}\mathbf{B}_{agg}\hat{\mathbf{y}}_{agg}\boldsymbol{\varepsilon}_1 + \mathbf{i}^T\left(\hat{\mathbf{v}}_{agg}\mathbf{B}_{agg}\hat{\mathbf{y}}_{agg}\right)^T\boldsymbol{\varepsilon}_1 - \left[diag\left(\hat{\mathbf{v}}_{agg}\mathbf{B}_{agg}\hat{\mathbf{y}}_{agg}\right)\right]^T\boldsymbol{\varepsilon}_1 \tag{9}$$

Integrating Gross Fixed Capital Formation of the Digital Economy in a Three-Industry Economy

Equation 9 captures all contemporaneous input-output transactions with respect to exogenous final demand. However, if in the current year an industry purchases capital goods from a nondigital industry to use as inputs for future production, the **Z** matrix will not be able to capture this, as formation of fixed capital is reflected in the final demand vector, **y**.[21]

---

[21] Capital goods refer to fixed assets, or assets intended for use in the production of other goods and services for a period of more than 1 year, as defined by the System of National Accounts (SNA) 2008.

While the contribution of fixed capital formation to current year's production is reflected in the **gva** matrix as consumption of fixed capital, it fails to account for the various sector contributions required to produce said fixed capital as an output in the market. To illustrate, suppose there is a three-industry economy with Industry 1 as a digital industry and Industry 2 and Industry 3 as nondigital. Suppose further that Industry 1 purchases capital goods from Industry 3. In a standard input-output framework, this purchase by Industry 1 will be reflected in **y**. To show this, if **y** is disaggregated across three final demand components, for simplicity: household final consumption expenditure (hfce), general government consumption expenditure (ggce), and gross fixed capital formation (gfcf), then:

$$\mathbf{y} = \begin{bmatrix} y_1 \\ y_2 \\ y_3 \end{bmatrix} = \mathbf{h} + \mathbf{g} + \mathbf{k} = \begin{bmatrix} hfce_1 \\ hfce_2 \\ hfce_3 \end{bmatrix} + \begin{bmatrix} ggce_1 \\ ggce_2 \\ ggce_3 \end{bmatrix} + \begin{bmatrix} gfcf_1 \\ gfcf_2 \\ gfcf_3 \end{bmatrix}$$

Further disaggregating vector **k** into a matrix with columns as the purchaser of capital and the rows as the seller of capital results in matrix **K**, where Industry 1's purchase of fixed capital from Industry 3 is equal to $gfcf_{31}$. Suppose $gfcf_{31}$ is the only capital investment in the economy for the period.

$$\mathbf{K} = \begin{bmatrix} gfcf_{11} & gfcf_{12} & gfcf_{13} \\ gfcf_{21} & gfcf_{22} & gfcf_{23} \\ gfcf_{31} & gfcf_{32} & gfcf_{33} \end{bmatrix} = \begin{bmatrix} 0 & 0 & 0 \\ 0 & 0 & 0 \\ gfcf_{31} & 0 & 0 \end{bmatrix}$$

While matrix **K** shows which industry sold the capital, it does not show how said capital was produced. Therefore, without explicitly integrating the production of gross fixed capital purchased by digital Industry 1, the computation of $GDP_{digital}$ will be understated. This is because the capital goods produced by Industry 3 and purchased by Industry 1 also derived value from other industries in the economy. Thus, other industries' value-added shares to Industry 3's final products indirectly enable the digital economy and should therefore be counted as part of $GDP_{digital}$. The $\mathbf{\hat{v}B\hat{y}}$ matrix already contains this information, but it still needs to be explicitly augmented to Equation 9.

To derive an equation that accounts for the backward linkage of fixed capital goods consumed by the digital industry (i.e., the GDP contribution of digitally enabling industries through capital formation), a single ratio for each of the columns corresponding to industries from which the digital sector purchased capital goods can be applied.[22]

---

[22] A single ratio would suffice, given technical coefficients are assumed to be fixed, following the Leontief insight (Leontief 1936).

In the previous illustration, multiplying the final product of Industry 3, $v_1 b_{13} y_3 + v_2 b_{23} y_3 + v_3 b_{33} y_3$, with a ratio, say r_3, will give the value of fixed capital investment by Industry 1, $gfcf_{31}$. Let $\mathbf{r}$ be the vector of ratios of gfcf used by the digital industry to corresponding final demand and $\hat{\mathbf{r}}$ be the diagonalized $\mathbf{r}$.

$$\mathbf{r} = \begin{bmatrix} r_1 \\ r_2 \\ r_3 \end{bmatrix}; \quad \hat{\mathbf{r}} = \begin{bmatrix} r_1 & 0 & 0 \\ 0 & r_2 & 0 \\ 0 & 0 & r_3 \end{bmatrix}$$

Post-multiplying $\hat{\mathbf{r}}$ to $\hat{\mathbf{v}}\mathbf{B}\hat{\mathbf{y}}$ gives:

$$\hat{\mathbf{v}}\mathbf{B}\hat{\mathbf{y}}\hat{\mathbf{r}} = \begin{bmatrix} v_1 b_{11} y_1 & v_1 b_{12} y_2 & v_1 b_{13} y_3 \\ v_2 b_{21} y_1 & v_2 b_{22} y_2 & v_2 b_{23} y_3 \\ v_3 b_{31} y_1 & v_3 b_{32} y_2 & v_3 b_{33} y_3 \end{bmatrix} \begin{bmatrix} r_1 & 0 & 0 \\ 0 & r_2 & 0 \\ 0 & 0 & r_3 \end{bmatrix} = \begin{bmatrix} r_1 v_1 b_{11} y_1 & r_2 v_1 b_{12} y_2 & r_3 v_1 b_{13} y_3 \\ r_1 v_2 b_{21} y_1 & r_2 v_2 b_{22} y_2 & r_3 v_2 b_{23} y_3 \\ r_1 v_3 b_{31} y_1 & r_2 v_3 b_{32} y_2 & r_3 v_3 b_{33} y_3 \end{bmatrix}$$

All elements in the first row and column of the $\hat{\mathbf{v}}\mathbf{B}\hat{\mathbf{y}}\hat{\mathbf{r}}$ matrix will already be accounted for by Equation 9 within forward and backward linkages, respectively, of the digital Industry 1. To prevent double counting of a portion of the forward linkage of the digital industry in $GDP_{digital}$, $(\mathbf{i} - \boldsymbol{\varepsilon}_1)^T$ is pre-multiplied to $\hat{\mathbf{v}}\mathbf{B}\hat{\mathbf{y}}\hat{\mathbf{r}}$:

$$(\mathbf{i} - \boldsymbol{\varepsilon}_1)^T \hat{\mathbf{v}}\mathbf{B}\hat{\mathbf{y}}\hat{\mathbf{r}} = \begin{pmatrix} 0 & 1 & 1 \end{pmatrix} \begin{bmatrix} v_1 b_{11} y_1 & v_1 b_{12} y_2 & v_1 b_{13} y_3 \\ v_2 b_{21} y_1 & v_2 b_{22} y_2 & v_2 b_{23} y_3 \\ v_3 b_{31} y_1 & v_3 b_{32} y_2 & v_3 b_{33} y_3 \end{bmatrix} \begin{bmatrix} r_1 & 0 & 0 \\ 0 & r_2 & 0 \\ 0 & 0 & r_3 \end{bmatrix}$$

$$\rightarrow (\mathbf{i} - \boldsymbol{\varepsilon}_1)^T \hat{\mathbf{v}}\mathbf{B}\hat{\mathbf{y}}\hat{\mathbf{r}} = \begin{pmatrix} \sum_{i \neq 1}^{3} vby_{i1} & \sum_{i \neq 1}^{3} vby_{i2} & \sum_{i \neq 1}^{3} vby_{i3} \end{pmatrix} \begin{bmatrix} r_1 & 0 & 0 \\ 0 & r_2 & 0 \\ 0 & 0 & r_3 \end{bmatrix}$$

$$\rightarrow (\mathbf{i} - \boldsymbol{\varepsilon}_1)^T \hat{\mathbf{v}}\mathbf{B}\hat{\mathbf{y}}\hat{\mathbf{r}} = \begin{pmatrix} r_1 \sum_{i \neq 1}^{3} vby_{i1} & r_2 \sum_{i \neq 1}^{3} vby_{i2} & r_3 \sum_{i \neq 1}^{3} vby_{i3} \end{pmatrix}$$

Since Industry 1 only invests in final products of Industry 3, r_2 will be equal to zero, which leaves the following:

$$(\mathbf{i} - \boldsymbol{\varepsilon}_1)^T \hat{\mathbf{v}}\mathbf{B}\hat{\mathbf{y}}\hat{\mathbf{r}} = \begin{pmatrix} r_1 \sum_{i \neq 1}^{3} vby_{i1} & 0 & r_3 \sum_{i \neq 1}^{3} vby_{i3} \end{pmatrix}$$

Another eliminator vector, $\boldsymbol{\varepsilon}_2 = \begin{pmatrix} 0 & 0 & 1 \end{pmatrix}^T$ is then post-multiplied to $(\mathbf{i} - \boldsymbol{\varepsilon}_1)^T \hat{\mathbf{v}}\mathbf{B}\hat{\mathbf{y}}\hat{\mathbf{r}}$

to get: $(\mathbf{i} - \boldsymbol{\varepsilon}_1)^T \hat{\mathbf{v}}\mathbf{B}\hat{\mathbf{y}}\hat{\mathbf{r}}\boldsymbol{\varepsilon}_2 = (\mathbf{i} - \boldsymbol{\varepsilon}_1)^T \hat{\mathbf{v}}\mathbf{B}\hat{\mathbf{y}}\hat{\mathbf{r}} \begin{pmatrix} 0 \\ 0 \\ 1 \end{pmatrix} = \begin{pmatrix} r_1 \sum_{i \neq 1}^{3} vby_{i1} & 0 & r_3 \sum_{i \neq 1}^{3} vby_{i3} \end{pmatrix} \begin{pmatrix} 0 \\ 0 \\ 1 \end{pmatrix}$

$$\rightarrow (\mathbf{i} - \boldsymbol{\varepsilon}_1)^T \hat{\mathbf{v}}\mathbf{B}\hat{\mathbf{y}}\hat{\mathbf{r}}\boldsymbol{\varepsilon}_2 = r_3 \sum_{i \neq 1}^{3} vby_{i3}$$

The eliminator vector $\boldsymbol{\varepsilon}_2$ has a value of 1 for the row corresponding to the industry from which the digital industry purchases fixed capital, except itself. Excluding own-account capital formation of the digital industry from the calculation is required to prevent double counting of a portion of the backward linkage of the digital industry in $GDP_{digital}$. Therefore, in the illustration, the element of $\boldsymbol{\varepsilon}_2$ corresponding to digital industry, $\boldsymbol{\varepsilon}_{2_1}$, is set to zero, as well as $\boldsymbol{\varepsilon}_{2_2}$. Only $\boldsymbol{\varepsilon}_{2_3} = 1$ because Industry 1 only purchases fixed capital from Industry 3. The term $r_3 \sum_{i \neq 1}^{3} vby_{i3}$ corresponds to the backward linkage of fixed capital goods consumed by digital Industry 1 from nondigital Industry 3.[23]

Quantifying the Digital Economy in an *n*-Industry Economy

The three-industry case is generalizable to an economy with n industries. To illustrate, the dimension of the vector of ratios, $\mathbf{r}$, is redefined to $n \times 1$. Correspondingly, this is diagonalized as $\hat{\mathbf{r}}$, to form an $n \times n$ matrix.

$$\mathbf{r} = \begin{bmatrix} r_1 \\ r_2 \\ \vdots \\ r_n \end{bmatrix}; \quad \hat{\mathbf{r}} = \begin{bmatrix} r_1 & 0 & 0 & 0 \\ 0 & r_2 & 0 & 0 \\ 0 & 0 & \ddots & 0 \\ 0 & 0 & 0 & r_n \end{bmatrix}$$

Likewise, the $\hat{\mathbf{v}}\mathbf{B}\hat{\mathbf{y}}\hat{\mathbf{r}}$ matrix will have a dimension of $n \times n$, as shown below.

$$\hat{\mathbf{v}}\mathbf{B}\hat{\mathbf{y}}\hat{\mathbf{r}} = \begin{bmatrix} v_1 b_{11} y_1 & v_1 b_{12} y_2 & \cdots & v_1 b_{1j} y_j & \cdots & v_1 b_{1n} y_n \\ v_2 b_{21} y_1 & v_2 b_{22} y_2 & \cdots & v_2 b_{2j} y_j & \cdots & v_2 b_{2n} y_n \\ \vdots & \vdots & \ddots & \vdots & \ddots & \vdots \\ v_j b_{j1} y_1 & v_j b_{j2} y_2 & \cdots & v_j b_{jj} y_j & \cdots & v_j b_{jn} y_n \\ \vdots & \vdots & \ddots & \vdots & \ddots & \vdots \\ v_n b_{n1} y_1 & v_n b_{n2} y_2 & \cdots & v_n b_{nj} y_j & \cdots & v_n b_{nn} y_n \end{bmatrix} \begin{bmatrix} r_1 & 0 & 0 & 0 & 0 & 0 \\ 0 & r_2 & 0 & 0 & 0 & 0 \\ 0 & 0 & \ddots & 0 & 0 & 0 \\ 0 & 0 & 0 & r_j & 0 & 0 \\ 0 & 0 & 0 & 0 & \ddots & 0 \\ 0 & 0 & 0 & 0 & 0 & r_n \end{bmatrix}$$

$$= \begin{bmatrix} r_1 v_1 b_{11} y_1 & r_2 v_1 b_{12} y_2 & \cdots & r_j v_1 b_{1j} y_j & \cdots & r_n v_1 b_{1n} y_n \\ r_1 v_2 b_{21} y_1 & r_2 v_2 b_{22} y_2 & \cdots & r_j v_2 b_{2j} y_j & \cdots & r_n v_2 b_{2n} y_n \\ \vdots & \vdots & \ddots & \vdots & \ddots & \vdots \\ r_1 v_j b_{j1} y_1 & r_2 v_j b_{j2} y_2 & \cdots & r_j v_j b_{jj} y_j & \cdots & r_n v_j b_{jn} y_n \\ \vdots & \vdots & \ddots & \vdots & \ddots & \vdots \\ r_1 v_n b_{n1} y_1 & r_2 v_n b_{n2} y_2 & \cdots & r_j v_n b_{nj} y_j & \cdots & r_n v_n b_{nn} y_n \end{bmatrix}$$

Now, suppose Industry 1 is a digital industry and that it purchases fixed capital from both Industry j and itself. Assume that only Industry 1 is digital, while the rest of the industries are nondigital. The $(\mathbf{i} - \boldsymbol{\varepsilon}_1)^{\mathrm{T}} \hat{\mathbf{v}} \mathbf{B} \hat{\mathbf{y}} \hat{\mathbf{r}}$ equation becomes

$$(\mathbf{i} - \boldsymbol{\varepsilon}_1)^{\mathrm{T}} \hat{\mathbf{v}} \mathbf{B} \hat{\mathbf{y}} \hat{\mathbf{r}} = \left(r_1 \sum_{i \neq 1}^{n} vby_{i1} \quad r_2 \sum_{i \neq 1}^{n} vby_{i2} \quad \cdots \quad r_j \sum_{i \neq 1}^{n} vby_{ij} \quad \cdots \quad r_n \sum_{i \neq 1}^{n} vby_{in} \right)$$

$$\rightarrow (\mathbf{i} - \boldsymbol{\varepsilon}_1)^{\mathrm{T}} \hat{\mathbf{v}} \mathbf{B} \hat{\mathbf{y}} \hat{\mathbf{r}} = \left(r_1 \sum_{i \neq 1}^{n} vby_{i1} \quad 0 \quad \cdots \quad r_j \sum_{i \neq 1}^{n} vby_{ij} \quad \cdots \quad 0 \right)$$

To eliminate the double counting of the backward linkage of own-account fixed capital formation in the digital industry, the $n \times 1$ eliminator vector $\boldsymbol{\varepsilon}_2$ is post-multiplied to $(\mathbf{i} - \boldsymbol{\varepsilon}_1)^{\mathrm{T}} \hat{\mathbf{v}} \mathbf{B} \hat{\mathbf{y}} \hat{\mathbf{r}}$ to arrive at a value for the backward linkage of fixed capital goods consumed by the digital industry.

$$(\mathbf{i} - \boldsymbol{\varepsilon}_1)^{\mathrm{T}} \hat{\mathbf{v}} \mathbf{B} \hat{\mathbf{y}} \hat{\mathbf{r}} \boldsymbol{\varepsilon}_2 = \left(r_1 \sum_{i \neq 1}^{n} vby_{i1} \quad 0 \quad \cdots \quad r_j \sum_{i \neq 1}^{n} vby_{ij} \quad \cdots \quad 0 \right) \begin{pmatrix} 0 \\ 0 \\ \vdots \\ 1 \\ \vdots \\ 0 \end{pmatrix}$$

---

[23] Only domestic purchases of fixed capital are included within the framework estimates, as imported gross fixed capital formation is not produced within the domestic economy.

The Core Digital Economy Equation

The core digital economy equation (Equation 10) is derived by consolidating Equation 9 with the value of the backward linkage of fixed capital goods consumed by the digital industry. In Equation 10, the "agg" subscripts are suppressed for notational simplicity, but note that aggregation (as discussed in Appendix 2) was done prior to calculations.

$$\text{GDP}_{\text{digital}} = \mathbf{i}^{\mathrm{T}}\hat{\mathbf{v}}_{\text{agg}}\mathbf{B}_{\text{agg}}\hat{\mathbf{y}}_{\text{agg}}\boldsymbol{\varepsilon}_1 + \mathbf{i}^{\mathrm{T}}\left(\hat{\mathbf{v}}_{\text{agg}}\mathbf{B}_{\text{agg}}\hat{\mathbf{y}}_{\text{agg}}\right)^{\mathrm{T}}\boldsymbol{\varepsilon}_1 - \left[\text{diag}\left(\hat{\mathbf{v}}_{\text{agg}}\mathbf{B}_{\text{agg}}\hat{\mathbf{y}}_{\text{agg}}\right)\right]^{\mathrm{T}}\boldsymbol{\varepsilon}_1$$
$$+ \left(\mathbf{i} - \boldsymbol{\varepsilon}_1\right)^{\mathrm{T}}\hat{\mathbf{v}}_{\text{agg}}\mathbf{B}_{\text{agg}}\hat{\mathbf{y}}_{\text{agg}}\boldsymbol{\varepsilon}_2$$

$$\text{GDP}_{\text{digital}} = \mathbf{i}^{\mathrm{T}}\hat{\mathbf{v}}\mathbf{B}\hat{\mathbf{y}}\boldsymbol{\varepsilon}_1 + \mathbf{i}^{\mathrm{T}}(\hat{\mathbf{v}}\mathbf{B}\hat{\mathbf{y}})^{\mathrm{T}}\boldsymbol{\varepsilon}_1 - [\text{diag}(\hat{\mathbf{v}}\mathbf{B}\hat{\mathbf{y}})]^{\mathrm{T}}\boldsymbol{\varepsilon}_1 + (\mathbf{i} - \boldsymbol{\varepsilon}_1)^{\mathrm{T}}\hat{\mathbf{v}}\mathbf{B}\hat{\mathbf{y}}\hat{\mathbf{r}}\boldsymbol{\varepsilon}_2 \qquad (10)$$

In Equation 10, the four terms respectively refer to the digital economy's (i) backward linkages; (ii) forward linkages; (iii) the double-counted term (i.e., the aggregate digital industry's value-added contribution to its own final products), and (iv) the nondigital products it capitalizes.

Methodological Requirements

Supply and Use Tables and Input-Output Tables

The principal sources of data for the digital economy framework are national supply and use tables (SUTs) and IOTs. The supply table details how goods and services are supplied in an economy, either by domestic production or imports. On the other hand, the use table demonstrates how these outputs are used in the same economy, either as intermediate consumption, final consumption (which includes household final consumption expenditure, non-profit institutions serving households final consumption expenditure, and government final consumption expenditure), capital formation, or exports. SUTs are the main bases for national economic accounting systems, as a dataset that describes interactions within an economy and as a balancing framework for GDP calculations. This makes it an attractive source for various kinds of analytical uses and satellite systems (UN 2018).

The IOT combines the identities in the supply table and the use table into a single identity (UN 2018). As discussed, the proposed framework methodology requires matrices and vectors directly extracted from IOTs. SUTs may be easily transformed into IOTs using a transformation model prescribed by Eurostat (2008). For this report, the "fixed product sales structure" assumption was used to transform SUTs to IOTs, which converts a product-by-industry SUT to an industry-by-industry IOT.[24]

---

24 Known as "Model D," this assumes that each product has its own specific sales structure, irrespective of the industry where it is produced (Eurostat 2008).

While IOTs allow a more organized application of Leontief's insight in analyses, SUTs provide greater detail on dynamics between products and industries at the rudimentary level. Thus, SUTs are particularly useful to capture the fourth term in the central formula (Equation 10), which incorporates the dependence of digital sectors on fixed capital. They may also be used for analyses concerning specific product-industry relationships, such as in assessing the digitalization of industries based on the use of digital products.

Uniformity Across National Tables

To ensure consistency with published aggregates, SUTs and/or IOTs are sourced from each economy's published tables on its respective national statistics office (NSO) website. Oftentimes, this entails further data collection and adjustment to apply the methodology as uniformly as possible across different economies. Three main concerns are considered to ensure uniformity and comparability of data: correspondence in classification systems, harmonization of SUT and IOT presentation format, and comparability in price and valuation.

Correspondence in classification systems

One major point of consideration is that different product and industry classification systems may be adopted by different economies. As such, identifying the exact same digital products and industries across economies requires close inspection and harmonization of these classification systems. For example, Canada uses the North American Industry Classification System, while Singapore uses its own Singapore Standard Industries Classification. Ensuring comparability between estimates of Canada's digital economy and that of Singapore requires an accurate correspondence between two different classification systems.

Another consideration is the varying levels of disaggregation of product and industry classification in SUTs or IOTs. Even when two economies adopt the same classification system, further data manipulation is necessary when disaggregation levels are not the same.

Harmonization of table presentation format

Another main concern is possible differences in the format by which SUTs and IOTs are presented for each economy. While presentation formats, in general, do not pose any real issue, problems arise when the variance pertains to difference in values contained in the $\mathbf{Z}$ matrix and $\mathbf{y}$ vector. For example, in the case of Japan, competitive imports are included in the intermediate consumption matrix. In the framework, the $\mathbf{Z}$ matrix only includes domestically produced inputs. Thus, appropriate adjustments must be made in such cases.

Comparability in price and valuation

Values in SUTs and IOTs may also be expressed in different prices (i.e., current prices or constant prices) and/or in different valuations (i.e., basic prices, producer's prices, or purchaser's prices). Tables at current prices are the bases of the main estimates produced by the framework. However, tables at constant prices are also employed when temporal analyses are made, such that only real changes are measured.

Furthermore, assuming that taxes, subsidies, and trade and transport margins are proportionately distributed across the products in an economy, estimates of $GDP_{digital}$ as a percentage of GDP calculated using tables valued in either basic, producer's, or purchaser's prices should not significantly differ from each other. Otherwise, when comparing across economies or time, it is preferred that the tables follow the same valuation.

The aforementioned are the most common differences observed across national tables. However, others may be encountered and should be appropriately addressed, especially when the inconsistency has a pervasive effect on the estimates. As long as the same methodology is applied given the available data, overall results per economy may be used for comparative analyses.

Disaggregating Products and Industries

Given the varying levels of product and industry disaggregation that economies present in their SUTs and IOTs, it is necessary to conduct a thorough evaluation of product and industry classification, then appropriately disaggregate the data. This poses a key challenge for tables with less than the desired level of detail, for which isolation of the exact digital activities identified for this methodology is crucial. As an example, software publishing is often combined with all publishing activities, and this needs to be extracted from other nondigital publishing activities.

Consing et al. (2020), a study that employed the same theoretical framework, examined and compared several data sources based on merits and drawbacks as a basis for disaggregation. Table 2 lists the established rankings of the top sources of data, from highest to lowest in terms of degree of reliability.

Table 2: Data Sources for Disaggregating Sectors

Source of Data	Merits	Drawbacks and/or Caveats
National statistics office	Highly reliable data consistent with the construction of SUT	Dependent on public availability of data or the NSO's responsiveness to queries
Relevant journals and published reports	Alternative of sourcing out if primary data are not available	Finding consistent and reliable data may be time-consuming, if even available
Supply table	Readily available in the SUT	Applies only if the desired degree of disaggregation among sectors is present
Operating revenue data from credible data resources	Readily available given permissions to access certain databases	May be limited by the amount of data collected by the resource
Data from donor economy	Based on an actual economy's industry disaggregation	Requires some degree of similarity in terms of structure between the two economies
Number of establishments from credible data resources	Readily available given permissions to access certain databases	Bias from an assumption of homogeneity

NSO = national statistics office, SUT = supply and use table.
Source: R. Consing III, M. Barsabal, J. Alvarez, and M. Mariasingham. 2020. The Wellness Economy, A Comprehensive System of National Accounts Approach. *Asian Development Bank Economics Working Paper* Series. No. 631. Manila: Asian Development Bank.

Using the best data disaggregation source available, a disaggregation ratio is calculated as the proportion of estimated digital activity (output) from the aggregate industry activity (output). The resulting percentage is then multiplied to all values in both the row and the column corresponding to the particular aggregate industry in the IOT. In effect, two subindustries replace the aggregate industry, expanding the dimension of the original IOT, but without changing its total measures and symmetry.

To illustrate, suppose there is the following 2 × 2 IOT:

	Industry 1	Industry 2	Final Demand	Gross Output
Industry 1	z_{11}	z_{12}	f_1	x_1
Industry 2	z_{21}	z_{22}	f_2	x_2
GVA	gva_1	gva_2		
Gross Output	x_1	x_2		

Suppose further that Industry 1 is an aggregate sector that contains both digital and nondigital subsectors. It is therefore necessary to disaggregate Industry 1 into two subindustries. Given the following revenue shares, derived from credible sources:

α which stands for the share of digital Industry 1a to Industry 1's total revenue, and

β which stands for the share of nondigital Industry 1b to Industry 1's total revenue.

where α + β = 1, a disaggregated 3 × 3 IOT is obtained as follows:

	Industry 1a	Industry 1b	Industry 2	Final Demand	Gross Output
Industry 1a	$\alpha\alpha z_{11}$	$\alpha\beta z_{11}$	αz_{12}	αf_1	αx_1
Industry 1b	$\beta\alpha z_{11}$	$\beta\beta z_{11}$	βz_{12}	βf_1	βx_1
Industry 2	αz_{21}	βz_{21}	z_{22}	f_2	x_2
GVA	αgva_1	βgva_1	gva_2		
Gross Output	αx_1	βx_1	x_2		

Several checks have to be implemented to ensure the accuracy of disaggregation. First, the resulting 3 × 3 IOT should be symmetric with respect to its gross output, as in the original 2 × 2 IOT. Second, total gross output must be exactly the same for the two tables.[25] Last, the sum of the technical coefficients for Industry 1a and Industry 1b should be the same as the technical coefficient of aggregate Industry 1.[26] Note that this disaggregation method can be extended to an *n*-industry setting.

Construction of the Multiregional Input-Output Tables with Digital Sectors

When measuring international linkages, particularly global value chains (GVCs) in the context of the digital economy, credible regional or inter-economy IOTs should be used instead of individual national IOTs. One useful resource in conducting such analyses is the Multiregional Input-Output Tables (MRIOTs) produced by the Asian Development Bank. However, the main hurdle prior to conducting any GVC analyses for the digital economy is the aggregation level of the MRIOTs. As such, one of the key efforts of this project is the construction of these tables with industries disaggregated up to the level required in the framework.

The MRIOT database contains information on the production, consumption, and trade linkages of 62 economies, and an aggregated economy for "the rest of the world." Each economy has 35 sectors[27] and five final demand components.[28] The MRIOTs generally follow the sources and methods used to construct the World Input Output Database (WIOD), handled by the University of Groningen.[29]

---

[25] To show that gross output is the same for the 2 × 2 and 3 × 3 IOTs:
$x_1 + x_2 = \alpha x_1 + \beta x_1 + x_2 \Longrightarrow x_1 + x_2 = (\alpha + \beta)x_1 + x_2 \Longrightarrow x_1 + x_2 = x_1 + x_2$ ∎

[26] To show that the sum of technical coefficients of Industries 1a and 1b is equal to the technical coefficient of Industry 1:
$\frac{z_{11}}{x_1} = \frac{\alpha\alpha z_{11}}{\alpha x_1} + \frac{\beta\alpha z_{11}}{\alpha x_1} = \frac{\alpha\beta z_{11}}{\beta x_1} + \frac{\beta\beta z_{11}}{\beta x_1} \Longrightarrow \frac{z_{11}}{x_1} = \frac{\alpha z_{11}}{x_1} + \frac{\beta z_{11}}{x_1} \Longrightarrow \frac{z_{11}}{x_1} = \frac{\alpha z_{11} + \beta z_{11}}{x_1} \Longrightarrow \frac{z_{11}}{x_1} = \frac{(\alpha + \beta)z_{11}}{x_1} \Longrightarrow \frac{z_{11}}{x_1} = \frac{z_{11}}{x_1}$ ∎

[27] Table A3.1 (Appendix 3) outlines the 35 MRIO sectors.

[28] The five final demand components include household final consumption expenditure (FCE), nonprofit institutions serving households (NPISHs) FCE, government FCE, gross fixed capital formation, and changes in inventories.

[29] See Timmer et al. (2012) for details on constructing the WIOD.

The MRIOT sectors Electrical and Optical Equipment (c14), Post and Telecommunications (c27), and Renting of Machinery & Equipment and Other Business Activities (c30) include the digital sectors identified in the framework, and were therefore each split into two subsectors to isolate these digital subsectors. Thus, instead of the usual 35 sectors, this study uses a 38-sector MRIOT for 2017–2019. Figure 3 shows the six new sectors as a result of isolating digital industries. For the MRIOT, the authors had to disaggregate the three sectors for each of the 63 economies (Figure 4).

Figure 3: Isolating Digital Sectors in the Multiregional Input-Output Tables

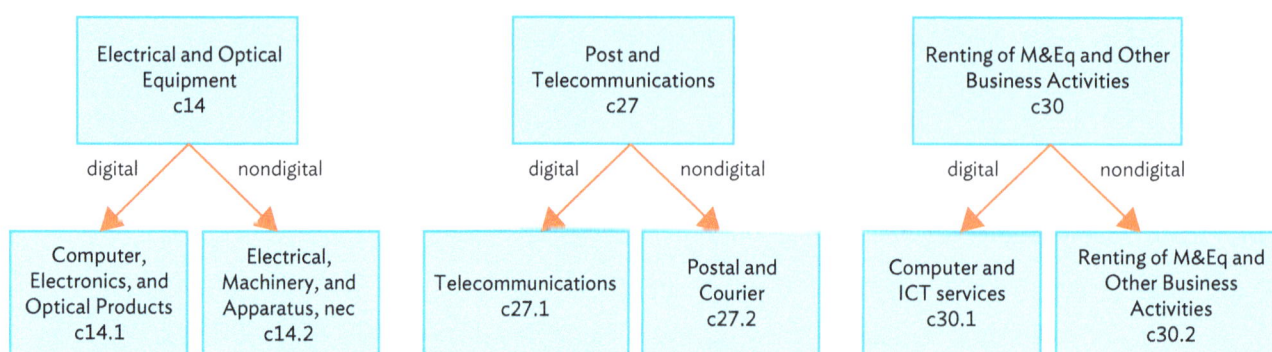

ICT = information and communication technology, M&Eq = machinery and equipment, nec = not elsewhere classified.
Source: Methodology of the Digital Economy Measurement Framework study team.

To isolate the digital component from c14, c27, and c30, column and row disaggregators were generated using multiple data sources. Column disaggregators gathered information from the WIOD and national SUTs to disaggregate the digital component in gross output, GVA, and imported inputs. The digital components for intermediate consumption and domestic inputs were calculated as a residual. Meanwhile, row disaggregators made use of bilateral exports and imports data by Broad Economic Categories classification[30] from the United Nations Commodity Trade (UN Comtrade) database (2017).[31] This information was converted into shares, which were subsequently used to split the rows and columns of the MRIO 63 × 35 tables into 63 × 38 tables. The authors then compared the resulting MRIOT values with the published NSO figures to ensure data consistency, and checked whether the table was balanced and/or symmetric.

---

[30] The broad economic categories fall under intermediate use, final consumption, or capital goods.

[31] The Comtrade database provides international trade data with variety in specification of product type, classification, year, and trade flow, among others (UN 2017).

Figure 4: The Multiregional Input-Output Disaggregation Process
(disaggregating the c2 sector)

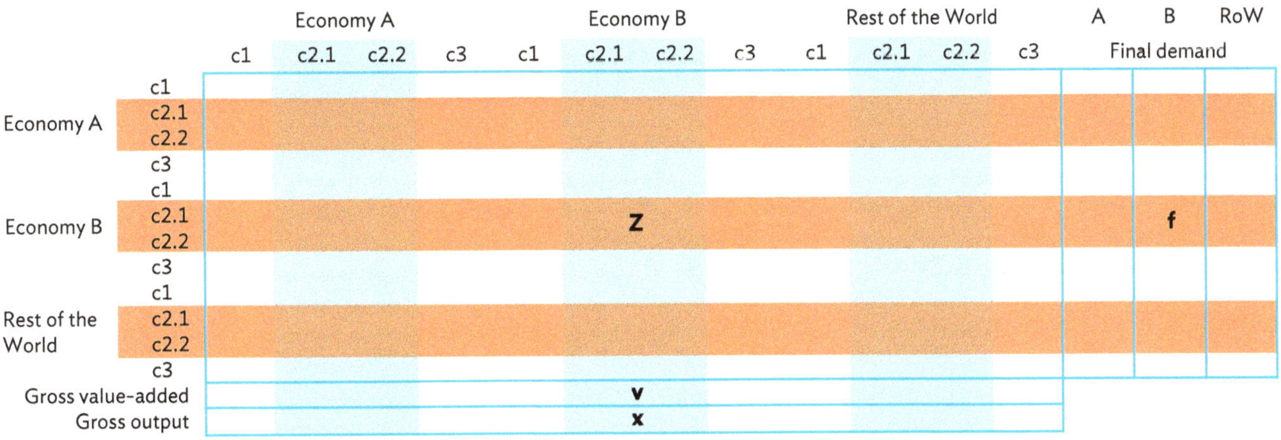

		Economy A				Economy B				Rest of the World				A	B	RoW
		c1	c2.1	c2.2	c3	c1	c2.1	c2.2	c3	c1	c2.1	c2.2	c3	Final demand		
Economy A	c1															
	c2.1															
	c2.2															
	c3															
Economy B	c1															
	c2.1						Z								f	
	c2.2															
	c3															
Rest of the World	c1															
	c2.1															
	c2.2															
	c3															
Gross value-added							v									
Gross output							x									

RoW = Rest of the World.
Note: **Z** = intermediate consumption matrix, **v** = value-added vector, **x** = gross output vector, and **f** = final demand matrix.
Source: Methodology of the Digital Economy Measurement Framework study team.

Limitations of the Framework

The framework presented in this study aims to be entirely data-driven and based on economically and statistically sound approaches. Data collection and analysis adopted a mainly top-down strategy, relying on secondary data published by official and credible sources. As such, a range of data limitations arise.

First, the accessibility to granular data is often limited. Therefore, to disaggregate high-level data, direct inquiries to the appropriate NSOs are necessary, further supplemented by subordinate methods to extrapolate the required data. Where there are available data, the format, structure, and statistical compilation methods used may vary widely by economy, thus requiring a significant amount of data cleaning and processing. Therefore, a constraint exists in ensuring consistency and accuracy of all data.

Second, exclusions from what is defined to be the digital economy may be interpreted as limitations in completeness. This framework considers the narrowest possible definition of digital products. For example, the entire value of an online sale of a nondigital commodity is not considered. Instead, only the value contribution of the digital products (or the digital industries producing these) involved in such a transaction is captured. A narrow definition is employed in order to avoid ambiguities that require some arbitrary judgment. As the scope of digital products is at the narrowest level, it excludes the digitally dependent economy, which comprises the value-added of the sectors that are critically dependent on digital sectors. Nonetheless, the measurement framework is flexible to accommodate the calculation of this.

Third, the measurement framework, which estimates the value of the digital economy as a percentage of national GDP, presents another area of limitation. Since economy-wide GDP excludes imports, estimates of the digital economy likewise exclude these. This might result in some underestimation of the digital economy, especially for economies with digital sectors that have relatively high imports such as Singapore; Malaysia; and Taipei,China, as shown in Figure 5.

Figure 5: Imports of Digital Sectors, 2019

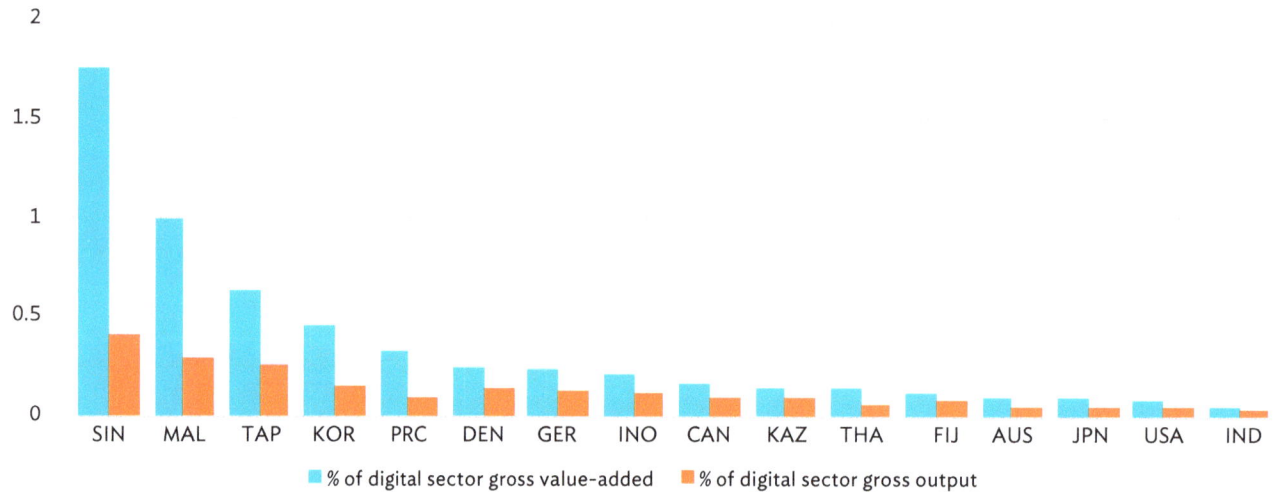

AUS = Australia; CAN = Canada; DEN = Denmark; FIJ = Fiji; GER = Germany; IND = India; INO = Indonesia; JPN = Japan; KAZ = Kazakhstan; KOR = Republic of Korea; MAL = Malaysia; PRC = People's Republic of China; SIN = Singapore; TAP = Taipei,China; THA = Thailand; USA = United States.
Note: Digital sectors include manufacture of computer, electronic and optical products; telecommunications; computer programming, consultancy, and related activities; and information service activities.
Source: Calculations of the Digital Economy Measurement Framework study team, using the 38-sector Asian Development Bank Multiregional Input-Output Tables 2019.

Therefore, economies that have high imports of digital products, as well as those with industries heavily reliant on core digital sectors, are likely to have small digital economy estimates relative to others. Supplementary analyses must be conducted for more expansive insights.

Finally, another limitation lies in the input-output model's assumption that production processes are fixed in the short-term or do not change within an accounting period. This ignores changes in production requirements that happen within 1 year, which is not an impossibility, given the fast-paced nature of digitalization and digital transformation.

Digital Economy Estimates

The framework methodology summarized in Equation 10 is applied to 16 economies: Australia; Canada; Denmark; Fiji; Germany; India; Indonesia; Japan; Kazakhstan; Malaysia; the PRC; the Republic of Korea (ROK); Singapore; Taipei,China; Thailand; and the US. These are economies belonging to eight regions and for which SUTs or IOTs are available: 11 of the 16 economies are within Asia and the Pacific (i.e., Central Asia, East Asia, South Asia, Southeast Asia, and the Pacific), since the authors of this study aimed to provide apt regional representation for the block. Estimations for additional OECD member economies located in Europe and North America, as well as Australia, were included to provide a more diverse set of economies and to enrich subsequent comparative analyses. A summary of the data sources by economy-year can be found in Table A4.4 (Appendix 4).

The preliminary estimates of $GDP_{digital}$ as a percentage of GDP, by economy, are summarized in Figure 6. It can be observed that the size of the digital economy as a percentage of GDP ranges from 2% to 9% for all economies examined.[32]

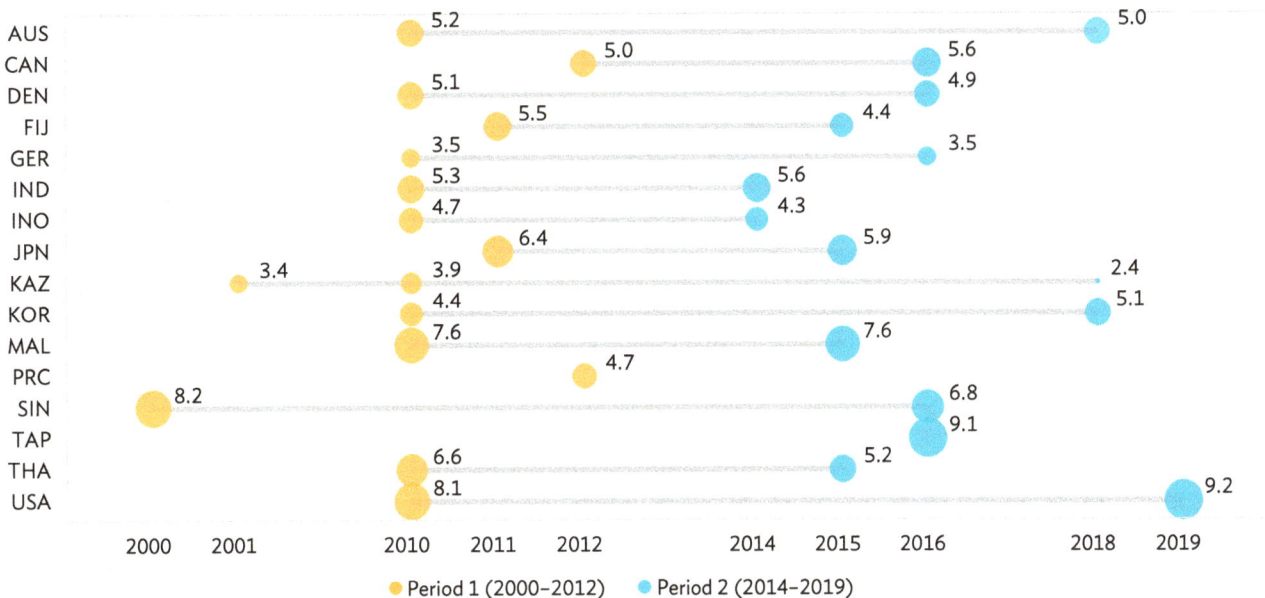

Figure 6: Digital Economy as a Proportion of Total Economy
(% of gross domestic product)

AUS = Australia; CAN = Canada; DEN = Denmark; FIJ = Fiji; GER = Germany; IND = India; INO = Indonesia; JPN = Japan; KAZ = Kazakhstan; KOR = Republic of Korea; MAL = Malaysia; PRC = People's Republic of China; SIN = Singapore; TAP = Taipei,China; THA = Thailand; USA = United States.
Note: Point size reflects size of the digital economy.
Source: Calculations of the Digital Economy Measurement Framework study team, using input-output and related data from various national statistics offices and international databases.

---

32 Using the 2019 MRIOTs, the global digital economy estimate is 8.8% of worldwide GDP.

A declining digital economy as a percentage of GDP is observed in all economies, except in Canada, India, the ROK, and the US (all of which increased), and Malaysia (which remained the same). While measures of the digital economy as a percentage of GDP generally declined, or posted only marginal increases through the years, this does not imply a declining impact on, and relevance to, the global economy. Because the SUTs and national IOTs examined in this report are stated in current prices, the measures derived do not allow for changes in prices of the core digital products. Looking at digital consumer products, there is no question that their prices have significantly declined over the past 2 decades. In the US alone—one of the world leaders in consumer electronics (Statista 2020)—the producer price index (PPI) of portable computers, laptops, tablets, and other single-user computers has fallen from a PPI of 804.9 in 2000 to a PPI of 15.6 in 2020 (USBLS 2021), a decline of approximately 98%.[33]

With the foregoing discussion in mind, estimates shown in Figure 6 cannot be analyzed temporally. Additionally, one must also take caution in applying spatial analyses across national economies because each faces varying prices of its core digital products. For instance, relatively more expensive digital products in an economy may bias the estimated size of its digital economy upwards. Therefore, when analyzing the size of the digital economy, one must apply caution and take note that the estimates do not allow for differences in prices over time and across economies. A temporal analysis of the digital economy will be tackled later in this study.

Contribution of the Digital Economy to Gross Domestic Product in Developing Economies

Because a complete time series of data is not available for all economies examined, the authors opted to divide the study range into two time periods (Period 1 and Period 2), based on the general development of the digital economy. Figure 7 and Figure 8 show a spatial representation of the size of the digital economy in absolute terms and as a percentage of GDP, respectively, for each comparative period. Figure 7 shows the size of the digital economy within each wider economy for a selected year in the period 2000 to 2012 (Period 1), when the digital economy was in its relative infancy. Figure 8 shows the size of the digital economy within each wider economy for a selected year from 2014 to 2019 (Period 2), when the size of the digital economy had been observed to grow at great speed.

Figure 7 shows that, in absolute terms in Period 1, the US (2010) overwhelmingly had the largest digital economy at approximately $1.2 trillion. This is followed by Japan (2011) and the PRC (2012) at $0.38 trillion and $0.37 trillion, respectively. In terms of share of GDP in Period 1, Singapore (2000) had the largest digital economy at 8.2%, followed closely by the US (2010) at 8.1%, then by Malaysia (2010) and Thailand (2010) at 7.6% and 6.6%, respectively.

---

[33] Base year is year 2007 prices.

Figure 7: Size of the Digital Economy, Period 1

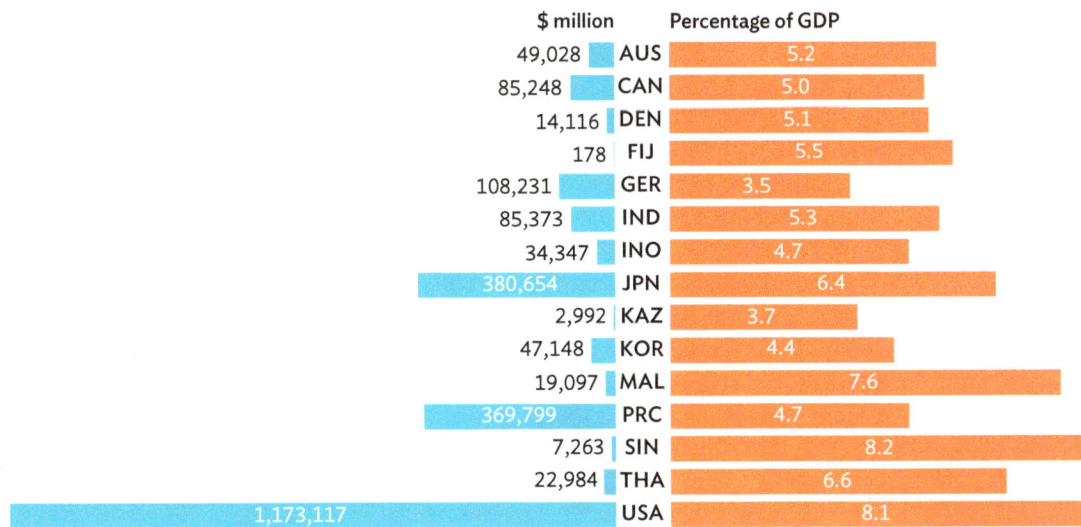

$ million		Percentage of GDP
49,028	AUS	5.2
85,248	CAN	5.0
14,116	DEN	5.1
178	FIJ	5.5
108,231	GER	3.5
85,373	IND	5.3
34,347	INO	4.7
380,654	JPN	6.4
2,992	KAZ	3.7
47,148	KOR	4.4
19,097	MAL	7.6
369,799	PRC	4.7
7,263	SIN	8.2
22,984	THA	6.6
1,173,117	USA	8.1

$ = United States dollars; AUS = Australia; CAN = Canada; DEN = Denmark; FIJ = Fiji; GDP = gross domestic product; GER = Germany; IND = India; INO = Indonesia; JPN = Japan; KAZ = Kazakhstan; KOR = Republic of Korea; MAL = Malaysia; PRC = People's Republic of China; SIN = Singapore; THA = Thailand; USA = United States.
Notes: Period 1 = 2007 to 2012. Period 1 for AUS, 2010; CAN, 2012; DEN, 2010; FIJ, 2011; GER, 2010; IND, 2010; INO, 2010; JPN, 2011; KAZ, 2001, 2010; KOR, 2010; MAL, 2010; PRC, 2012; SIN, 2000, THA, 2010; and USA, 2010. The average is presented in economies for which calculations include multiple years.
Source: Calculations of the Digital Economy Measurement Framework study team, using input-output and related data from various national statistics offices and international databases.

Figure 8: Size of the Digital Economy, Period 2

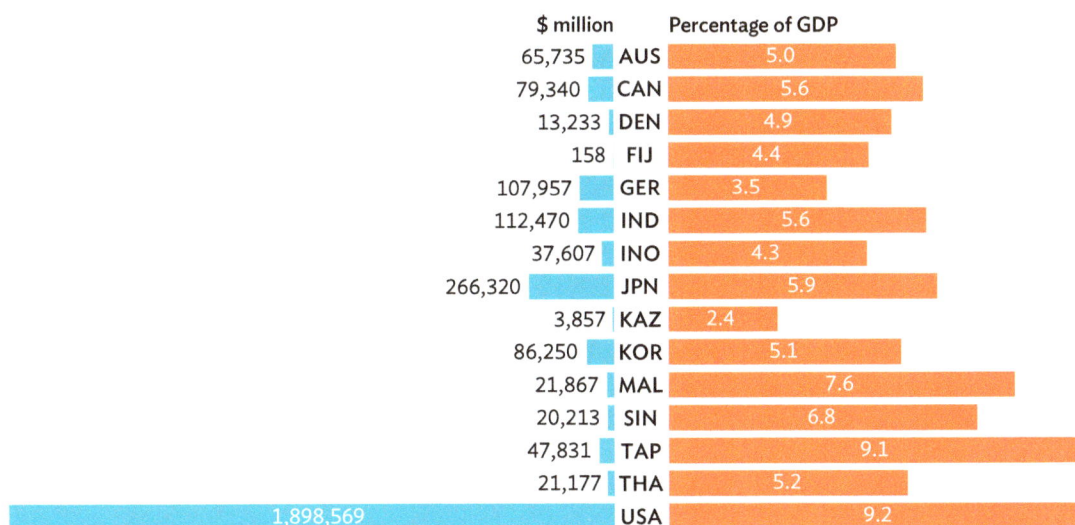

$ million		Percentage of GDP
65,735	AUS	5.0
79,340	CAN	5.6
13,233	DEN	4.9
158	FIJ	4.4
107,957	GER	3.5
112,470	IND	5.6
37,607	INO	4.3
266,320	JPN	5.9
3,857	KAZ	2.4
86,250	KOR	5.1
21,867	MAL	7.6
20,213	SIN	6.8
47,831	TAP	9.1
21,177	THA	5.2
1,898,569	USA	9.2

$ = United States dollars; AUS = Australia; CAN = Canada; DEN = Denmark; FIJ = Fiji; GDP = gross domestic product; GER = Germany; IND = India; INO = Indonesia; JPN = Japan; KAZ = Kazakhstan; KOR = Republic of Korea; MAL = Malaysia; SIN = Singapore; TAP = Taipei,China; THA = Thailand; USA = United States.
Notes: Period 2 = 2014 to 2019. Period 2 for AUS, 2018; CAN, 2016; DEN, 2016; FIJ, 2015; GER, 2016; IND, 2014; INO, 2014; JPN, 2018; KAZ, 2018; KOR, 2018; MAL, 2015; SIN, 2015; TAP, 2016; THA, 2015; and USA, 2019. The average is presented in economies for which calculations include multiple years.
Source: Calculations of the Digital Economy Measurement Framework study team, using input-output and related data from various national statistics offices and international databases.

Figure 8 shows that the US (2019) digital economy was still largest in absolute terms in Period 2, at approximately $1.9 trillion. Japan (2015) and India (2014) followed at $0.27 trillion and $0.11 trillion, respectively.[34] In percentage of GDP terms, digital economy shares in Period 2 were highest in the US (2019) at 9.2%; Taipei,China (2016) at 9.1%; and Malaysia (2015) at 7.6%.

In both periods, it is apparent that estimates of the digital economy as a percentage of GDP is in the upper range for several developing economies, such as Fiji (5.5% and 4.4%), India (5.3% and 5.6%), Malaysia (7.6% for both periods), and Thailand (6.6% and 5.2%). The relatively high shares of the digital economy to GDP in these economies signify aggressive contributions of core digital products and industries to each economy's output.

Declining Prices and Increasing Productivity of Core Digital Products

As mentioned, the share of the digital economy to GDP fell for most economies over time. In absolute US dollar terms, Figures 7 and 8 also show either a decline in digital economy estimates or a marginal increase through the years examined. Because digital economy estimates are possibly affected by dollar exchange rates per economy, the study authors stated digital economy estimates in local currency units (LCU) and calculated the corresponding compound annual growth rate (CAGR). The CAGR assumes that digital GDP increases at a constant rate each year.[35] Two types of CAGR per economy are presented in Figure 9. One is the CAGR of digital GDP in absolute LCU terms and the other is digital GDP as a percentage of GDP in LCU.

In absolute LCU terms, all economies except Thailand exhibited a positive CAGR, with several economies' digital GDP growing more exceptionally than others. India, Indonesia, Kazakhstan, Malaysia, and the ROK all registered digital GDP CAGR of more than 6%. The CAGR of other economies such as Australia, Canada, Denmark, Fiji, Germany, Japan, Singapore, and the US posted more modest increases, ranging between 1% and 6% CAGR. Observably, it is developing economies (except the ROK) that had high digital GDP growth, and this is possibly correlated to the digital economy's rapidly growing output as these economies have a lower GDP base.

The CAGR of digital GDP as a percentage of GDP in LCU shows the annual growth as a more normalized measure of digital GDP across economies. In sharp contrast with the CAGR in absolute terms, most economies posted negative growth rates.

---

[34] Because of limitations in data availability, the authors of this study were not able to obtain digital economy estimates for Taipei,China in Period 1 or for the PRC in Period 2.

[35] The CAGR is calculated as $CAGR = \left(\frac{GDP_{Digital^T}}{GDP_{Digital^0}} \right)^{\frac{1}{n}} - 1$, where $GDP_{Digital^T}$ is the latest year's estimation of digital GDP, $GDP_{Digital^0}$ is the first year's estimation of digital GDP, and n is the number of years in between.

Figure 9: Compound Annual Growth Rates of the Digital Economy

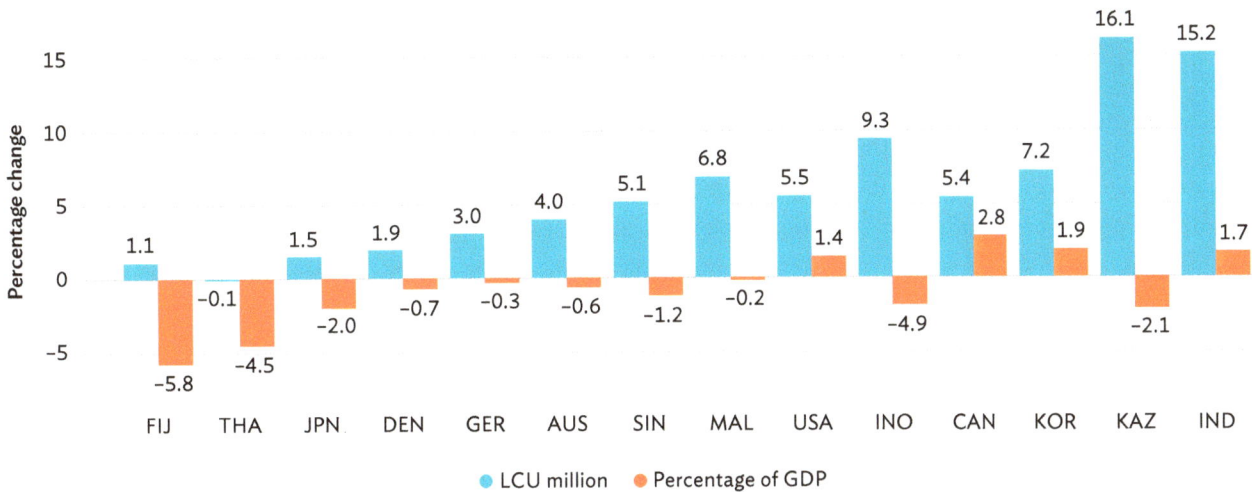

AUS = Australia; CAN = Canada; DEN = Denmark; FIJ = Fiji; GDP = gross domestic product; GER = Germany; IND = India; INO = Indonesia; JPN = Japan; KAZ = Kazakhstan; KOR = Republic of Korea; LCU = local currency unit; MAL = Malaysia; SIN = Singapore; THA = Thailand; USA = United States.

Note: The first and latest years used to calculate the compound annual growth rate are: AUS, 2010, 2018; CAN, 2012, 2016; DEN, 2010, 2016; FIJ, 2011, 2015; GER, 2010, 2016; IND, 2010, 2014; INO, 2010, 2014; JPN, 2011, 2015; KAZ, 2001, 2018; KOR, 2010, 2018; MAL, 2010, 2015; SIN, 2000, 2016; THA, 2010, 2015; USA, 2010, 2019.

Source: Calculations of the Digital Economy Measurement Framework study team, using input-output and related data from various national statistics offices and international databases.

Only Canada, India, the ROK, and the US reported a positive CAGR. Fiji's CAGR of the normalized measure contracted at a significantly higher rate than the rest, dropping by 5.8% annually from 2011 to 2015 (a thorough discussion is provided in the next section, approaching the analysis by component of the digital GDP equation). In contrast, Canada experienced the highest annual growth rate at 2.8% from 2012 to 2016. Kazakhstan is an interesting case, as it posted the greatest CAGR in absolute terms (16.1%), but reported a –2.1% CAGR in percentage of GDP terms. This suggests that economy-wide GDP in Kazakhstan grew at a faster rate (18.7%) than digital GDP. However, this does not automatically imply that digital GDP is declining in importance as a contributor to the output of Kazakhstan (or any other economy).

One reason why the GDP share of the digital economy is declining, or is increasing at a slower rate, is because of the falling prices of core digital products. Another reason is the increasing productivity of digital products over time. For example, the processing capacity of a single laptop computer in 2020 might be comparable to the capacity of multiple computers in 2000. Thus, the digital economy in more recent years is characterized by cheaper digital products that can process information more efficiently, contributing to its declining share in economy-wide GDP. In addition, the transition of business models toward offering goods-as-services in recent years is further exacerbating this phenomenon. This is particularly apparent in digital products, such as software, conventionally capitalized but now increasingly sold as services (e.g., cloud computing services), and subsequently recorded as intermediate consumption in national accounts. This leads to a lower value-added for corresponding industries (OECD 2019).

Another noteworthy case is the US, which, despite its sizeable GDP, still registered a positive CAGR for both absolute (5.5%) and normalized terms (1.4%).[36] This is not surprising as the US has highest concentration of digital platform companies, representing about 70% of platforms' market capitalization worldwide (UNCTAD 2019a). In addition, majority of the top visited websites globally are hosted in the US (Mueller and Grindal 2018). The remarkable growth of few large technology firms and widespread use of social media and content has raised considerable policy interest in monitoring digital platforms' economic activity in recent years (Box 2).

Box 2: Does Gross Domestic Product Capture "Free" Digital Media?

Internet use, which began in the early 2000s as a way to access emails and information, has now evolved into more sophisticated consumption, including social networking, media, and gaming (OECD 2020). The utility derived from these services is potentially far higher compared to their more expensive analog predecessors. However, peculiar to this phenomenon is that most of what we do online is generally assumed to be free. Social media, entertainment videos, maps, news, and other types of information are usually accessible at no cost to end users. Yet, choice experiments indicate that there is a massive economic value to digital media consumed by end users at "zero cost," raising the question as to whether this value is captured at all in gross domestic product (GDP) measurements (Brynjolfsson and Collis 2019).

This discovery did not bode well for GDP, especially at a time when productivity levels were slowing at the peak of the digital wave (Byrnjolfsson, Collis, and Eggers 2019; Brynjolfsson and Steffenson McElerhan 2017; Corrado et al. 2016). These concerns prompted a review of statistical concepts and practices, such as quality adjustments in deflators and gaps in measuring online platform activities (IMF 2018). While this issue remains open, findings suggest that mismeasurement alone does not explain the productivity slowdown (Ahmad and Schreyer 2016; Bryne, Fernald, and Reinsdorf 2016; Ahmad, Ribarsky, and Reinsdorf 2017); and, when measured, the "free" digital component of the economy does little to pull up measures of productivity (Nakamura, Samuels, and Soloveichik 2016; IMF 2018).

Furthermore, a closer review suggests that GDP does in fact capture "free" digital platform services to the extent that they generate revenues. For example, seven leading platform companies—Alibaba, Alphabet, Amazon, Apple, Facebook, Microsoft, and Tencent— earned about $1.2 trillion in 2020 (or roughly 28% of the global digital platform market). To operate, the digital services of these firms are financed by a paying side of the platform, so that the subsidized side of the platform can continue to enjoy content at no direct cost (Reinsdorf 2020; Mitchell 2020; Ahmad and Ribarsky 2018; Ravets 2016). This model is similar to how digital platforms' analog counterparts, such as television and radio, are financed by advertising and are hence recorded in economic accounts (Ahmad and Schreyer 2016; Nguyen and Paczos 2020; Li, Nirei, and Yamana 2018; ISWGNA 2020; Mitchell 2020).

To illustrate the chain of transactions, it is useful to form a three-party set up: the user, platform, and advertiser. First, the digital platform charges advertisers for its services at a rate high enough to sustain its operations. This is recorded as output on the resource side of the economy (i.e., the platform's revenues), and intermediate consumption on the use side (i.e., advertising expense of the firm). Second, firms, in their sale of goods or services, would recoup this advertising cost in the form of higher prices to final consumers. This sale is recorded as an output of the selling firm, which correspondingly shows up as final household consumption. In effect, "free" services financed by advertising are implicitly carried over to purchases of advertised products by households themselves.

continued on next page.

---

[36] In 2012, the GDP of the US was 96% higher than that of the PRC, the next largest economy among those examined in this report.

Box 2 *continued.*

Other things being equal, overall GDP levels are not understated by the amount of "free" digital services. Following the current approach under the System of National Accounts, an analysis of company data of the seven largest platforms shows gross value-added of about $519 billion in 2020 or about 0.6% of global GDP in 2020.[a] Extrapolating the results, the global digital platform industry is estimated to have contributed $1.84 trillion worth of gross value-added, or 2.2% of world GDP in 2020.[b] So long as digital platforms are covered by business surveys, their activity is highly likely to appear in these figures. Identifying these transactions separately is not yet widespread practice, but progress towards a framework for Digital Economy Satellite Accounts indicates a demand to monitor platforms' economic activities moving forward.

[a] Similar estimate for 2016 brings these digital platforms' share to 0.31% of world GDP. This figure is higher than the business value-based share of 0.02% estimated by Ahmad, Ribarsky, and Reinsdorf (2017). It should be noted however that latter estimates do not yet incorporate data from Alibaba, Amazon, Apple, Microsoft, and Tencent.

[b] For perspective, 8.5% of global GDP constitutes industries in which digital platforms are likely to operate, such as electronic shopping and mail-order houses (NAICS 454110); data processing, hosting, and related services (518210); prepackaged software and software publishing (511210); and all other information services (519190). A narrower band of information service industries (ISIC 4 section J) represented 4.2% of global GDP in 2014 (Timmer et al. 2015).

References:
N. Ahmad and P. Schreyer. 2016. Measuring GDP in a Digitalised Economy. *OECD Statistics Working Papers*. No. 7.
N. Ahmad, J. Ribarsky and M. Reinsdorf. 2017. Can Potential Mismeasurement of the Digital Economy Explain the Post-Crisis Slowdown in GDP and Productivity Growth? *OECD Statistics Working Papers*. https://doi.org/10.1787/18152031.
D. Byrne, J. Fernald, and M. Reinsdorf. 2016. Does the United States have a Productivity Slowdown or a Measurement Problem? *Brookings Paper on Economic Activity*. Spring 2016. http://www.brookings.edu/about/projects/bpea/papers/2016/byrne-et-al-productivity-measurement.
E. Brynjolfsson and A. Collis. 2019. November. How Should We Measure the Digital Economy? *Harvard Business Review*. November–December. https://hbr.org/2019/11/how-should-we-measure-the-digital-economy.
E. Byrnjolfsson, A. Collis, and F. Eggers. 2019. Using Massive Online Choice Experiments to Measure Changes in Well-Being. *Proceedings of the National Academy of Sciences*. 116. pp. 7250–7255.
C. Corrado, J. Haskel, C. Jona-Lasinio, and M. Iommi. 2016. Intangible Investment in the EU and US Before and Since the Great Recession and its Contribution to Productivity Growth. *European Investment Bank Working Papers*, 8.
International Monetary Fund (IMF). 2018. *Measuring the Digital Economy*. IMF Policy Papers: Washington, D.C. https://www.imf.org/en/Publications/Policy-Papers/Issues/2018/04/03/022818-measuring-the-digital-economy.
Inter-Secretariat of Working Group on National Accounts (ISWGNA). 2020. Recording and Measuring Data in the System of National Accounts. 14th Meeting of the Advisory Expert Group on National Accounts.
W.C.Y. Li, M. Nirei, and K. Yamana. 2018. Value of Data: There's No Such Thing as a Free Lunch in the Digital Economy. *Sixth IMF Statistical Forum*. November 8. Washington, D.C.: International Monetary Fund.
J. Mitchell. 2020. *Guidelines for Supply-Use tables for the Digital Economy*. OECD Informal Advisory Group on Measuring GDP in a Digitalised Economy.
L. Nakamura, J. Samuels, and R. Soloveichik. 2016. Valuing Free Media in GDP: An Experimental Approach. *BEA Working Papers*. 0133. Bureau of Economic Analysis. https://ideas.repec.org/p/bea/wpaper/0133.html.
Organisation for Economic Cooperation and Development (OECD). 2020. ICT Access and Usage by Households and Individuals. https://stats.oecd.org/Index.aspx?DataSetCode=ICT_HH2 (accessed April 2021).
C. Ravets. 2016, April. *The Internet Economy*. Presented at the 10th Meeting of the Advisory Expert Group on National Accounts. https://unstats.un.org/unsd/nationalaccount/aeg/2016/4_Internet_Economy.pdf.
M. Reinsdorf. 2020. *Status Report on the Work of the Subgroup on the Treatment of Free Products*. United Nations Economic Commission for Europe. October 5. https://unece.org/statistics/events/webinars-group-experts-national-accounts.

The Digital Economy as a Supplier and User of Goods and Services

Drivers of the digital economy can more richly be analyzed in terms of forward and backward linkages. Figure 10 shows the disaggregation of digital economy GDP for the 16 studied economies from 2010 to 2019, assessed across the four terms that make up the core digital economy equation, Equation 10. Respectively, these terms represent the following in relation to an economy's digital sector: (i) its backward linkages, (ii) its forward linkages, (iii) the double-counted term (i.e., the digital sector's value-added contribution to its own final products), and (iv) the nondigital products it capitalizes.

Figure 10: Disaggregation of the Digital Economy by Terms of Equation 10

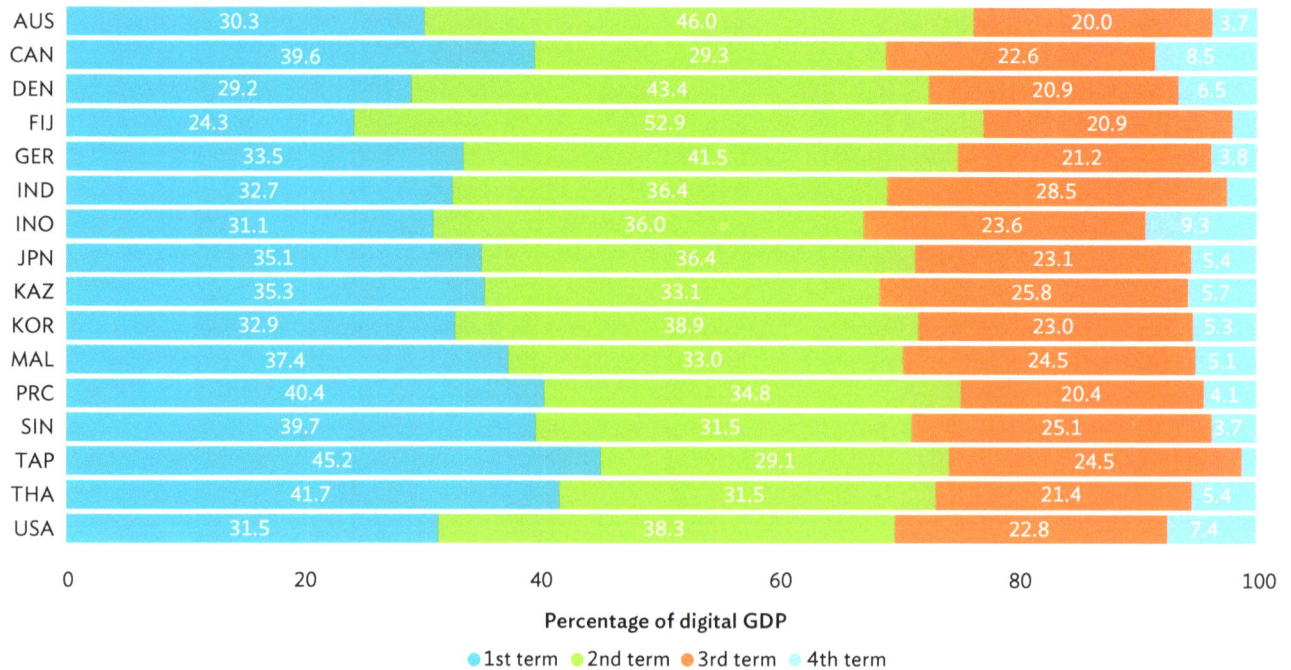

	1st term	2nd term	3rd term	4th term
AUS	30.3	46.0	20.0	3.7
CAN	39.6	29.3	22.6	8.5
DEN	29.2	43.4	20.9	6.5
FIJ	24.3	52.9	20.9	
GER	33.5	41.5	21.2	3.8
IND	32.7	36.4	28.5	
INO	31.1	36.0	23.6	9.3
JPN	35.1	36.4	23.1	5.4
KAZ	35.3	33.1	25.8	5.7
KOR	32.9	38.9	23.0	5.3
MAL	37.4	33.0	24.5	5.1
PRC	40.4	34.8	20.4	4.1
SIN	39.7	31.5	25.1	3.7
TAP	45.2	29.1	24.5	
THA	41.7	31.5	21.4	5.4
USA	31.5	38.3	22.8	7.4

Percentage of digital GDP

● 1st term ● 2nd term ● 3rd term ● 4th term

AUS = Australia; CAN = Canada; DEN = Denmark; FIJ = Fiji; GDP = gross domestic product; GER = Germany; IND = India; INO = Indonesia; JPN = Japan; KAZ = Kazakhstan; KOR = Republic of Korea; MAL = Malaysia; PRC = People's Republic of China; SIN = Singapore; TAP = Taipei,China; THA = Thailand; USA = United States.
Notes: Years included are AUS 2010, 2018; CAN, 2012, 2016; DEN, 2010, 2016; FIJ, 2011, 2015; GER, 2010, 2016; IND, 2010, 2014; INO, 2010, 2014; JPN, 2011, 2015; KAZ, 2010, 2018; KOR, 2010, 2018; MAL, 2010, 2015; PRC, 2012; SIN, 2016; TAP, 2016; THA, 2010, 2015; USA, 2010, 2019. Equation 10 = $GDP_{digital} = \mathbf{i^T\hat{v}B\hat{y}\varepsilon_1} + \mathbf{i^T}(\mathbf{\hat{v}B\hat{y}})^T\mathbf{\varepsilon_1} - [diag(\mathbf{\hat{v}B\hat{y}})]^T\mathbf{\varepsilon_1} + (\mathbf{i} - \mathbf{\varepsilon_1})^T\mathbf{\hat{v}B\hat{y}\hat{r}\varepsilon_2}$. 1st term = backward linkage of the digital sector, 2nd term = forward linkage of the digital sector, 3rd term = double-counted term or the digital sector's value-added contribution to its own final goods, 4th term = the nondigital products capitalized by the digital sector. When the 2nd term is greater than the 1st term, the digital economy takes a supply-side role. When the 1st term is greater than 2nd term, the digital economy takes a demand-side role. The average is presented in economies for which calculations include multiple years.
Source: Calculations of the Digital Economy Measurement Framework study team, using input-output and related data from various national statistics offices and international databases.

As Figure 10 shows, a major proportion of the digital GDP of Australia, Denmark, Fiji, and Germany can be attributed to forward linkages (second term—green bars), accounting for more than 40% of each economy's digital GDP. This means that, in these economies, the digital sector more prominently acts as a supplier of value-added to domestic nondigital sectors. For example, Germany has developed a comparative advantage in global ICT services, supplying key service inputs, such as IoT components, to automotive industries (UNCTAD 2019; MacDougall 2018). Comparing these economies with Taipei,China; Thailand; and the PRC, the latter economies have a greater fraction (above 40%) of their digital GDP contributed by backward linkages (first term—dark blue bars). In these economies, the digital sector is more notably a user of value-added from domestic nondigital sectors. This is attributable to the presence of major computer brands in these economies, which naturally require various parts and components from different suppliers in the production chain.

Across all individual economies, the double-counted term or the contribution of the digital sector to itself (third term—orange bars) comprises around 20% to 29% of the digital GDP of all economies. This suggests that the reliance of the aggregate digital sector on itself is of nearly equal weight across all economies examined. Dependence on nondigital gross fixed capital formation or GFCF (fourth term—light blue bars) appears to be the smallest share for all economies' digital GDP, with the largest shares observed for Indonesia at 9.3% and Canada at 8.5%.

The earlier calculations of the CAGR of the whole digital economy are augmented by the CAGR of the disaggregated digital GDP. Doing so enables one to identify which specific component of digital GDP drove down the CAGR of the whole digital economy as a percentage of economy-wide GDP.

Figure 11 shows the CAGR of each term comprising digital GDP expressed as a percentage of economy-wide GDP. The chart reveals that the largest changes were dealt by the GFCF from nondigital sectors (fourth term—light blue bars) in a majority of the studied economies. Fiji's fourth term changed by –44.2% annually (and –42.5% when expressed in local currency value), indicating that its purchase of nondigital GFCF decreases at a rate significantly higher than any other economy's. This can be explained by a large decrease in construction GFCF purchased by digital industries,

Figure 11: Compound Annual Growth Rates of Normalized Digital Gross Domestic Product
(disaggregated by term)

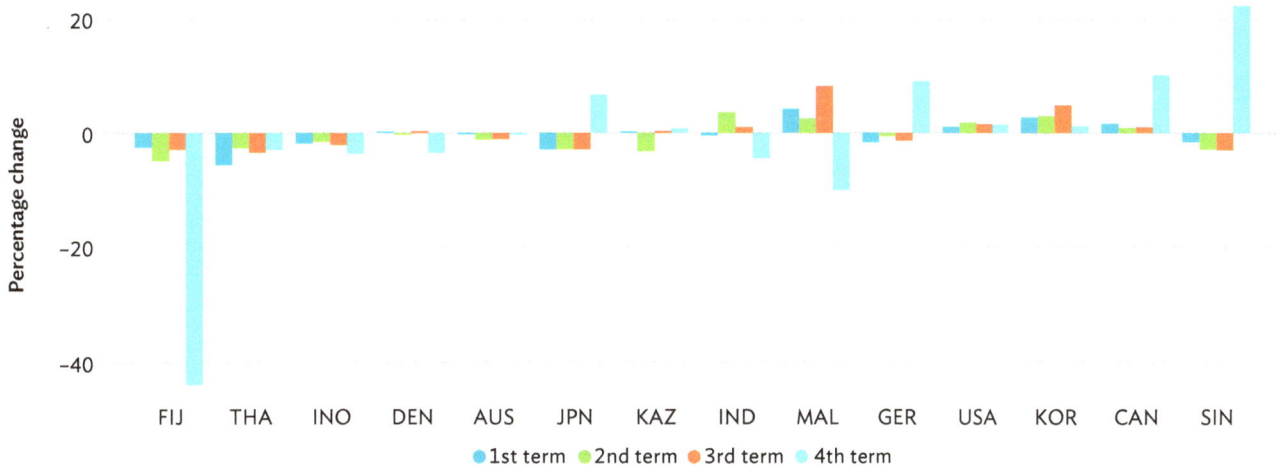

AUS = Australia; CAN = Canada; DEN = Denmark; FIJ = Fiji; GER = Germany; IND = India; INO = Indonesia; JPN = Japan; KAZ = Kazakhstan; KOR = Republic of Korea; MAL = Malaysia; SIN = Singapore; THA = Thailand; USA = United States.
Notes: Normalized digital gross domestic product (GDP) = digital GDP as a percentage of economy-wide GDP. First and latest years used to calculate compound annual growth rates are AUS, 2010, 2018; CAN, 2012, 2016; DEN, 2010, 2016; FIJ, 2011, 2015; GER, 2010, 2016; IND, 2010, 2014; INO, 2010, 2014; JPN, 2011, 2015; KAZ, 2001, 2018; KOR, 2010, 2018; MAL, 2010, 2015; SIN, 2000, 2016; THA, 2010, 2015; USA, 2010, 2019. 1st term = backward linkage of the digital sector, 2nd term = forward linkage of the digital sector, 3rd term = double-counted term or the digital sector's value-added contribution to its own final goods, 4th term = the nondigital products capitalized by the digital sector.
Source: Calculations of the Digital Economy Measurement Framework study team, using input-output and related data from various national statistics offices and international databases.

Box 3: Estimation of Denmark's Digital Economy over 20 Years

Only a few of the economies examined in this study make publicly available a complete time series of input-output data. One of these economies is Denmark. Available input-output tables, with consistent structure and sufficiently detailed data, from the Denmark Statistics website span from 1966 until 2016. (Data to disaggregate the digital portion of information service activities were not explicit and, thus, were not considered.) With the assumption that significant development of digital technology and innovation began at some point in the 1990s, the proposed framework to measure the digital economy was applied to the period 1996–2016 to produce a time series of Denmark's digital gross domestic product (GDP) for 20 years.

The resulting estimates show steady growth of Denmark's digital economy as a percentage of GDP from 1996 to 2001, rising from 3.25% to 4.82%. In subsequent years, the estimates display more volatility, reaching a peak of 5.1%, after which digital GDP posted a share to GDP ranging between 4.4% and 4.6% for the next 6 years. Interestingly, economy-wide GDP in absolute terms was relatively constant from 1996 to 2001, indicating that the early years of digital expansion contributed immensely to economy-wide GDP. Only after 2001 did GDP rise, up until the years leading to the global financial crisis. Beyond 2008, growth of GDP in absolute terms was less robust, as seen by alternating years of contraction and expansion.

Denmark's Economy-wide Gross Domestic Product versus Digital Gross Domestic Product

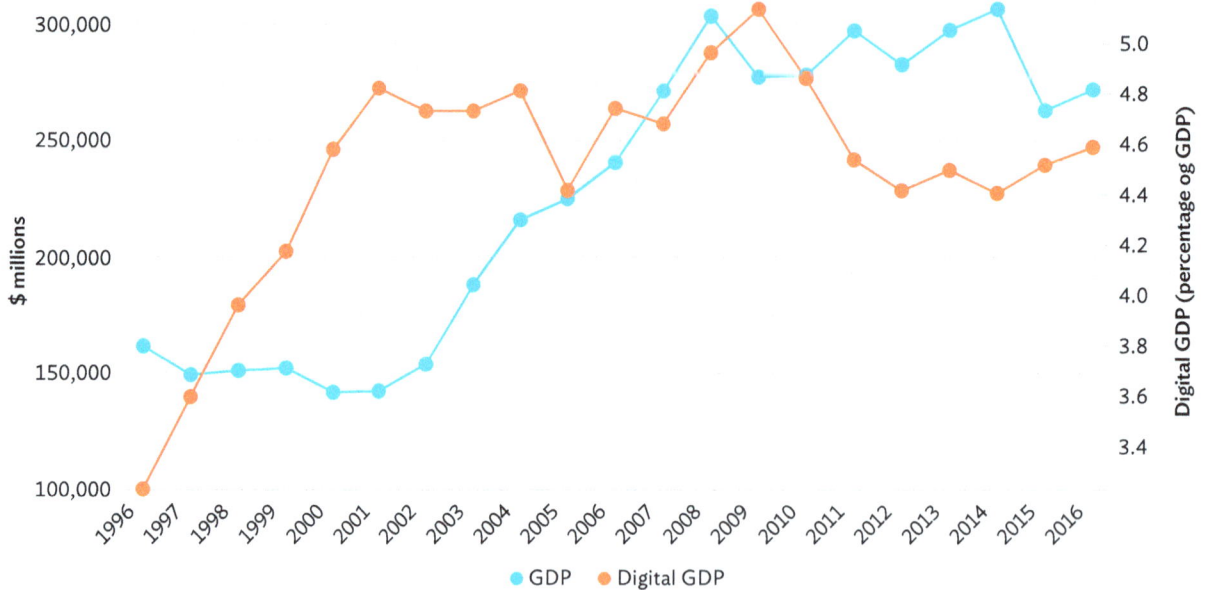

GDP = gross domestic product.
Note: Digital GDP for this time-series was calculated excluding the digital portion of Denmark's information service activities industry in order to keep the application consistent for all years, as disaggregated data prior to 2010 are lacking. The data used are in current prices.
Source: Calculations of the Digital Economy Measurement Framework study team, using data from Statistics Denmark.

Structurally, Denmark's digital GDP can be mostly attributed to its forward linkages, as illustrated below, indicating the strong role of Denmark's digital sectors as a supplier of value-added to nondigital sectors. Over the 20 years, the trends of the first to third terms follow that of the economy-wide GDP: the high growth rates during the first decade, peaking at around 2009 to 2010, then reaching a plateau toward the latter years. The fourth term is expectedly more volatile compared to other terms. It is clear, however, that after the global financial crisis, there is a declining dependence of the digital economy on nondigital gross fixed capital formation.

continued on next page.

Box 3 *continued.*

Structure of Denmark's Digital Gross Domestic Product by Term

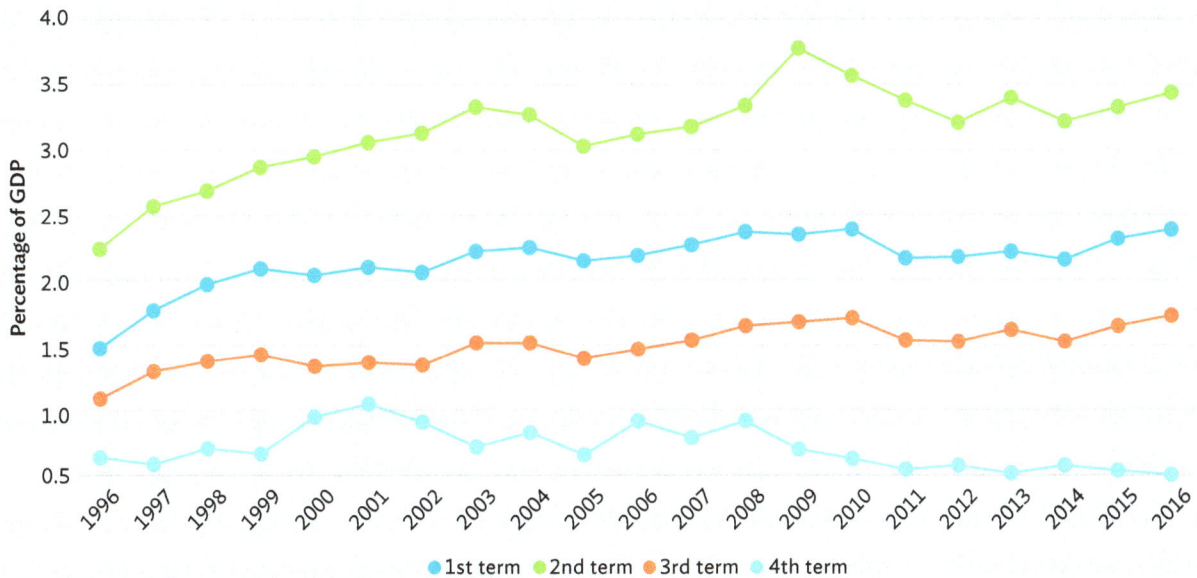

GDP = gross domestic product.
1st term = backward linkage of the digital sector, 2nd term = forward linkage of the digital sector, 3rd term = double-counted term or the digital sector's value-added contribution to its own final goods, 4th term = the nondigital products capitalized by the digital sector.
Note: Digital GDP for this time-series was calculated excluding the digital portion of Denmark's information service activities industry in order to keep the application consistent for all years, as disaggregated data prior to 2010 are lacking. The data used are in current prices.
Source: Calculations of the Digital Economy Measurement Framework study team, using data from Statistics Denmark.

FJ\$326,330 in 2015 compared to FJ\$22,486,237 in 2011 (FBS 2014, 2018).[37] The inverse is true for economies such as Canada, Germany, and Singapore, for which nondigital GFCF is increasingly purchased by digital industries. In the case of Canada, telephone apparatus had the biggest growth as a percentage of final demand from 2012 to 2016, increasing by 10.5 percentage points.

Varying Concentration of the Digital Economy across Digital Subsectors

The aggregate digital sector is comprised of subsectors with varying characteristics. It is therefore vital to characterize the concentration of the digital economy to contextualize why the digital sector of economies act mainly as a supplier of value-added, while others are primarily a user of value-added.

---

[37] GFCF across time periods tends to be volatile due to its long-use nature, such that large investments made in one year may serve for multiple years thereafter. Therefore, declining shares of nondigital capital purchases do not necessarily indicate declining dependence on them. In the case of Fiji, much larger investments were made in digital hardware after 2011 (FBS 2014, 2018), which would not be captured in the 4th term.

Figure 12 presents a disaggregation of the digital sector (in percentage of GDP terms) by economy. It can be seen that each economy's digital sector is concentrated in different subsectors. In Singapore; Taipei,China; and Thailand, hardware comprises a sizable share of the respective digital economy. The size of Taipei,China's hardware industry—of which approximately 80% is computer production—is unsurprising given that the economy supplies 90% of all laptops sold worldwide (Sui 2013). This provides context as to why Taipei,China's digital economy is more prominently a user of value-added, as the hardware subsector is relatively downstream and closer to final consumption. The digital economies of Singapore and Thailand are likewise characterized as users of the value-added of nondigital sectors. Meanwhile, specialized and support services are relatively large contributors in Denmark and India. This explains why the digital economies of both Denmark and India more prominently take a supply-side role, where their forward linkage is greater than their backward linkage.

Software publishing and web publishing take a more subsidiary portion of the digital economy in most economies. However, software publishing is generally greater in more advanced economies, such as Germany, Japan, the ROK, and the US. Moreover, it is notably the largest digital subsector for the ROK. Based on data published by Orbis, in 2018, the top software companies in the ROK produced financial, automotive, and mobile gaming software (Bureau van Dijk 2018). Germany, Japan, the ROK, and the US are shown to take more of a demand-side role, as users of nondigital sectors' value-added.

Figure 12: Disaggregation of the Digital Economy by Digital Subsector

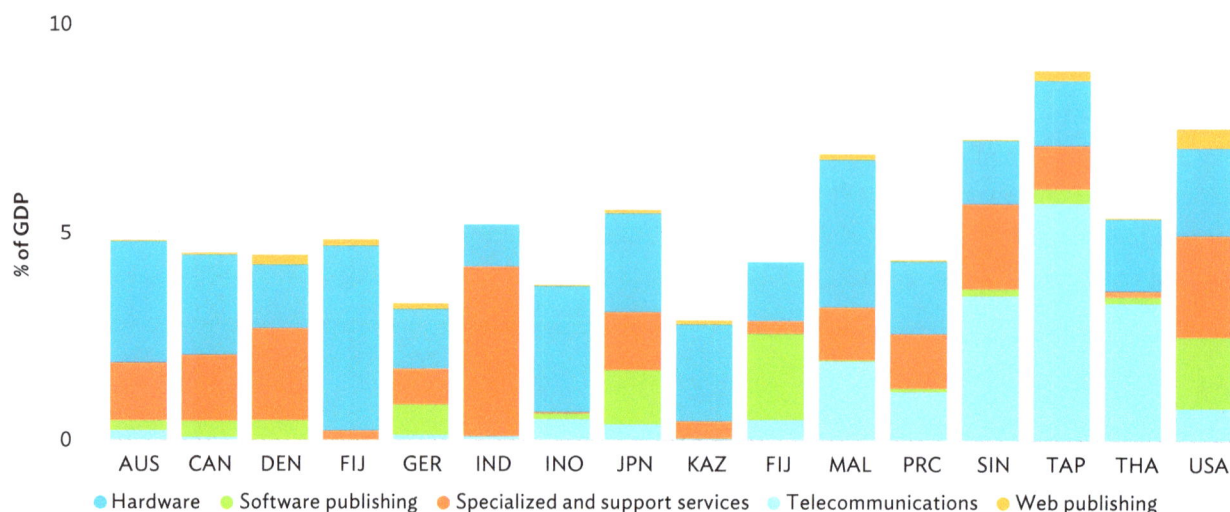

AUS = Australia; CAN = Canada; DEN = Denmark; FIJ = Fiji; GER = Germany; IND = India; INO = Indonesia; JPN = Japan; KAZ = Kazakhstan; KOR = Republic of Korea; MAL = Malaysia; PRC = People's Republic of China; SIN = Singapore; TAP = Taipei,China; THA = Thailand; USA = United States.
Notes: Years included are AUS, 2010, 2018; CAN, 2012, 2016; DEN, 2010, 2016; FIJ, 2011, 2015; GER, 2010, 2016; IND, 2010, 2014; INO, 2010, 2014; JPN, 2011, 2015; KAZ, 2001, 2010, 2018; KOR, 2010, 2018; MAL, 2010, 2015; PRC, 2012; SIN, 2000, 2016; TAP, 2016; THA, 2010, 2015; USA, 2010, 2019. The average is presented in economies for which calculations include multiple years.
Source: Calculations of the Digital Economy Measurement Framework study team, using input-output and related data from various national statistics offices and international databases.

In Fiji, Indonesia, and Kazakhstan, telecommunications account for the overwhelmingly majority of the digital economy. A similar case, but to a lesser extent, is observed in Australia, Canada, and Malaysia, where telecommunications account for a vast share of each economy's respective digital GDP. It is not clear whether a digital sector concentrated in telecommunications takes more of a supply-side or a demand-side role. Some are mainly suppliers (Australia, Fiji, and Indonesia) and some are primarily users (Canada, Kazakhstan, and Malaysia), which implies that telecommunication activities vary in their role, depending on the economic structure of a jurisdiction.

It is also interesting to observe in Figure 12 that, while the US' digital economy is not dominated by any one subsector, it is mainly concentrated in the services subsectors. Software publishing, specialized and support services, and telecommunications almost equally comprise the US' digital economy. The greater share of the digital services sector is an indicator of a more mature economic system, as is expected from the US. Hardware and web publishing take minor portions of the digital GDP of the US.

Note that Fiji has neither hardware nor software publishing as part of its digital economy. This does not mean the absence of these products in the Fijian economy, rather it merely reflects the absence of domestic production of these products. The supply of these digital products and services are reliant on imports, which are not included in the digital economy equation. Thus, further analyses outside the scope of the framework is necessary to examine this.

Impact of Sector Linkages of Digital Sectors

While the digital economy has been shown to make significant contributions to the GDP of various economies, another key characteristic of the digital economy is its potentially disruptive effects. Current technologies, such as cloud computing, blockchain, big data, artificial intelligence, and IoT, have been generating massive economic transformation (IDB 2018) and their effects, while perceptible, have yet to be precisely quantified.

Prior to quantifying the economic transformation allowed by digital technologies, it is imperative that sector linkages of the digital economy are determined, particularly the extent to which the digital economy shapes the digitally dependent economy. Additionally, the potential impacts of digital sectors across economies are analyzed using output and value-added multipliers.

The Digitally Dependent Economy

While the previous chapter examined the relative sizes of core digital industries in various economies, this section aims to explore the roles that digital industries play in economic production. Estimates show that dependence on core digital products vary at the economy-level, while at the sector level, some appear to be more affected by digitalization than others. Sectors such as wholesale, retail, and finance are more likely to be dependent than other sectors, across different approaches of analysis.

Identifying Digitally Enabled Sectors Using Forward Linkages

The digitally enabled economy (alternatively, the digitally dependent economy) was earlier defined as the value-added of the sectors that are critically dependent on digital sectors. This is captured by the second term of the core digital economy equation (Equation 10), which represents the forward linkages of the digital sectors. Sector analysis of the digital sector's forward linkages allows the identification of the digitally enabled economy and its relative size.

In order to come up with a comparable scale across the economies in this study, forward linkage values per economy are normalized based on the aggregate digital sector to itself, i.e., the value of the third term of the equation. To demonstrate this, the matrix of a sample three-industry economy can be reviewed below:

$$\hat{v}B\hat{y} = \begin{bmatrix} v_1b_{11}y_1 & v_1b_{12}y_2 & v_1b_{13}y_3 \\ v_2b_{21}y_1 & v_2b_{22}y_2 & v_2b_{23}y_3 \\ v_3b_{31}y_1 & v_3b_{32}y_2 & v_3b_{33}y_3 \end{bmatrix} \quad \text{Forward linkages}$$

Assuming Industry 1 is the aggregate digital sector, its forward linkages would be the sum of the first row, representing the entire digitally enabled economy. Suppose $v_1 b_{11} y_1$, $v_1 b_{12} y_2$, and $v_1 b_{13} y_3$ have values of 25, 10, and 15, respectively. As $v_1 b_{11} y_1$ is the digital sector's value-added contribution to its own final goods production, this can be assumed to be the maximum value of digitalization that can exist in any industry, therefore it represents 100% digitally enabled. Rescaling the possible range of digitalization for all sectors in the economy, $v_1 b_{12} y_2$ and $v_1 b_{13} y_3$ normalized values are calculated by dividing 10 and 15 by 25, which is 40% and 60%, respectively. These can be taken as a measure of digitalization of an industry with respect to the total economic digitalization.

The 10 industries with the highest forward linkages from the aggregate digital industry per economy were normalized. These sectors were then harmonized across economies for comparability, based on ISIC Revision 3.1. For economies with more highly disaggregated industries belonging to the same broader industry (e.g., the wholesale industry and the retail industry), the sum in level terms is taken before normalization. The results by economy are shown in Figure 13.

Emergence of E-Commerce and E-Government in a Majority of Economies

Collectively, the most digitally enabled industries using forward linkages are (i) wholesale and retail trade; (ii) public administration and defense; compulsory social security; (iii) electronic, electrical, and optical equipment; (iv) financial intermediation, and (v) construction. Across time periods, most of the economy-sectors shown in Figure 13 increase in digitalization.

The use of online platforms has revolutionized wholesale and retail trade, as firms increasingly turn to shopping websites and apps instead of brick-and-mortar stores. In 2017, Credit Suisse predicted the closure of 20%–25% of malls in the US by 2022 (Wertz 2020). An analysis between time periods shows that the use of digital technologies within wholesale and retail trade, in the form of e-commerce, varies across economies by depth and speed of adoption. Nonetheless, a later section on the impact of the COVID-19 pandemic shows how e-commerce adoption accelerated to play a central role in cushioning the negative impacts of the pandemic.

Government activities also continue to be digitally transformed, with many public service transactions and processes being shifted to electronic formats. Denmark is consistently one of the top-ranked economies by the Digital Economy and Society Index, especially in the area of e-government (EU 2020), owing possibly to transformational government strategies and high budget allocations by local

Figure 13: Top Domestic Digitally Enabled Sectors Based on Forward Linkages
(normalized %)

Industry	AUS	CAN	DEN	FIJ	GER	IND	INO	JPN	KAZ	KOR	MAL	PRC	SIN	TAP	THA	USA
Agriculture, hunting, forestry, and fishing				5.5												5.7
Air transport				8.4			2.1						1.3			
Architectural and engineering activities			3.2		0.9				3.0		0.5	2.6				
Construction	6.5	3.7	2.5	8.1		2.5	11.9	1.7	1.0	2.2	0.9	12.3	0.7	0.6		
Education	4.4		3.1	4.8			4.7		2.8	3.9	1.6	2.1	0.7	0.7	1.9	
Electronic, electrical, and optical equipment					3.2	1.9				4.6	9.6	15.3	1.6	0.6	19.4	1.6
Financial intermediation	19.2	9.1	3.2	7.9	3.8		1.8	4.9		5.0	4.4		2.1		1.6	
Food, beverages, and tobacco				10.0		2.1	3.6	1.3			1.8					
Furniture						1.6										
Health and social work	5.9	1.9	5.5		3.7			4.1		1.9		2.0		0.8		2.4
Hotels and restaurants				18.0	3.5			2.6		2.2	0.5			1.4	1.8	
Information services					4.9											
Inland transport						2.2			1.7							
Leather, leather products, and footwear															1.4	
Machinery, nec					4.1	1.7		1.2				5.1		0.7		
Manufacturing, nec; recycling															0.7	
Mining and quarrying									3.6							
Other community, social, and personal services								0.8			1.8					2.6
Other supporting and auxiliary transport activities; activities of travel agencies				11.4												
Pharmaceuticals			3.7													
Post and telecommunications										2.9						
Public administration and defense; compulsory social security	15.5	12.3	11.3	9.6	5.8		3.5	5.5	7.2	4.6	4.6	5.8	3.5	1.9		6.0
Real estate activities	5.2	2.1	4.9					1.5	0.7							
Renting of M&Eq and other business activities	3.8										1.1		1.1		3.8	
Research and development					3.4			4.2			3.1					
Textiles and textile products						2.3	1.7									
Transport equipment					5.0	1.6				2.4		2.6				6.4
Water transport													0.6			
Wholesale and retail trade	17.5		15.8	30.9	9.3		3.4	11.7	4.7	11.2	3.2		4.9	2.1	2.4	2.5
Wood and products of wood and cork																2.9

AUS = Australia; CAN = Canada; DEN = Denmark; FIJ = Fiji; GER = Germany; IND = India; INO = Indonesia; JPN = Japan; KAZ = Kazakhstan; KOR = Republic of Korea; MAL = Malaysia; nec = not elsewhere classified; PRC = People's Republic of China; SIN = Singapore; TAP = Taipei,China; THA = Thailand; USA = United States.
Notes: Years included are AUS, 2010, 2018; CAN, 2012, 2016; DEN, 2010, 2016; FIJ, 2011, 2015; GER, 2010, 2016; IND, 2010, 2014; INO, 2010, 2014; JPN, 2011, 2015; KAZ, 2010, 2018; KOR, 2010, 2018; MAL, 2010, 2015; PRC, 2012; SIN, 2000, 2016; TAP, 2016; THA, 2010, 2015; USA, 2010, 2019. The average is presented in economy-sectors for which calculations include multiple years. The aggregate is presented in economy-sectors that encompass multiple top original sectors after industry harmonization using International Standard Industrial Classification Revision 3.1.
Source: Calculations of the Digital Economy Measurement Framework study team, using input-output and related data from various national statistics offices and international databases.

government units toward digitalization (Scupola 2019).[38] Financial technology or "fintech," the incorporation of digital products into financial services for both business-to-consumer and business-to-business models, has resulted in innumerable online avenues for bills payment, management of funds and insurance, crowdfunding, and stock-trading (Sraders 2020) as well as the rise of blockchain networks and crypto-assets (Box 4).

---

[38] The Digital Economy and Society Index summarizes and measures changes in a range of indicators relevant to digital performance and competitiveness of EU Member States (EU 2020).

Box 4: Treatment of Digital Currencies in the System of National Accounts

Since the launch of bitcoin in 2008, blockchain technology has become a record-keeping and database innovation, with impacts expected to extend well beyond the financial industry (The Economist 2015). With the world's growing interest in blockchain and its resulting cryptocurrencies and digital tokens, concerns about how to treat such "digital currencies" in national accounts have naturally arisen.

Based on the System of National Account (SNA) 2008, the infrastructure behind the blockchain system should be capitalized in the same manner as software and databases. There is a consensus among expert groups that the articles produced by these ledgers (digital currencies and tokens) are considered assets, due to their use as a storage of value and long-term nature with respect to the holding period. However, two things remain to be topics of debate: whether they should be considered financial or nonfinancial assets, and, if considered nonfinancial, whether they are produced or non-produced assets (IMF and OECD 2020).

The authors of this report are in agreement with the Advisory Expert Group on National Accounts' proposed classification of digital currencies and tokens, which generally depends on the identity of the issuer (IMF and OECD 2020). If they are issued by a national government or central bank, they should be treated as a financial asset (currency or share). Otherwise, they should be treated as a separate category under nonfinancial produced asset, similar to the recording of valuables in the production account.

Furthermore, the authors of this report recommend that "data mining", the process used to generate cryptocurrencies through blockchain networks, should fall under data processing, with payments to "miners" recorded as part of value-added. Should institutions, such as banks or online platforms, mediate these transactions, the recording of their services would similarly depend on whether financial assets or nonfinancial produced assets are being transacted. If the former, these would be considered financial intermediation services directly or indirectly measured and, if the latter, a transaction fee for a nonfinancial service.

Recently, the People's Republic of China became the first major economy to issue its own digital currency, the digital yuan, with some theorizing its potential to revolutionize cross-border currency movements, thus leading to substantial political implications (Areddy 2021). However, it is currently unclear if the digital yuan relies on the same blockchain technology as other decentralized cryptocurrencies. What is known is that it will be issued by the People's Bank of China, the country's central bank (Kharpal 2021). As such, when officially traded, the digital yuan would be considered a financial asset based on the abovementioned classification. It appears other economies are keen or starting to follow suit, with ongoing initiatives toward digital currency issuance by the United States, the United Kingdom, and the European Union. Much debate has surrounded the topic of government-issued digital currencies, which contests the product's decentralized origins, due to its considerable implications on retail banking, geopolitics, and citizen autonomy (The Economist 2021).

References:
J.T. Areddy. 2021. China Creates Its Own Digital Currency, a First for Major Economy. *Wall Street Journal*. 5 April. https://www.wsj.com/articles/china-creates-its-own-digital-currency-a-first-for-major-economy-11617634118
International Monetary Fund (IMF) and Organisation for Economic Co-operation and Development (OECD). 2020. *The Recording of Crypto Assets*. 14th Meeting of the Advisory Expert Group on National Accounts, Virtual Meeting.
Kharpal. 2021. China Has Given Away Millions in its Digital Yuan Trials: This is How it Works. *Consumer News and Business Channel*. https://www.cnbc.com/2021/03/05/chinas-digital-yuan-what-is-it-and-how-does-it-work.html.
The Economist. 2015. The Great Chain of Being Sure About Things. https://www.economist.com/briefing/2015/10/31/the-great-chain-of-being-sure-about-things
The Economist. 2021. The Digital Currencies That Matter. https://www.economist.com/leaders/2021/05/08/the-digital-currencies-that-matter.

While digitalization of sectors such as public administration, defense, electronic equipment, and finance may be evident to most consumers, the same might not be so apparent for construction. For most of the selected economies, telecommunications accounted for the majority of digital products intermediately consumed by the construction industry. The use of mobile phones and apps has greatly aided internal communication vital to contractors, while newer technologies, such as analytics, virtual reality, and artificial intelligence, have benefitted traditional operations with cost reductions, safety, and efficiency (LetsBuild 2019).

Agriculture appears in the top 10 digital industries only for the US and Fiji. For the former, this is unsurprising given that digital solutions are used by more than two thirds of US farmland (Bryan et al. 2020). The latter can be explained by national policies to digitalize the sector, including promotion of the use of geographic information systems and drought-monitoring software, among others (Chand n.d.).

Digitally Disrupted Sectors

Using the framework provides a holistic measure of industries most impacted by digitalization in each economy. Meanwhile, other organizations have classified activities significantly affected by digitalization across all economies. The Advisory Expert Group on National Accounts (2019) considers 10 sectors as increasingly digitally disrupted (Table 3). It can be observed that, except for financial and insurance services, these do not completely coincide with the five sectors considered most highly digitalized according to the analysis in Figure 13.

Applying the same framework (Equation 10) to the identified digital sectors and digitally disrupted sectors would give an approximate estimate of the entire digitally dependent economy. As this would be one standard set of industries across economies, there would be almost no variation among the criteria set (apart from some missing detailed sectors by economy),[39] which allows comparability among them.[40]

As a percentage of economy-wide GDP, the largest digitally dependent economies were those of Fiji, Australia, and Thailand (Figure 14). The share of Fiji's accommodation services, comprising an average of 9.1% of GDP across the two time periods, was significantly larger than that of other economies (the next highest was 3.1% for Thailand in 2015). In general, financial and insurance services accounted for the largest share of the digitally dependent economy at an average of 7.1% of GDP across economy-years, the highest of which was Australia's at 10.7%.

Table 3: Most Digitally Disrupted Sectors, Classification of Products by Activity

Code	Description
49	Land transport services and transport services via pipelines
55	Accommodation services
56	Food and Beverage serving services
58	Publishing services
59	Motion picture, video and television programme production services, sound recording and music publishing
K	Financial and insurance services
73	Advertising and market research services
79	Travel agency, tour operator and other reservation services
P	Education services
92	Gambling and betting services

Source: Advisory Expert Group on National Accounts (2019).

---

[39] Most of these refer to travel agencies, tour operators, and other reservation services; gambling and betting services; and advertising and market research services.

[40] Due to data limitations, the framework is calculated excluding the 4th term of the core equation, i.e., capital purchased by sector from sectors other than itself.

Figure 14: Degree of Digital Dependence by Economy

(% of gross domestic product)

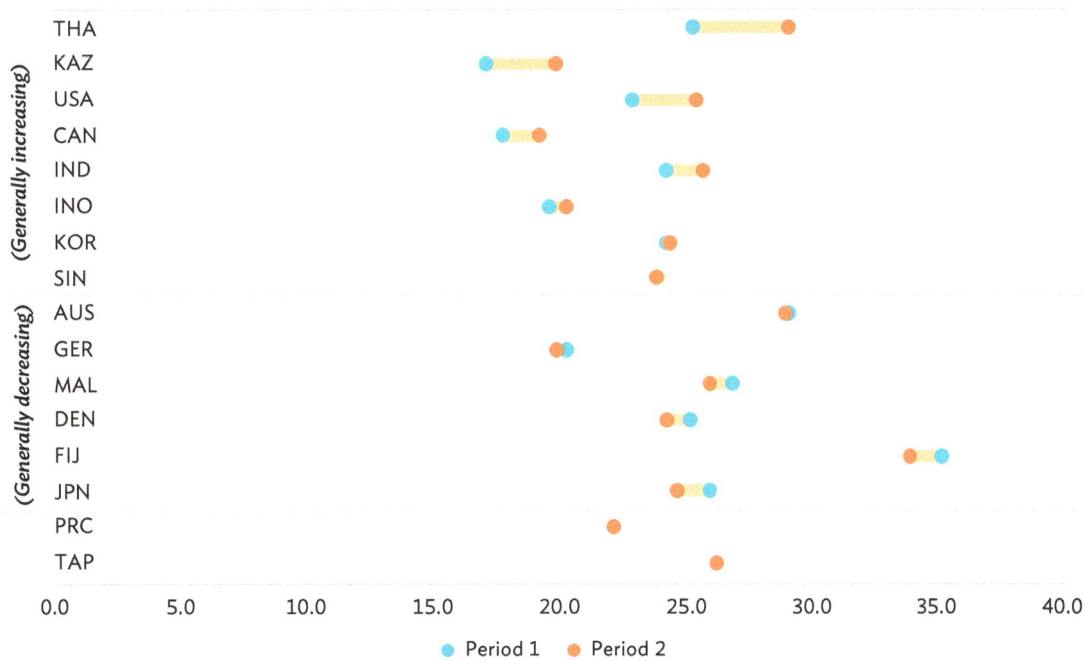

AUS = Australia; CAN = Canada; DEN = Denmark; FIJ = Fiji; GER = Germany; IND = India; INO = Indonesia; JPN = Japan; KAZ = Kazakhstan; KOR = Republic of Korea; MAL = Malaysia; PRC = People's Republic of China; SIN = Singapore; TAP = Taipei,China; THA = Thailand; USA = United States.
Notes: Period 1 is AUS, 2010; CAN, 2012; DEN, 2010; FIJ, 2011; GER, 2010; IND, 2010; INO, 2010; JPN, 2011; KAZ, 2001; KOR, 2010; MAL, 2010; SIN, 2000; THA, 2010; USA, 2010. Period 2 is AUS, 2018; CAN, 2016; DEN, 2016; FIJ, 2015; GER, 2016; IND, 2014; INO, 2014; JPN, 2015; KAZ, 2018; KOR, 2018; MAL, 2015; PRC, 2012; SIN, 2016; TAP, 2016; THA, 2015; USA, 2019.
Source: Calculations of the Digital Economy Measurement Framework study team, using input-output and related data from various national statistics offices and international databases.

Using CAGR, annual growth of the digitally dependent economy between Period 1 and Period 2 was fastest for Thailand (2.9%), Canada (2.0%), Kazakhstan (1.9%), and the US (1.2%). The growth of the digitally dependent economy within the developing economies of Thailand and Kazakhstan is contrary to the declining growth of their digital economies, at –4.5% and –2.1%, respectively. Economies with a slowdown in their CAGR, most apparent in Japan (–1.3%) and Fiji (–0.9%), similarly face a downtrend in their respective digital economy estimates (–2.0% and –5.8%).

Through the $\hat{v}B\hat{y}$ matrix, the measurement framework allows the isolation of the digital sectors' contribution to the 10 digitally dependent sectors identified in Table 3. The resulting value is an indicator of the depth of digitalization by digitally dependent sector. This can be calculated by taking the share of the value-added contribution of the collective digital sector to the nondigital (digitally dependent) sector, i.e., the forward linkage, out of the latter's overall size. While in the previous analysis, forward linkages were used to identify and rank the digitally dependent sectors, in this analysis, they are used to determine the depth of digitalization among the 10 digitally dependent sectors across select economy-years, and the results are shown in Figure 15.

Figure 15: Digitally Disrupted Sectors by Size of Digital Forward Contribution
(averaged % of respective sector size)

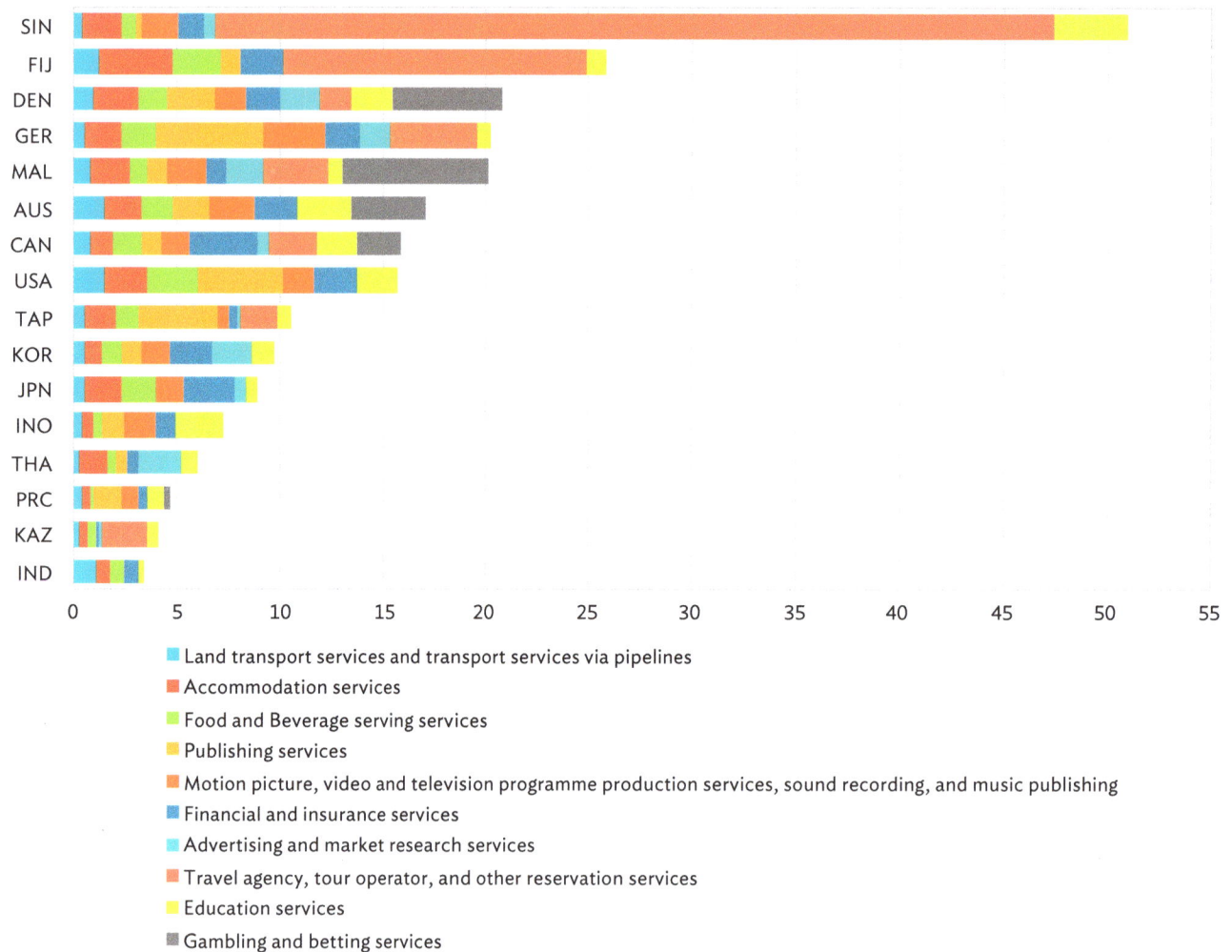

Land transport services and transport services via pipelines
Accommodation services
Food and Beverage serving services
Publishing services
Motion picture, video and television programme production services, sound recording, and music publishing
Financial and insurance services
Advertising and market research services
Travel agency, tour operator, and other reservation services
Education services
Gambling and betting services

AUS = Australia; CAN = Canada; DEN = Denmark; FIJ = Fiji; GER = Germany; IND = India; INO = Indonesia; JPN = Japan; KAZ = Kazakhstan; KOR = Republic of Korea; MAL = Malaysia; PRC = People's Republic of China; SIN = Singapore; TAP = Taipei,China; THA = Thailand; USA = United States.
Note: Years included are AUS, 2010, 2018; CAN, 2012, 2016; DEN, 2010, 2016; FIJ, 2011, 2015; GER, 2010, 2016; IND, 2010, 2014; INO, 2010, 2014; JPN, 2011, 2015; KAZ, 2010, 2018; KOR, 2010, 2018; MAL, 2010, 2015; PRC, 2012; SIN, 2000, 2016; TAP, 2016; THA, 2010, 2015; USA, 2010, 2019.
Source: Calculations of the Digital Economy Measurement Framework study team, using input-output and related data from various national statistics offices and international databases.

The most digitally disrupted economy-sectors, by significant margins, were the "travel agency, tour operator, and other reservation services" sectors of Singapore and Fiji. This is indicative of how the tourism industry in these economies has been substantially shaped by digital transformation. Singapore ranks first in travel and tourism competitiveness in Southeast Asia and 17th globally, with one of the leading contributors being ICT readiness (WEF 2019). Fiji is a tourism-dependent economy (Kaufmann and Nakagawa 2015), where the top two digitally disrupted sectors were travel agencies and accommodation services.

The next most affected economy-sectors were the gambling and betting services sectors of Denmark and Malaysia. Gambling has a long-standing prevalence in Malaysia, home to one of the biggest casino groups worldwide, Genting Group, and a growing internet gambling market (Dhillon et al. 2021). Denmark's online gaming industry has expanded steadily year-on-year since 2012 as a result of online avenues opening up, making its participation rate in online gambling higher than its physical counterpart, and the second highest in Europe (O'Boyle 2020).

Germany's publishing services sector follows. The economy's book industry is the second biggest worldwide, with digital publishing rising in popularity and e-books taking 4.3% of overall book turnover in 2014 (Süßmann 2015). The sector also leads in digitalization for the US and Taipei,China.

For the analysis conducted thus far, it must be noted that some of industries are heavily affected by their corresponding values in the value-added coefficient vector $\mathbf{v}$ and final demand vector $\mathbf{y}$. Moreover, the $\mathbf{\hat{v}B\hat{y}}$ matrix only accounts for domestic production using the domestic transactions matrix $\mathbf{z}$, which means the contribution of digital imports cannot be readily traced. Analysis of the intermediate consumption matrix of an economy's use table or IOT, including noncompetitive imports, would provide another angle, i.e., the direct usage of digital products or industries by nondigital industries on digital products or industries, both domestically produced and imported.

Increasing Overall Direct Digital Dependence among Economies

Intermediate consumption of core digital products measures the extent of digital technology use in the economy. These expenditures, such as data storage, processing, and IT consulting, may be used to gauge "direct" digital dependence. In other words, higher purchases of both domestic and imported digital products relative to other inputs in the production process indicate a greater degree of direct digital dependence, and vice versa. However, this direct or intermediate use approach does not take into account a sector's domestic investments related to digital technologies as these are already included in the preceding sections. In addition, issues related to data assets increasingly being held by firms are currently flagged for discussion at the System of National Accounts research agenda (Box 5).

The intermediate use approach becomes more relevant with the increase of "pay-as-you-go" schemes in selling digital products. In more recent years, digital goods and services have been offered on a flexible basis, with software licenses sold in shorter life periods depending on the customer's needs. Aside from software, companies are also forgoing investments in private services for data storage and processing, and are opting to purchase access to servers from external providers, as in the case of cloud computing (OECD 2019). This business strategy is often adopted on account of cash flow considerations (i.e., it reduces upfront financing needs for hardware and software) and the scalability of cloud services. In national accounts, this implies a switch from fixed investment to intermediate consumption of digital products.

Box 5: Recording and Measuring Data

A complete understanding of value creation of digital platforms requires measuring data as an input to production. Recent years have shown that data helps drive the outcomes of advertisements, and therefore increases the premiums earned by more data-driven platforms. In fact, businesses recognize the demand for measuring the value of data as evidenced by huge investments in data infrastructure. For instance, the international bandwidth usage of a few large tech firms—such as Alibaba, Amazon, Facebook, Google, Microsoft, and Tencent—has become almost on par with that of internet backbone providers (UNCTAD 2019b; Mauldin 2017). These companies own or lease more than half of the submarine cable networks through where 99% of international data transmissions run (Bischof, Fontugne, and Bustamante 2018).

While there is an agreement that data constitute a significant role in production, there is far less consensus about whether data should be recorded as an asset in the System of National Accounts (SNA). Currently, the SNA only records, as gross fixed capital formation (GFCF), expenditures related to the *"cost of preparing the data in the appropriate format, but not the cost of acquiring or producing the data"* (SNA 2008, para. 10.113). That is not to say that datasets have no value, but rather their contribution is implicit, and only appears residually as goodwill when a sale of entire company occurs (SNA 2008, para. 10.196–10.199). Consider Facebook's high-profile acquisitions of Instagram in 2012 and WhatsApp in 2014. After removing the value of trademark, technology, patents, and user base, the calculation leaves intact about 74% and 84% of the acquisition values of both cases, respectively. These substantial shares to total value are not surprising as an increasing number of tech mergers and acquisitions are data-motivated (Nguyen and Paczos 2020). This treatment as goodwill, however, recognizes data as de facto non-produced assets and therefore does not affect gross domestic product (GDP) (Ahmad and van de Ven 2018).

Investments in Data, Databases, and Data Science in India
(₹ billion)

	2011	2013	2015	2017	2019
Total of all data-related categories					
Lower range value	914	867	1,040	1,407	1,663
Upper range value	1,102	1,045	1,256	1,702	2,004
"Data"					
Lower range value	496	466	567	811	980
Upper range value	624	587	715	1,021	1,225
"Databases"					
Lower range value	201	189	217	267	373
Upper range value	225	211	243	299	418
"Data science"					
Lower range value	217	212	256	329	310
Upper range value	253	247	298	383	361
Net capital stock of all data-related categories					
Lower range value	2,944	3,392	3,802	4,540	5,511
Upper range value	3,631	4,189	4,701	5,610	6,794
Economy-wide gross fixed capital formation	29,977	35,156	39,571	48,156	58,513
of which: Intellectual property products	2,169	3,577	4,853	5,627	7,627

₹ = Indian rupees.
Note: Figures of economy-wide gross fixed capital formation refer to current price figures published by India's Ministry of Statistics and Programme Implementation (MOSPI) available from http://mospi.nic.in/ (accessed April 2021).
Source: Calculations of the Digital Economy Measurement Framework study team, following the approach of Statistics Canada (2019) and using 2011 Census data from India's Office of the Registrar General and Census Commissioner, employment statistics from the International Labor Organization, technical coefficients from the Asian Development Bank Multiregional Input-Output Database, and national accounts data from MOSPI (India).

Data, however, should not be confused with observable phenomena. An observable phenomenon is taken simply as an occurrence of an event or piece of information (ISWGNA 2020). For this observation to be digitized, a firm must hire qualified staff and mobilize resources and technology systems to capture and store observations. This process of collecting, recording, organizing, and storing implies that a productive activity has occurred. Therefore, there is a strong argument that data are produced, and what is non-produced in the 2008 SNA has come to refer to observable phenomenon (ISWGNA 2020).

continued on next page.

Box 5 *continued.*

While the recording of data is still an open issue, its valuation is compounding this challenge. Largely, the valuation issues relate to the heavy context-dependent uses of data, and that the standard units of data (bytes, megabytes, etc.) do not automatically translate to data's underlying monetary value. Fortunately, experimental estimates provide starting point for gauging the stock of data assets. At the forefront is Statistics Canada's (2019) approach, which evaluates investment as a sum of labor costs; associated indirect labor; and other costs such as electricity, building maintenance, and telecommunication services.

The same approach is replicated in a developing economy context for India. Results in the table below show that (current price) investments on data, databases, and data science in India ranged from ₹1,633 ($23.6) billion to ₹2,004 ($28.5) billion in 2019, or 2.8% to 3.4% of economy-wide GFCF. These cost-based estimates of India's data assets grew at a compound annual growth rate (CAGR) of 7.8% from 2011 to 2019. This is slightly lower than the economy-wide investment growth of 8.7% for all assets over the same period. Extending the analysis, net capital stocks of data-related assets in India were estimated to range from ₹5,511 ($78.3) billion to ₹,794 ($96.5) billion in 2019. Figures show that data-related stocks grew at a CAGR of 8.2% from 2011 to 2019, below par for the economy-wide rate of 10.6%.

While it has yet to be determined to what extent data will be added to the asset boundary of the SNA, this exercise is nonetheless informative of the scale of the issue. With this caveat in mind, estimated GFCF related to data, databases, and data science could range from 0.82% to 0.98% of GDP in 2019. Again, the estimates cannot be readily added to current GDP figures due to the potential overlap with the coverage of GFCF in official estimates. As such, future studies should measure this overlap, if any, in addition to refining the key parameters in the method.

The above estimates indicate that data-related assets in India are not yet growing at a rate above the overall investment growth, as observed in the advanced economy example of Canada. However, there is an indication that these assets are growing in tandem with other types of investments. In addition, sum-of-cost estimates are invariably expected to produce lower-bound figures compared to market-based valuations. Nevertheless, the estimates are intended as a step towards understanding the order-of-magnitude of emerging digital assets in a developing economy context.

₹ = Indian rupees, $ = United States dollars.

References:
N. Ahmad and P. van de Ven. 2018. *Recording and Measuring Data in the System of National Accounts.* Paris: OECD Publishing.
Z. Bischof, R. Fontugne, and F. Bustamante. 2018. Untangling the World-Wide Mesh of Undersea Cables. *Proceedings of the 17th ACM Workshop on Hot Topics in Networks HotNets-XVII.* IIJ Innovation Institute.
Inter-Secretariat of Working Group on National Accounts (ISWGNA). 2020. *Recording and Measuring Data in the System of National Accounts.* 14th Meeting of the Advisory Expert Group on National Accounts.
A. Mauldin. 2017. *A Complete List of Content Providers' Submarine Cable Holdings.* TeleGeography. 9 November. https://blog.telegeography.com/telegeographys-content-providers-submarine-cable-holdings-list.
D. Nguyen & Paczos, M. 2020. *Measuring the Economic Value of Data and Cross-Border Data Flows: A Business Perspective.* Paris: OECD Publishing.
Statistics Canada. 2019. *The Value of Data in Canada: Experimental Estimates.* 22 April 2021.
United Nations Conference for Trade and Development (UNCTAD). 2019b. *Digital Economy Report 2019: Value Creation and Capture—Implications for Developing Countries.* https://unctad.org/system/files/official-document/der2019_en.pdf.
United Nations, European Commission, International Monetary Fund, Organisation for Economic Co-operation and Development, and World Bank. 2009. *System of National Accounts 2008.* New York: United Nations.

Given this conjecture, the analysis is supplemented by looking at changes in digital input use by sectors. The approach differs in that digital dependence is taken directly as a ratio of intermediate inputs of digital products to total inputs (whereas earlier measures also considered indirect linkages with the core digital economy).

Figure 16 plots each economy's direct digital dependence averaged across the sectors listed in Table 3. It can be observed that the direction of trends is similar to the economic size of the digitally dependent sectors in Figure 14. Remarkable increases in digital dependence are seen in Indonesia and Thailand; driven mostly by changes in motion picture and related services in the former, and education services (CPA P) in the latter. Fiji's decrease in digital dependence, meanwhile, is reflective of the lower relative digital input purchases of travel agencies, accommodation services, and advertising sectors. While the activities of travel agencies in Germany increased in digital dependence between the two periods, publishing services decreased its share of digital inputs. With the latter sector occupying a larger portion of the digitally disrupted economy in Germany, decline in this sector outweighed the deepening digital dependence in other sectors.

Figure 16: Average Share of Digital Inputs to Total Intermediate Inputs for Digitally Dependent Sectors

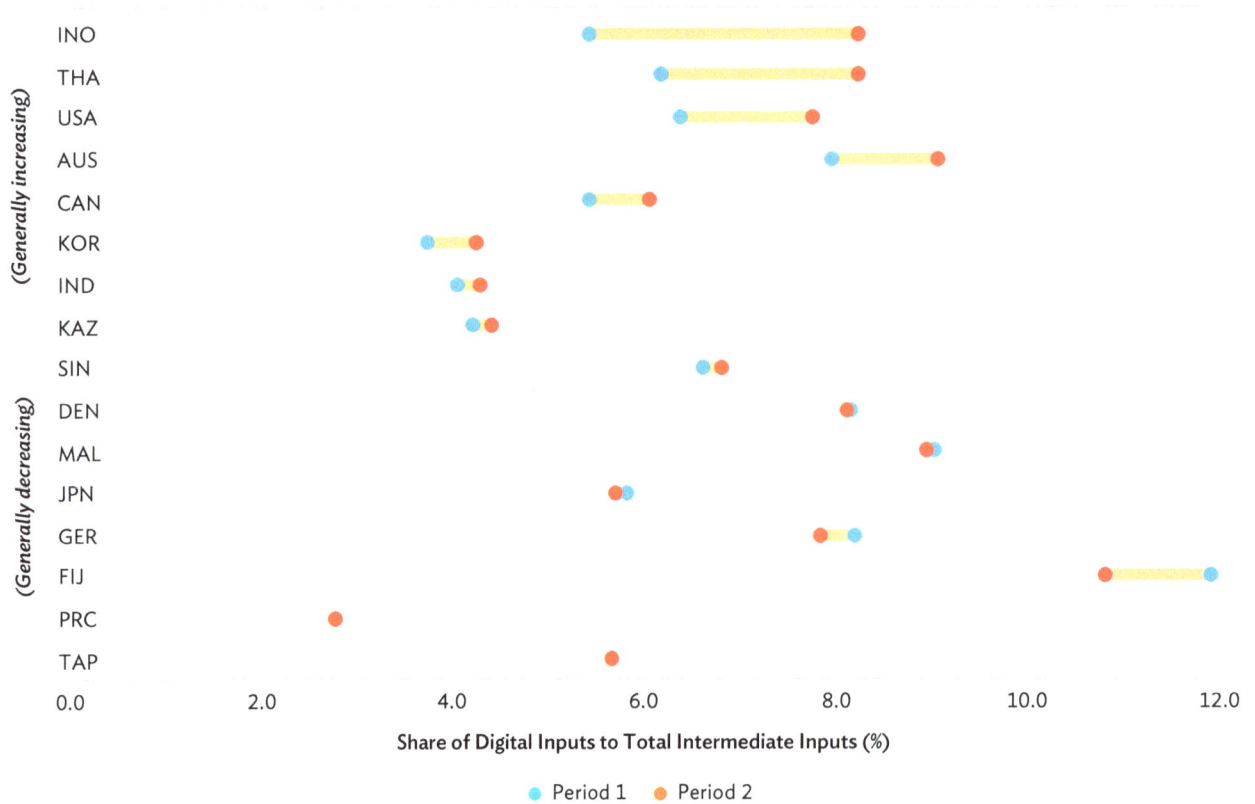

AUS = Australia; CAN = Canada; DEN = Denmark; FIJ = Fiji; GER = Germany; IND = India; INO = Indonesia; JPN = Japan; KAZ = Kazakhstan; KOR = Republic of Korea; MAL = Malaysia; PRC = People's Republic of China; SIN = Singapore; TAP = Taipei,China; THA = Thailand; USA = United States.
Notes: Period 1 is AUS, 2010; CAN, 2012; DEN, 2010; FIJ, 2011; GER, 2010; IND, 2010; INO, 2010; JPN, 2011; KAZ, 2001; KOR, 2010; MAL, 2010; SIN, 2000; THA, 2010; USA, 2010. Period 2 is AUS, 2018; CAN, 2016; DEN, 2016; FIJ, 2015; GER, 2016; IND, 2014; INO, 2014; JPN, 2015; KAZ, 2018; KOR, 2018; MAL, 2015; PRC, 2012; SIN, 2016; TAP, 2016; THA, 2015; USA, 2019.
Source: Calculations of the Digital Economy Measurement Framework study team, using input-output and related data from various national statistics offices and international databases.

On a per sector basis, direct digital dependence across economies increased from 4.9% in Period 1 to 5.3% in Period 2 (Figure 17). However, growth was not observed uniformly across sectors. Financial and insurance services sectors, which are associated with high digital dependence in economies such as Australia, Canada, and Japan, slightly eased in Period 2. Meanwhile, a notable increase in digital dependence in publishing and media (e.g., motion pictures and television programs) helped more than offset the finance sector's decline in Australia and Canada. Japan's media services slightly eased from 2011 to 2015. The coexistence of nondigital and digital processes in anime production, for instance, experienced major constraints as demand shifted from television to the packaged video market (the so-called "anime bubble", which persisted until 2013). This implied higher quality standards for which a constrained domestic capacity deemed it more practical to outsource production to the PRC and the ROK (Hanzawa 2019). Concurrently, the ROK's motion picture and television sector saw a remarkable increase in digital dependence from 2010 to 2018. Despite a rise in digital dependence in the ROK, it must be noted that Japan's media industry still leads in terms of direct digital dependence in advanced Asian economies.

The increase in Indonesia's direct digital dependence can also be attributed to the motion picture, video, and television program sector. In 2014, almost one third of that sector in Indonesia was entirely comprised of digital inputs. This deepening digitalization of the industry coincides with the implementation of National Creative Industry Development Plan from 2009 to 2015. The animation and film industry of Indonesia formed about 10% of the economy's exports in 2010, destined for the markets of Europe and the US. During this period, the quality of production was raised on par with that of Taipei,China and the ROK as a result of adoption of digital technologies, which render films at higher frames per second (Simatupang et al. 2012). This sharp industry focus and government support encouraged firms in the creative industries to adopt digital processes in production techniques.

Figure 17: Average Share of Digital Inputs to Total Intermediate Inputs by Sector (%)

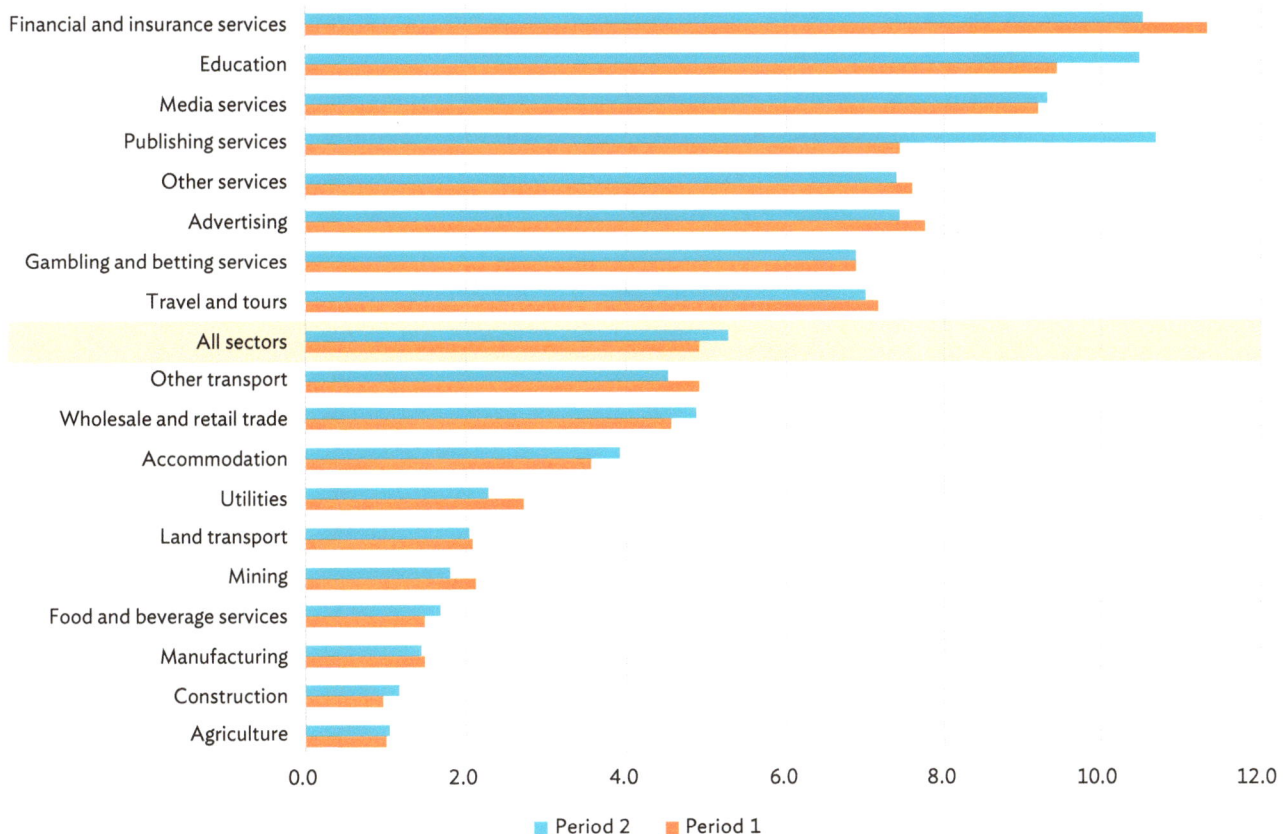

Period 2   Period 1

Notes: Economies covered and their years for Period 1 and Period 2 are Australia (2010, 2018); Canada (2012, 2016); Denmark (2010, 2016); Fiji (2011, 2015); Germany (2010, 2016); India (2010, 2014); Indonesia (2010, 2014); Japan (2011, 2015); Kazakhstan (2001, 2018); Republic of Korea (2010, 2018); Malaysia (2010, 2015); People's Republic of China (2012); Singapore (2000, 2016); Taipei,China (2016); Thailand (2010, 2015); and the United States (2010, 2019). Sectors' digital input shares are averaged across sectors for Period 1 and Period 2.
Source: Calculations of the Digital Economy Measurement Framework study team, using input-output and related data from various national statistics offices and international databases.

Generally, this section has explored the contribution of core digital technologies' enabling role in production processes of other nondigital sectors using existing macroeconomic frameworks. Estimates show that digitally dependent sectors, including digital sectors, represent a sizable share of economies, ranging from 17% to 35% of GDP in both periods examined. Results also indicate that more service-oriented economies tend to have deeper forward linkages with the core digital economy. Digitalization in services is also evident in direct measures of dependence using intermediate digital products' relative shares of total inputs. Examination of these inputs for more recent years also supports the observation of service sectors' relatively higher digital dependence.[41] While digital dependence deepened in sectors related to wholesale and retail, accommodation, and entertainment-related industries, there are signs of maturity in sectors that were generally the first to digitalize, such as finance and advertising.

In the next section, the core digital industry's role is examined further from a demand-side perspective. It analyzes the extent to which other sectors in the economy contribute to the production of digital products. In addition, it demonstrates how the strength of these linkages can be quantified and therefore provide an indication of potential spillover impacts from the digital economy.

Digital Multiplier Analysis

Multipliers are useful when simulating the impact of an exogenous demand-side shock coursed through certain sectors in the IOTs. In particular, multipliers measure the impact of a unit change in the final demand for digital sectors' output on either the gross output or the total value-added of an economy. The impact of the exogenous demand-side shock consists of the direct and knock-on effects due to industrial interlinkages. For this section, the simple output and value-added multipliers for the 16 economies studied are calculated using their national input-output tables (NIOTs). These are then compared with the multipliers calculated using the 38-sector MRIOT for 2019.

The simple output multiplier captures the total direct and indirect effects of a unit change in final demand on the total value of production in an economy. For example, if an economy has a 1.5 output multiplier for computer equipment, then a $1 increase in final demand for computer equipment generates an additional $1.50 gross output for this economy. The value-added multiplier, meanwhile, gives the value created in

---

[41] Same analysis of direct digital dependence was conducted for 2017 and 2019 using the MRIOTs. A wider set of economies recorded an average digital dependence rate of 7.6%. While global average digital dependence barely moved from 2017 to 2019, financial sectors decreased their digital inputs share by -0.6 percentage points. Meanwhile, the wholesale and retail sector exhibited the largest increase across other sectors in this period. While travel and tours are not separately identified as a sector in the MRIOTs, at higher aggregation, this sector showed an increase in digital dependence of +0.23 percentage points. The related sector of accommodation services also increased its dependence by 0.21 percentage points.

an economy (gross output less intermediate consumption) due to a unit change in final demand. Analogous with an output multiplier, if an economy has a value-added multiplier of 0.9 for telecommunications, then a $1 increase in telecom sales generates a $0.90 increase in the total value-added of an economy.[42]

Digital Sectors in the National Economy

Figure 18 shows the output and value-added multipliers for two periods for the digital sector in the 16 economies studied. Notably, many economies exhibited lower output multipliers for the latter periods across digital sectors. This indicates either an increased dependence on the external economy (imported inputs) or, more generally, the dilution of domestic linkages in the digital sector. Meanwhile the value-added multipliers for each economy were more stable over time, as indicated by the overlapping blue and green points in Figure 18.

For hardware, the output multipliers of the PRC, at 2.9 in 2012 and 3.1 in 2019, were far ahead of other economies for both periods. This means that a $1 increase in the demand for hardware products in the PRC generates about thrice its value in domestic gross output, suggesting strong local linkages of hardware manufacturing in the economy. Thailand follows the PRC with its output multiplier of 2.2 in 2010 and 2.0 in 2015. Japan and India likewise registered output multipliers of around 2.1 to 2.2 per $1 increase in hardware demand, although Japan in 2015 posted a slightly lower output multiplier of 1.9. Looking at the value-added multipliers, the US had the highest multipliers across economies for both periods, whereby for every $1 increase in the final demand for hardware, the US generated around $0.90 additional value to the economy in 2019 and in 2010. More interestingly, Singapore's hardware sector registered the lowest period 1 and 2 value-added multipliers at 0.2 and 0.3, respectively, signaling its high use of foreign intermediate products in production. Low value-added multipliers for any economy-sector mean high vertical integration of the domestic sector to foreign sectors, which implies that the income earned per dollar or unit of demand will be increasingly shared between the domestic and foreign economy.

Taipei,China; Germany; and Indonesia had the highest output multipliers for software publishing products at around 1.9 in both periods. However, turning to value-added multipliers, the US, Denmark, and the ROK registered the highest among the economies, at around 0.9 value-added for every $1 increase in the final demand for

---

[42] Appendix 1 details the preliminary steps in calculating the output and value-added multipliers of any economic system described by an IOT. Using the Leontief inverse matrix $L = (I - A)^{-1}$, the output multiplier of each sector is derived by taking the column sum (across rows) of L. In mathematical terms, a vector of output multipliers is given by $m_o = i' L$. Meanwhile, the value-added multiplier of each sector is computed by first pre-multiplying the diagonalized value-added coefficient vector $\hat{v} = diag(gva') \hat{x}^{-1}$ by Leontief inverse matrix, and then getting the column sum (across rows) of the matrix product. In mathematical terms, a vector of value-added multipliers is given by $m_v = i' (\hat{v}L)$.

Figure 18: Digital Sector Output and Value-Added Multipliers Based on National Input–Output Tables

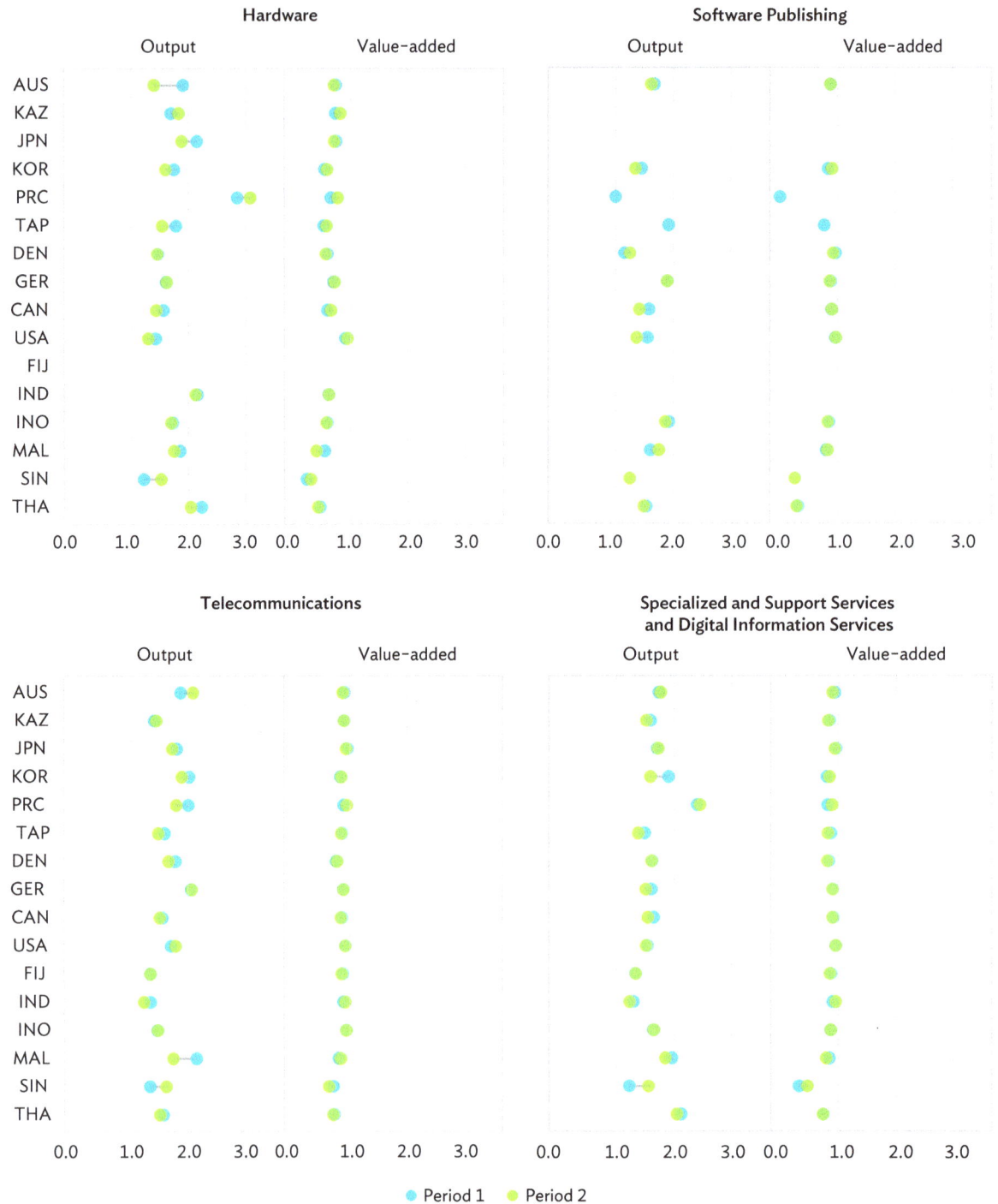

● Period 1   ● Period 2

Notes: Economies covered and their years for Period 1 and Period 2 are Australia (2010, 2018); Canada (2012, 2016); Denmark (2010, 2016); Fiji (2011, 2015); Germany (2010, 2016); India (2010, 2014); Indonesia (2010, 2014); Japan (2011, 2015); Kazakhstan (2001, 2018); Republic of Korea (2010, 2018); Malaysia (2010, 2015); People's Republic of China (2012); Singapore (2000, 2016); Taipei,China (2016); Thailand (2010, 2015); and the United States (2010, 2019). Period 2 national input-output tables for the People's Republic of China and Taipei,China were extracted from the 2019 multiregional input-output analysis. For economies with more than four core digital sectors in their national input-output tables, the weighted average of their multipliers was taken using gross output shares to get the multipliers for the four digital sectors used in this analysis.
Source: Calculations of the Digital Economy Measurement Framework study team, using input-output and related data from various national statistics offices and international databases.

software products. This supports the earlier observation that software publishing is generally more value-adding to the economy and with greater domestic linkages in advanced economies. Developing economies, such as Fiji and Kazakhstan, did not have values for software publishing, possibly because products of the sector are not produced or not identified in these economies.

For digital services sectors, telecommunications and specialized and support services and digital information services, the results of the estimates did not have a clear delineation among advanced and developing economies. For telecommunications, Malaysia had the highest multiplier for the first period, at $2.10 additional gross output for every $1 increase in telecom services demand for 2010, but its output multiplier declined to 1.7 in 2015. Germany, the PRC, the ROK, and Australia followed Malaysia, with telecom output multipliers of around 1.9 to 2.1 in both periods. In terms of value-added, Japan, the PRC, and Indonesia demonstrated the largest multipliers at around $0.90 to $1 value-added generated for every $1 increase in the demand for telecom services. On specialized and support services and digital information services, the PRC generated the highest output multiplier at 2.4 in 2012 and 2.5 in 2019 per $1 increase in demand, while the US generated the most value-added to its economy per $1 increase in demand, at $0.95 in 2010 and $0.96 in 2019. Singapore's specialized and support services and digital information services sector again exhibited low value-added multipliers of 0.3 and 0.5 for its periods 1 and 2, respectively, indicative of the strong vertical integration of the sector to foreign sectors.

Digital Economy-Sectors in the Global Economy

Figure 19 visualizes MRIOT-based and NIOT-based output multipliers of the digital sector in the 16 economies studied.[43] These multipliers were calculated using the 2019 MRIOT. Impacts of MRIOT-based multipliers are interpreted relative to the global economy. For instance, if sector k in economy i has an output multiplier of 1.5, then a $1 increase in its global final demand would induce a $1.50 increase in the global gross output. Multipliers calculated using an MRIOT (MRIOT-based multipliers) are generally higher than multipliers calculated using NIOTs (NIOT-based multipliers) as the former captures international dependencies that may lead to interregional spillovers.

In terms of the output multipliers of the three digital subsectors—manufacture of computer, electronic, and optical products ("manufacture of computers"); telecommunications ("telecom"); and computer programming, consultancy, and related activities, and information service activities ("information services")—in the 2019 MRIOT, Singapore led the 16 economies in its telecom and information services sectors, bearing output multipliers of 2.7 and 2.8, respectively (Figure 19). Singapore's information services sector stands out against other selected economies (except for the PRC, which has an output multiplier of 2.7 for the same sector), whereby a $1 increase

---

43   For MRIOT-based output multipliers, a global Leontief inverse was used, thus explicitly considering interregional linkages.

in the final demand of Singapore's information services would increase the global output by $2.80. Analogously, a $1 increase in the final demand of Singapore's telecom would induce a $2.70 increase in global output. The PRC's manufacture of computers sector had the highest output multiplier (3.7) among the 16 economies. This is also the highest of all the economy-digital subsector output multipliers presented in Figure 19.

In terms of economic size, Singapore and the PRC—leaders in digital sectors' output multipliers—are starkly different. In 2019, Singapore reported GDP in current prices of $372 billion, while the PRC posted $14,343 billion (ADB 2020). This suggests one important feature of multipliers as a policy variable: they do not only signify the economic significance of an economy-sector in terms of size; they also provide a measure of how deeply linked an economy-sector is to other economy-sectors. In the case of Singapore, its high output multipliers may be indicative of the latter feature. Singapore's comparably lower output multipliers based on the NIOTs, which only capture the domestic direct and indirect effects, also confirm this.

Figure 19: Digital Sector Output Multipliers Based on Multiregional and National Input-Output Tables, 2019

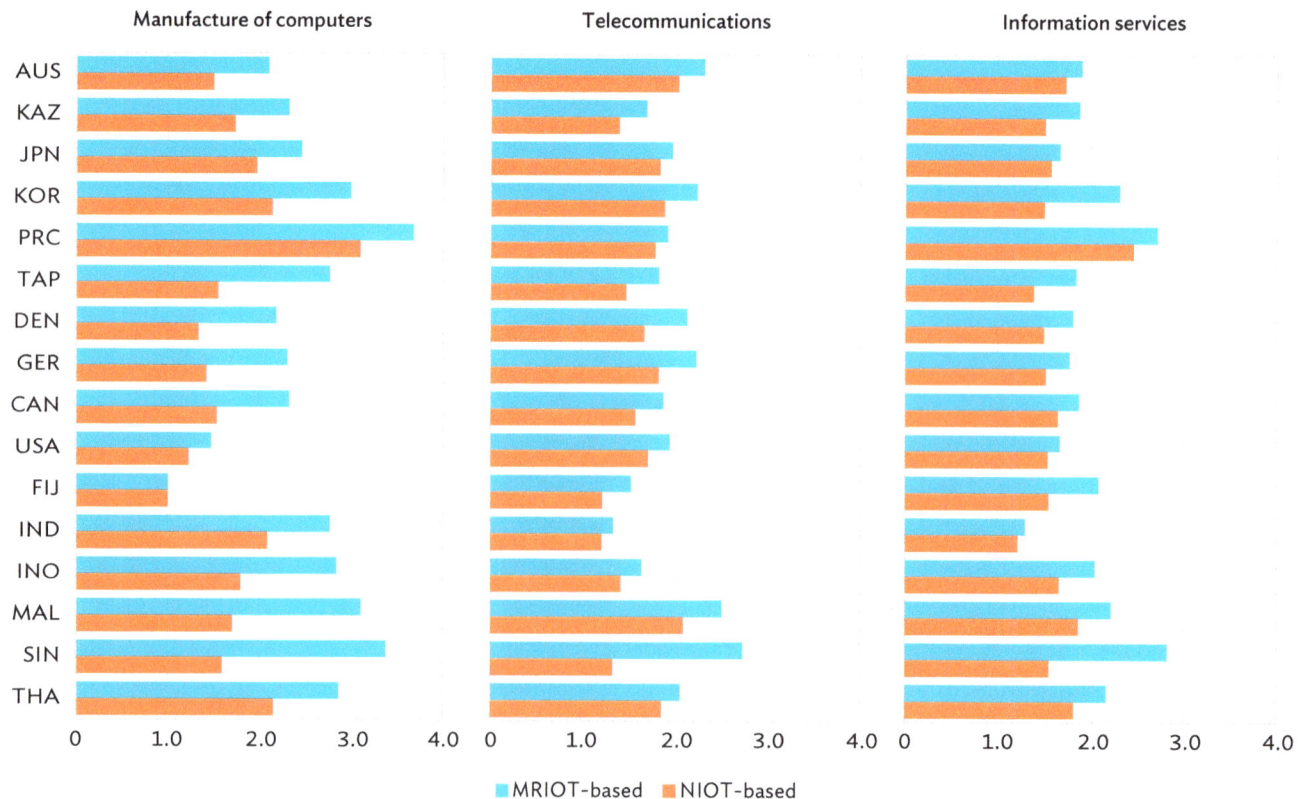

AUS = Australia; CAN = Canada; DEN = Denmark; FIJ = Fiji; GER = Germany; IND = India; INO = Indonesia; JPN = Japan; KAZ = Kazakhstan; KOR = Republic of Korea; MAL = Malaysia; MRIOT = multiregional input-output table; NIOT = national input-output table; PRC = People's Republic of China; SIN = Singapore; TAP = Taipei,China; THA = Thailand; USA = United States.
Note: NIOT-based multipliers were calculated using the NIOT extracted from the 38-sector MRIOTs for 2019, for sector and temporal comparability to MRIOT-based multipliers.
Source: Calculations of the Digital Economy Measurement Framework study team, using the 38-sector Asian Development Bank MRIOT for 2019.

Comparing Figure 18 and Figure 19 provides a richer picture of domestic and international linkages of the digital sector. Multipliers shown in Figure 18 provide a temporal comparison of NIOT-based multipliers between two periods using detailed NIOTs published by national statistics offices. Meanwhile, those shown in Figure 19 provide a comparison of MRIOT-based and NIOT-based multipliers generated using the 2019 MRIOT. In Figure 18, it can be observed that domestic output multipliers for hardware declined relatively significantly for Australia; Japan; and Taipei,China between the two periods. Observing Figure 19 for the manufacture of computers, a gap between the MRIOT-based and NIOT-based output multipliers are naturally seen in these economies, possibly relating the decline observed in Figure 18 to thicker international linkages. The gap is largest for Taipei,China, providing stronger evidence in this economy that the decline in domestic output multipliers is due to increasing international linkages across the years. Figure 18 also shows that Malaysia's telecom output multiplier declined between the two periods and, as Figure 19 reveals, the decrease might be related to stronger international linkages. However, the evidence for this is not as strong as Taipei,China's hardware sector, because the gap between the NIOT-based and MRIOT-based multipliers for Malaysia's telecommunications sector is not as defined as Taipei,China's hardware sector.

As is observed in Figure 19, MRIOT-based multipliers are generally higher than NIOT-based ones, because the former nuances the sources of imports and destination of exports, thus allowing the calculation of interregional spillovers. To disentangle international and domestic impacts on gross output, Figure 20 shows a disaggregation of the gross output that is induced by the 2019 final demand for digital output in the 2019 MRIOT. Box 6 describes the disaggregation methodology.

Figure 20 shows that, in 2019, a majority of the output induced by the digital sectors of Kazakhstan; Singapore; and Taipei,China were derived from linkages with external economies through (i) impacts from local digital demand on the rest of the world (open-loop), and (ii) impacts of the rest of the world's digital demand on local economies (closed-loop). The impacts from local digital demand on the rest of the world (open-loop) was especially great for Singapore. In particular, Figure 20 shows that $1 of final demand for Singapore's digital products induced additional output of $1.70 from the rest of this world (comprising 46% of total output induced by $1 of Singapore's digital final demand), further confirming the deep links of Singapore's digital sector to the rest of the world. In Taipei,China, $1 of digital product final demand induced an output spillover of $1 to the rest of the world (open-loop), which further generated an output feedback of $1.30 to the Taipei,China economy (closed-loop)—a total of $2.30 interregional spillover induced.

Box 6: Multiplier Decompositions across Transfer, Open-Loop, and Closed-Loop Effects

The output multiplier can be decomposed into three components based on the drivers of the demand for production: the transfer effect M_1, the open-loop effect M_2, and the closed-loop effect M_3. The equation to decompose the multiplier is given by $L = M_3 * M_2 * M_1$

The transfer effect M_1 captures the impacts of domestic digital demand on the domestic economy, while the next two components give the effects of interregional production and trade linkages on the economies. Specifically, the open-loop effect M_2 captures the additional production required from the rest of the world to meet local digital demand. This additional production in the rest of the world could, however, result in additional domestic economic activity to the extent that relevant producers import inputs from the domestic economy. This feedback from the rest of the world to the domestic economy is captured in the closed-loop effect M_3. For example, a local brand of laptop bought in Taipei,China is produced by a domestic manufacturing firm, which purchases inputs of electronics components from a local supplier (transfer effect). This local electronics supplier in turn orders an assembly plant in Thailand to manufacture and ship raw components to Taipei,China (open-loop effect). To undertake this production order, the firm in Thailand purchases other related inputs from another firm in Taipei,China (closed-loop effect). This relationship is further illustrated below.

For ease of calculation, the 2019 Asian Development Bank Multiregional Input-Output Table is simplified into a two-region input-output table to decompose the multipliers, where one region refers to the domestic economy while the other region is the aggregate of all the other economies, i.e., the rest of the world. The multipliers for each economy are thereafter calculated and decomposed using this two-region table.

Flow Chart of Multiplier Decomposition

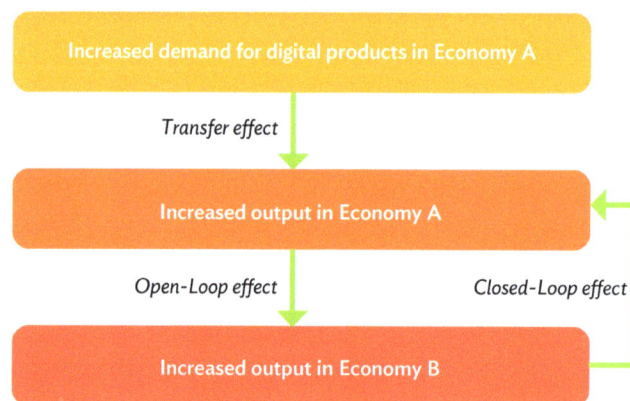

Source: R. Miller and P. Blair. 2009. Input-Output Analysis Foundations and Extensions (2nd ed.). Cambridge: Cambridge University Press.

The output induced for every \$1 of the PRC's digital final demand stands out across all economies in terms of direct impacts on the domestic economy. In the domestic economy alone, each dollar of the PRC's digital final demand generated \$2.80, which is 77% of the total output induced and hints at the strong production capacity of the PRC economy.

Figure 20: Gross Output Induced by Each Dollar of Digital Final Demand, 2019

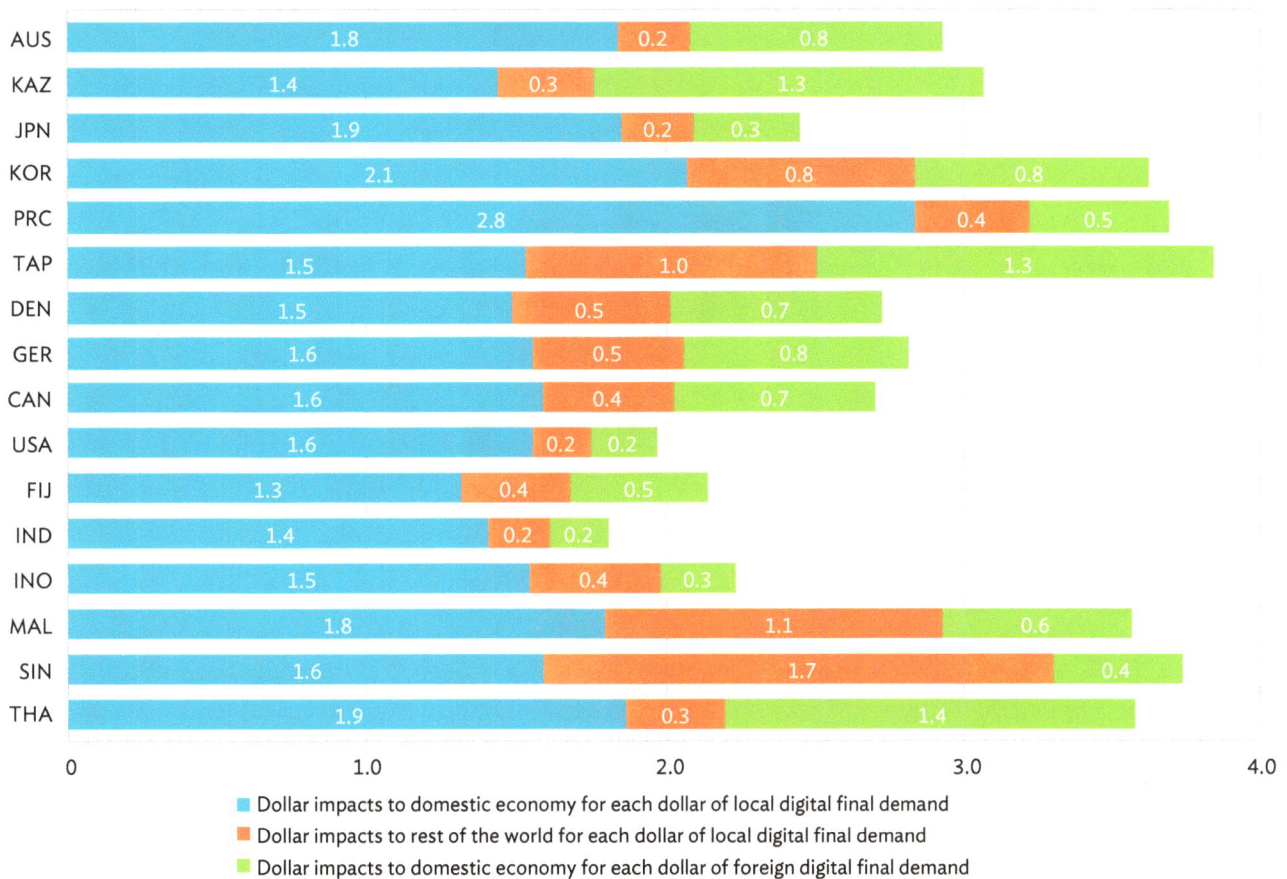

Dollar impacts to domestic economy for each dollar of local digital final demand

Dollar impacts to rest of the world for each dollar of local digital final demand

Dollar impacts to domestic economy for each dollar of foreign digital final demand

AUS = Australia; CAN = Canada; DEN = Denmark; FIJ = Fiji; GER = Germany; IND = India; INO = Indonesia; JPN = Japan; KAZ = Kazakhstan; KOR = Republic of Korea; MAL = Malaysia; PRC = People's Republic of China; SIN = Singapore; TAP = Taipei,China; THA = Thailand; USA = United States.

Notes: Impacts from local digital demand to domestic economy = transfer effects; impacts from local digital demand to rest of the world = open-loop effects; impacts of the rest of the world's digital demand to local economy = closed-loop effects. Digital sector includes manufacture of computer, electronic and optical products; telecommunications; and computer programming, consultancy, and related activities, and information service activities.

Source: Calculations of the Digital Economy Measurement Framework study team, using the 38-sector Asian Development Bank Multiregional Input-Output Table for 2019.

Digital–Nondigital Output Multiplier Gaps across Economies

Apart from analyzing digital output multipliers temporally (between two time periods) and spatially (across digital subsectors), comparing digital output multipliers against nondigital output multipliers sheds light on the transcendence of digital sectors in terms of output growth. Figure 21 juxtaposes the MRIOT-based digital output multipliers against those of nondigital sectors by economy for 2019.

Observably, the digital–nondigital gaps in output multipliers vary across economies. On the one hand, economies such as the Malaysia; the PRC; the ROK; Singapore; and Taipei,China display large positive gaps, i.e., digital output multipliers are greater than

Figure 21: Output Multipliers of Digital and Nondigital Sectors Based on Multiregional Tables, 2019

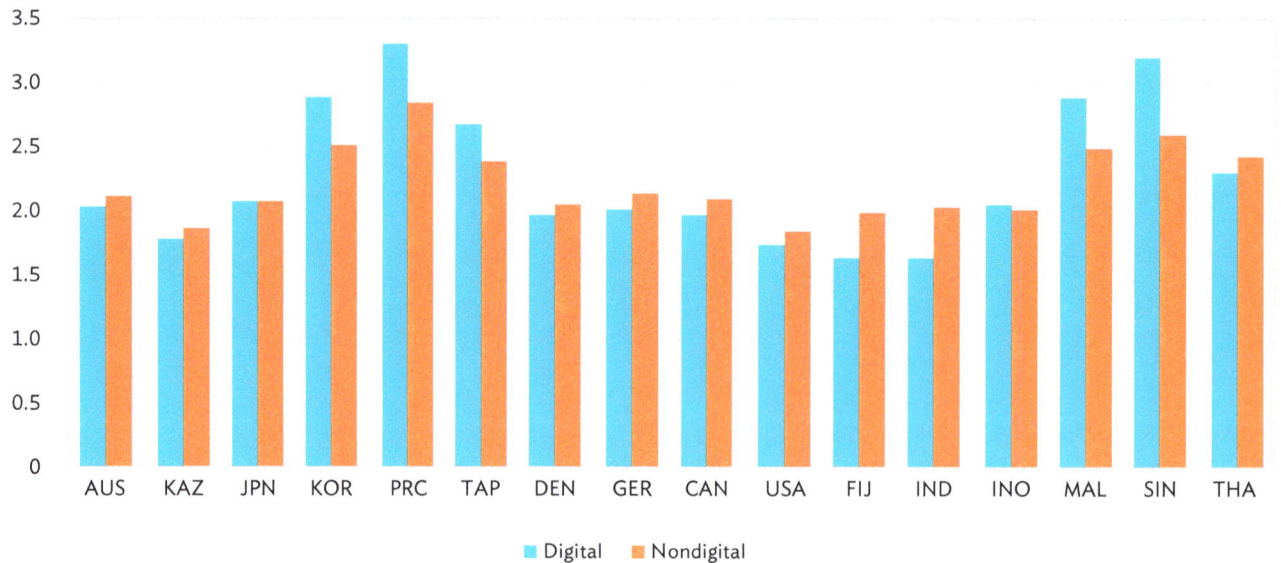

AUS = Australia; CAN = Canada; DEN = Denmark; FIJ = Fiji; GER = Germany; IND = India; INO = Indonesia; JPN = Japan; KAZ = Kazakhstan; KOR = Republic of Korea; MAL = Malaysia; PRC = People's Republic of China; SIN = Singapore; TAP = Taipei,China; THA = Thailand; USA = United States.
Notes: Output multipliers of digital and nondigital sectors are derived by taking the average of the output multipliers of each sector's subsectors, weighted against gross output. The digital sector includes manufacture of computer, electronic and optical products; telecommunications; and computer programming, consultancy, and related activities, and information service activities. The nondigital sector comprises of the rest of the sectors in the Asian Development Bank Multiregional Input-Output Table for 2019.
Source: Calculations of the Digital Economy Measurement Framework study team, using the 38-sector Asian Development Bank Multiregional Input-Output Table for 2019.

those of nondigital sectors. Digital sectors in these economies also registered the highest output multipliers among the 16 economies examined. On the other hand, economies such as Fiji and India exhibit large negative gaps, possibly indicating that digital sectors in these economies are not as transformative in terms of output induced, compared with nondigital sectors. Meanwhile, other economies show narrow digital–nondigital gaps, which means that output induced by digital and nondigital sectors are nearly on par.

Because multipliers may act as an indicator for sector linkages (assuming these interdependencies are robust across periods), they possess considerable policy relevance, particularly in economic planning. For instance, multipliers may be used by policymakers to understand where to channel investments to increase final demand for sectors that have the highest direct and indirect effects on the economy. Additionally, they can be used to anticipate the effects of exogenous shocks such as pandemics and natural disasters, holding other things constant. Additional insights may be gleaned if more refined or expanded multiplier indicators are calculated for the economies. One such method is calculating for multipliers of an economy based on the social accounting matrix, which is explored in Box 7. Though this matrix is more data intensive than the IOTs, it extends the IOTs by including information about the production processes and interinstitutional transactions that take place in an economy, which allows for more meaningful policy insights.

Box 7: Distributional Impacts of Digitalization using Social Accounting Matrices:
The Case of Canada and Armenia

A social accounting matrix (SAM) records the transactions of agents within the circular flow of an economy (ILO 2019). In addition to capturing production process linkages, a SAM includes information on the flow of resources among institutions such as households, corporations, and government. The disaggregation of household and labor accounts in the SAM allows us to delve into the distributional effects of certain policies. The total SAM multiplier for the digital economy measures value of all the effects on production and income in the economy brought by an increase of one local currency unit in the exogenous demand for digital sector commodities.

Social Accounting Matrix Multiplier Analysis using Canada 2016 Data

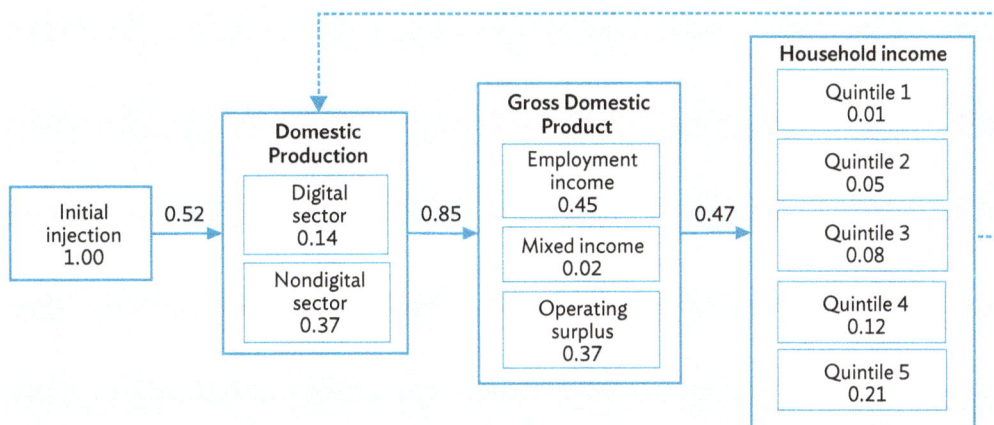

Deriving the SAM multiplier follows the same steps as getting the input-output multiplier, i.e., calculating for the Leontief inverse **L**, except that the user should first specify which accounts in the SAM are considered endogenous or exogenous. In practice, accounts for industries, labor, capital, and households are considered endogenous. Canada's 2016 SAM and Armenia's 2017 preliminary SAM are used for the digital multiplier calculations.[a]

Calculations suggest that the total SAM multiplier for Canada's digital sector is Can$3.79. This multiplier is larger when compared to Canada's 2016 input-output-based simple output multiplier of Can$1.52, which may be expected as the SAM takes into account the knock-on effects of exogenous changes on an expanded matrix of information.

Multiplier Effect in Urban and Rural Areas of Armenia, 2017
(by household income quintile)

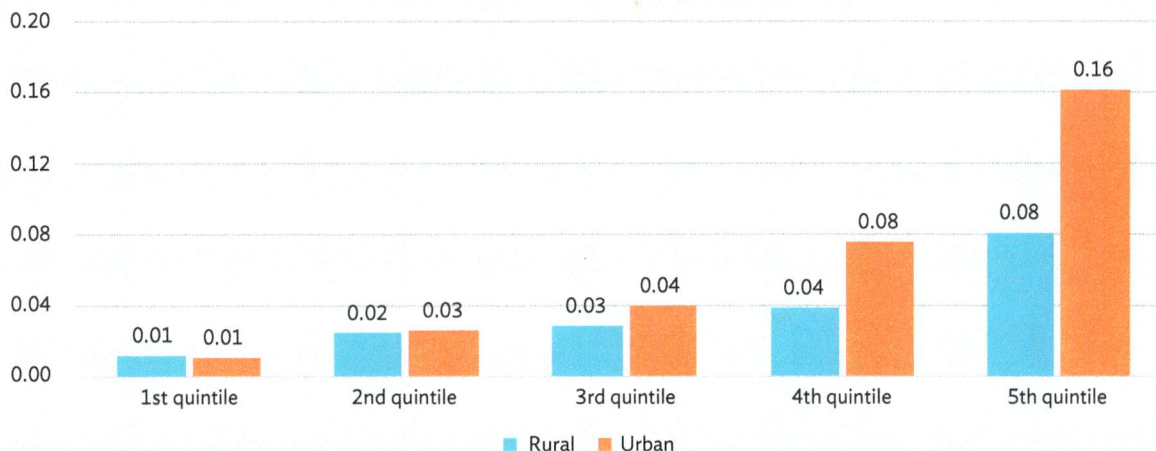

Source: Calculations of the Digital Economy Measurement Framework study team, using Armstat data.

continued on next page.

Box 7 *continued.*

Using the Stone Additive Decomposition method (Defourny and Thorbecke 1984), the total SAM multiplier can be further decomposed to examine the various mechanisms and linkages through which an exogenous shock contributes to the economy. The diagram above shows how the effect of a dollar increase in the demand for digital products affects the entire economy. A Can$1 increase in the exogenous demand for digital products is expected to boost domestic production by Can$0.52. In particular, Can$0.14 is the expected increase in the domestic production of digital products. Due to the production linkages of the digital sector, output of other industries in the economy is expected to rise by Can$0.37. The increase in domestic production in the economy will also increase gross domestic product (GDP) by Can$0.85, which will consequently increase household income by Can$0.47. This increase in household incomes will then induce another round of increases in domestic production, GDP, and income. In terms of its distributional effect, the initial injection in the demand for digital products is estimated to disproportionately benefit households in the richest quintile.

With the inclusion of feedback effects (as depicted by the dashed lines in the diagram), a dollar increase in the exogenous demand for digital products is expected to increase domestic output by Can$2.02, GDP by Can$1.12, and household income by Can$0.65.

For Armenia, preliminary results indicate that the 2017-based total SAM multiplier is AMD4.47 per AMD1 increase in exogenous demand for digital products. As a comparison, the 2017 input-output-based simple output multiplier for Armenia is AMD1.22 and, if household spending is endogenized, AMD1.63. The column chart above visualizes the effect of an AMD1 increase in the demand for digital products by household income quintile and by rural and urban areas in Armenia. The demand increase for digital products is likewise estimated to disproportionately benefit the households in the richest quintile and those living in urban areas.

---

a   The supply-and-use and input-output tables used in deriving the activities account in Armenia's SAM are preliminary balanced. Initial discrepancies were counted as changes in inventories.

References:
J. Defourny and E. Thorbecke. 1984. Structural Path Analysis and Multiplier Decomposition within a Social Accounting Framework. The Economic Journal. 94 (373). pp. 111–136.
International Labour Organization (ILO). 2019. Assessing the Effects of Trade on Employment: An Assessment Toolkit. Geneva, Switzerland: International Labour Organization Office.
W. Leontief. 1936. Quantitative Input and Output Relations in the Economic System of the United States. Review of Economics and Statistics. 18.

Generally, results indicate strong heterogeneity of digital multipliers across several economies and digital subsectors. These differences are driven by varying degrees of participation of economic sectors to the production of core digital products. While these impacts mean that growth in the digital sector extends the benefits to a wider range of other sectors, it also means that potential risks in core digital industries could spill over to other industries as well.

A Temporal Comparative Analysis of the Digital Economy

In the previous chapters, estimates of the digital economy made use of IOTs in current prices. This makes temporal analyses trickier, as value changes within each economy across time cannot be systematically differentiated between price changes and volume changes. Only the latter is considered a "real" change, so the impact of changes in prices must be removed from IOTs in order to make meaningful temporal analyses.

Using current-price tables is common among input-output studies for a couple of reasons. First, application is usually done without much consideration for the time dimension: in essence, the model is static. Ensuring that price changes do not influence results is therefore given less of a priority, compared to other data considerations such as extent of representativeness, level of aggregation, and applicability to the scope of analysis, among others. Second, constructing constant-price tables (if they are not readily available) is quite costly and, at times, unfeasible as they require rich data on price indices, careful setting of correspondences, and rebalancing, which takes significant time and resources for potential researchers.

In this chapter, the temporal comparative analysis of the digital economy using NIOTs in constant prices is explored. The overall objective is to demonstrate how conversion of transactions to volume terms, via adjustments for potential price effects, may influence results in terms of levels, trends, and rankings. This issue is important to investigate, especially when it comes to the digital sector, as the primary goods and services associated with it have undergone performance boosts and stark improvements in manufacturability over time. Case in point are laptops, which in the late 2016s were both more powerful and 96% cheaper than models released in the early 1990s (Perry 2016).

Table 4 shows the economies and years considered in this chapter, with the base year set to 2015. Criteria for selection included the availability of adequately spaced (i.e., 5 years or more) NIOTs, good-quality price indices, and regional representation. A detailed breakdown of how this study stated current-price NIOTs in constant prices is provided in Appendix 3.

Table 4: Economies with Constant National Input-Output Tables
(2015 = 100)

Economy	Year 1	Year 2
Canada	2010	2016
Germany	2010	2016
Japan	2000	2015
Malaysia	2010	2015
United States	2010	2016

Source: Published national input-output tables at current prices, stated in constant prices using double-deflation methodology.

Expansion of the Digital Economy in Volume Terms

From a static perspective, the size of each of the five economies' digital GDP as a percentage of economy-wide GDP varied between value (current-price) and volume (constant-price) terms in the two periods examined (Figure 22). In Period 1, the digital economy estimates were modestly higher using constant price NIOTs in Canada (+0.2 percentage points [pp] in 2010), Germany (+0.9 pp in 2010), and the US (+0.3 pp in 2010), while appreciably lower in Japan (–2.2 pp in 2000) and Malaysia (–1.4 pp in 2010). In Period 2, positive differences were observed in Germany and the US at higher margins (+1.4 pp and +0.4 pp, respectively, both in 2016), while only a slight negative difference is seen in Canada (–0.3 pp in 2016). For Japan and Malaysia NIOTs, Period 2 is the base year (2015), which is why its current and constant price estimates are equal.

From a dynamic perspective, the growth of digital GDP per economy likewise varied between value and volume terms. As discussed earlier in this report, growth in the digital economy as a percentage of GDP calculated using current-price NIOTs was negative for most of the economies studied. In the previous chapter, this result is attributed to falling prices and growing productivity within the digital sectors across economies and over time. Using constant price NIOTs, the former was established, as, in volume terms, the digital economy as a percentage of GDP grew at a positive rate for all five economies examined (Figure 22). Using current-price NIOTs, the digital economy of Japan as percentage of GDP became significantly smaller over time (–1.5 pp), while that of Germany and Malaysia shrunk marginally (both by –0.1 pp).

Figure 22: The Digital Economy as a Percentage of Economy-Wide Gross Domestic Product
(current prices versus constant prices)

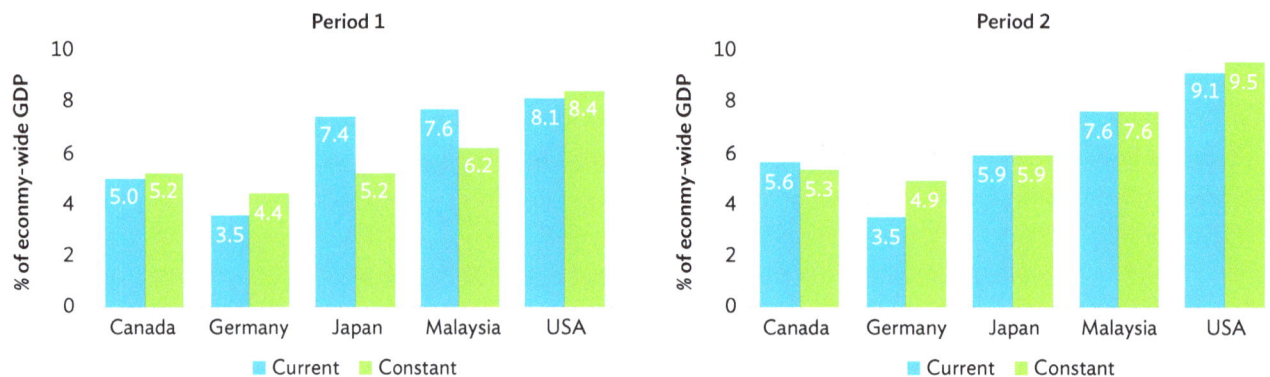

GDP = gross domestic product; USA = United States.
Note: Period 1 and Period 2 are represented by the following years: Canada, 2010, 2016; Germany, 2010, 2016; Japan, 2000, 2015; Malaysia, 2010, 2015; US, 2010, 2016. Base year of constant price estimates is 2015.
Source: Calculations of the Digital Economy Measurement Framework study team, using input-output and related data from various national statistics offices and international databases. Published input-output related data from national statistics offices were stated in constant prices using the double deflation methodology.

Increases were observed in the US (+1.0 pp) and Canada (+0.6 pp). A shift in the narrative was observed alongside a change of perspective to volume terms as the digital economy of Malaysia registered fastest growth (+1.4 pp) followed by the US (+1.1 pp), while Germany and Japan displayed growths of +0.5 pp and +0.7 pp respectively, outranking Canada's growth of +0.1 pp.

While the digital economy as a percentage of GDP had been growing in volume terms, the speed of growth varied across economies. Canada's digital economy as a percentage of GDP grew the slowest in volume terms between the 2 time periods (5.2% to 5.3%), much slower than its corresponding growth in value terms (5% to 5.6%) (Figure 22). This phenomenon can be partially attributed to the rising prices of the economy's digital products, relative to other economies. UN Comtrade database shows that across all five economies examined, it was only Canada's unit prices of automatic data-processing machines (Harmonized Commodity Code 8471) that registered a positive CAGR of 0.7% during the previous 2 decades. In contrast, the US showed declining unit prices at a CAGR of –3.3%, along with Japan (–3.1%), Germany (–2.4%), Malaysia (–0.5%). In addition, according to data from the International Telecommunication Union (2021b), fixed broadband prices in Canada increased from 2008 to 2017. Across all five economies, Canada had the second-highest rate of users for fixed broadband subscriptions, next to Germany. However, compared to the latter, the increase in prices for Canada was higher at a CAGR of 2.3%, while Germany's fixed broadband prices remain almost flat at 0.8% annually.

Japan's digital economy in value and volume terms is a stark contrast with Canada. There is a substantial gap between value and volume estimates of Japan's core digital economy in Period 1 (2000), which is due to the steeper decline in ICT prices in the economy. This could be tied to the developments in the economy during the late 1990s and early 2000s. Using the same dataset from UN Comtrade as mentioned above, unit prices dramatically rose from 1996, peaked in 2005, and have since declined at a rapid rate of –6.4% to 2020. These developments are affected by a confluence of factors, most notably the prolonged recession in the 1990s, or the so called "lost decade." Another major event was the entry into force of the Information Technology Agreement in 1996, initially subscribed to by 29 economies, including Japan. During this period, Japan recorded a sharp decline in the quantity of exported computers, partly due to greater competition from other economies. In addition, IT supply chains in Asia underwent major restructuring, as Japan occupied higher value-adding activities in downstream segments from a previously upstream position (WTO 2017). As a result, there was an upward pressure on prices as the market started to adjust. Taken together, these domestic conditions, in addition to the changes in the external environment, rendered prices of digital products in the early 2000s to be significantly higher in Japan than they were in more recent years.

Linkages with Digitally Enabled Sectors Robust to Price Changes

Zoning in on specific economies and dissecting the interindustry linkages from the perspective of the digital sector also leads to some interesting results. In general, the set of key industries with strong backward and forward linkages to digital sector are preserved, regardless if one is using current price or constant price NIOTs, hinting that prices only marginally affect digital economy linkages. However, it is important to note that the order of significance of linkages to the digital economy (i.e., the rankings) vary between current price and constant price NIOTs.

Figure 23 provides the mean absolute deviation (MAD) and the variance of the differences between rankings in forward and backward linkages of the digital economy using a current and a constant price framework. The MAD is the average of the absolute value of the difference between the ranks derived, while the variance is a measure of dispersion. Rankings based on forward and backward linkages only differ by an average of 0.03–2.36 and 0.87–2.73, respectively, across all economies considered. Except for the US in 2010, differences in backward linkage rankings generally outweigh those of forward linkages, as shown in Figure 23. Higher MAD and variances for backward linkage rankings suggest that relationships of the digital sector with digitally enabling sectors is less robust to changes in prices, compared to its relationship with

Figure 23: Mean Absolute Deviation and Variance of Differences in Rankings of Forward and Backward Linkages
(current prices versus constant prices)

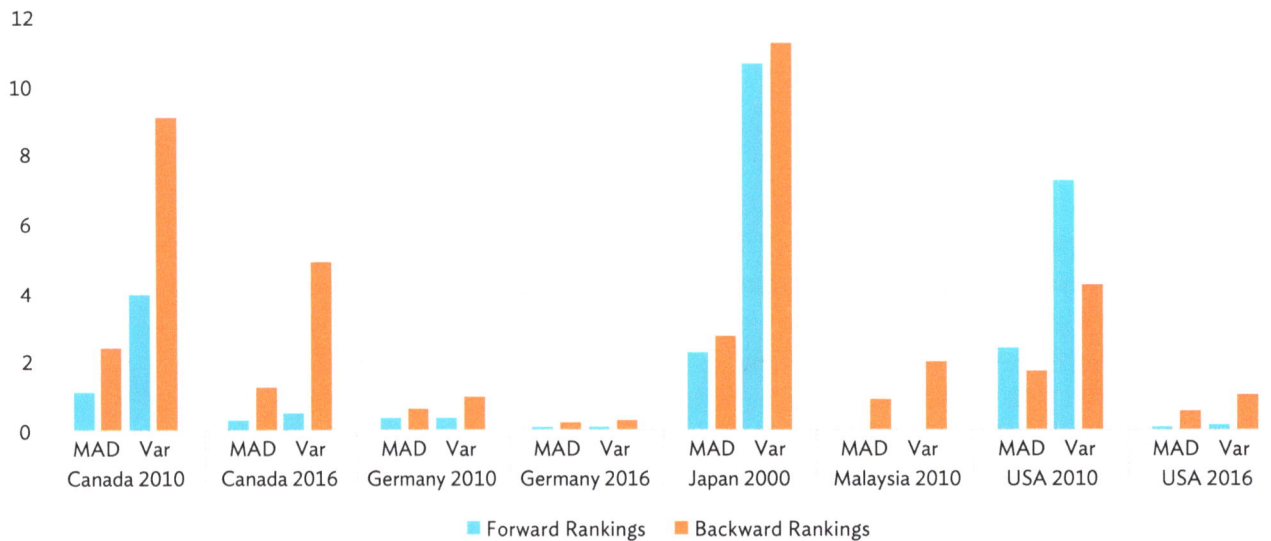

MAD = mean absolute deviation; Var = variance; USA = United States.
Note: Base year of constant price estimates is 2015.
Source: Calculations of the Digital Economy Measurement Framework study team, using input-output and related data from various national statistics offices and international databases. Published input-output related data from national statistics offices were stated in constant prices using the double deflation methodology.

digitally enabled sectors (forward linkages). This translates to good prospects for digital sectors, as its robust forward linkages imply that, despite price changes, digital sectors are taking primary roles within the digitally dependent economy, as was discussed in the previous chapter.

Over time, variability of both forward and backward rankings is seen to decline in Canada, Germany, and the US between 2010 and 2016, indicating that prices have less impact on the relative significance of a sector's linkage with the digital economy in more recent years. An important implication of this is that when one only seeks to determine the relative significance of a digitally enabling sector or a digitally enabled sector, using current price NIOTs may suffice, as sector rankings are preserved regardless of the price framework chosen.

Nonetheless, the usage of constant price data gives new context to the statistics generated earlier in this study. In this chapter, temporal analyses using constant price NIOTs allow not just the investigation of volume indicators, but of the related price dimension as well. As the digital economy and digitally dependent economy is expanding in volume, it raises an inquiry on how digital technologies are affecting conventional production structures, particularly the share of labor in production. In the next chapter, the dimension of temporal analyses is extended to assess the disruptive impacts of digital technologies on employment.

Jobs in the Digital Economy

Improvements in technology, such as the rise of digital data and digital platforms, are transforming relationships between producers and consumers across the globe (Mühleisen 2018). Consequently, this expansion in the digital economy has produced significant disruption in employment. On the one hand, digitalization and improvements in ICT have been associated with increased diversification and productivity, which in turn could lead to employment creation (UNCTAD 2019b). On the other hand, automation may result in the loss of jobs in certain sectors (ILO 2020; OECD and IDB 2016). Overall, changes in the digital economy are expected to produce structural transformation in labor markets, both in the short-run and in the long-run.

This chapter dissects the changes in employment in the digital economy. Employment in the digital economy is taken to mean employment in both core digital sectors and digitally enabled sectors. The former case looks at the trends in the number of employed in the digital sectors, while the latter pertains to how changes in the digital sectors have affected employment in other sectors dependent on digital sectors. Overall, this chapter focuses on how technological change in the digital economy has influenced net gains or losses in overall employment in digital and digitally enabled sectors. It also expands the analysis by looking at how sectors in the digital economy have generated jobs for the overall economy using employment multipliers.

Overall Employment Growth in the Digital Economy

Discussions surrounding employment often involve structural events that lead to the creation and/or loss of jobs. In the digital economy, new jobs are created directly through increased demand for labor in digital sectors, and indirectly through higher labor demand in digitally enabled sectors. Conversely, jobs losses arise due to the nature of technological changes in the digital economy. As firms shift to more automated processes, production may become less labor-intensive, which can impact economies with a comparative advantage in low-cost labor (ILO 2020). Moreover, digitalization's impact on employment goes beyond job creation and loss. Labor markets are transformed through changes in the skill requirements brought about by technological improvements in digital and nondigital sectors alike. In some cases, digitalization allows firms to outsource jobs outside the domestic market, implying that labor markets across economies are becoming increasingly integrated (OECD and IDB 2016).

Employment in the digital economy can be comprised of employment in the core digital sector itself and employment in the wider range of digitally enabled sectors (UNCTAD 2019b; OECD and IDB 2016). This section defines employment in the digital sector as total employed persons in the following sectors: hardware, software publishing, web publishing, telecommunications, and specialized support services (i.e., the core digital sectors). Meanwhile, the definition from the European Commission's Prospective Insights on R&D and ICT (PREDICT) database is used to define the scope of digitally enabled sectors (Mas et al. 2018).[44] The PREDICT database classifies employment in digitally enabled sectors into employment in the media content sector and the retail sales sector. The media content sector includes publishing of books, periodicals, and other publishing activities; audiovisual and broadcasting activities; and other information service activities. The retail sales sector pertains to retail sales via mail-order houses or via the internet. While it is possible to expand the list of digitally enabled sectors, limited data on employment in digital sectors and digitally enabled sectors make comparisons across economies challenging.

Using the PREDICT dataset, Figure 24 maps total employment in digital sectors for eight selected economies. Total employment in digital sectors is relatively higher in India and the US, reflecting their larger labor forces compared to other economies. India's employment in digital sectors has increased significantly since 2008 (2008–2015 CAGR of 7.6%), which is driven primarily by employment in telecom and specialized support services. Employment in digital sectors in the US had experienced a decline during the 2008–2010 Global Financial Crisis (GFC) and thereafter grew only minimally from 2010 to 2015 (CAGR of 2.2%). Meanwhile, employment increased at varying rates for the other economies: Austria (CAGR of 2.5%), Canada (CAGR of 2.4%), Germany (CAGR of 2.1%), Republic of Korea (1.7%), and Denmark (CAGR of 0.1%) from 2010 to 2015. Over the same period, Japan experienced a decline (CAGR of –0.9%).

Employment impacts of digitalization extend beyond core digital industries. Arguably, a narrow focus on employment in core digital sectors underestimates the total impacts brought about by digitalization. Figure 25 shows that, on average, employment in digitally enabled sectors (orange and green bars) was equivalent to approximately

Figure 24: Employment in Core Digital Sectors
('000)

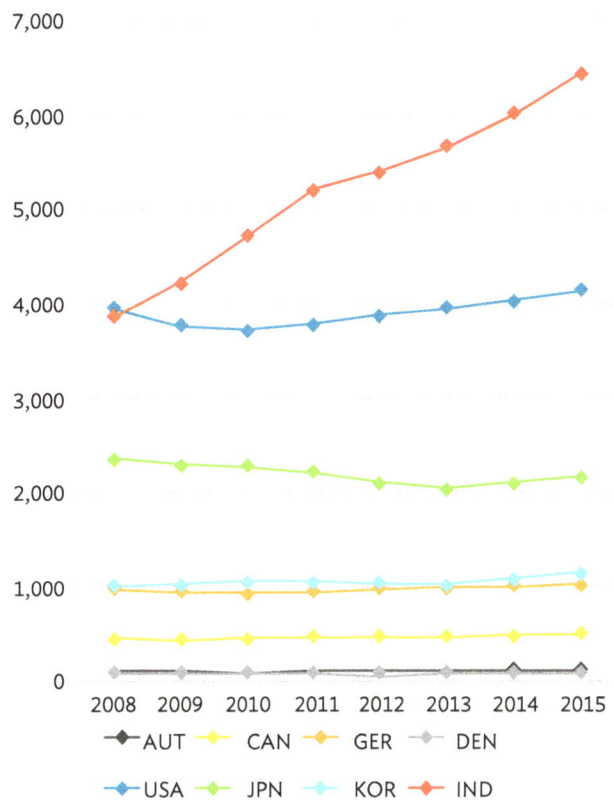

AUT = Austria; CAN = Canada; DEN = Denmark; GER = Germany; IND = India; JPN = Japan; KOR = Republic of Korea; USA = United States.
Note: Core digital sectors = hardware, software publishing, web publishing, telecommunications, and specialized support services.
Source: European Commission, Prospective Insights on R&D and ICT (PREDICT) Database 2018 (accessed 11 May 2021).

---

44 The PREDICT database has collected ICT-related information in 40 advanced and emerging economies since 2006. The database can be accessed at the following location: https://data.europa.eu/data/datasets/jrc-predict-2018-core?locale=nl.

Figure 25: Structure of Employment in the Digital Economy, 2015

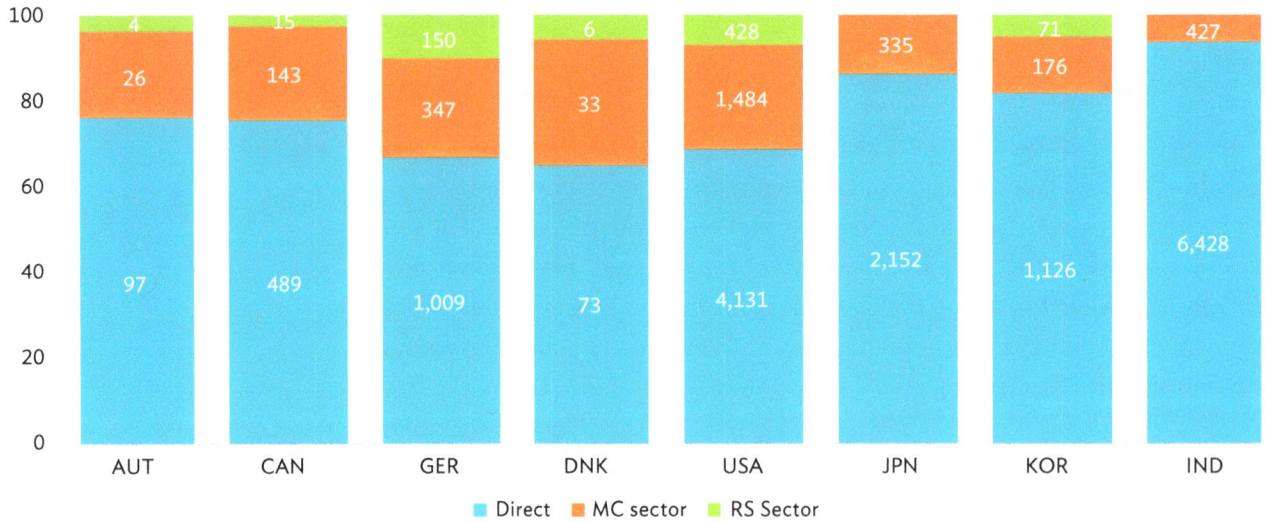

AUT = Austria; CAN = Canada; DEN = Denmark; GER = Germany; IND = India; JPN = Japan; KOR = Republic of Korea; MC = media content; RS = retail sales; USA = United States.
Notes: Data labels in thousands. Retail sales comprise those made via mail-order houses or the internet.
Source: European Commission, Prospective Insights on R&D and ICT (PREDICT) Database 2018 (accessed 11 May 2021)

one-third of the employment of digital sectors (blue bars). Therefore, employment indigitally enabled sectors constituted a significant portion of the employment in the digital economy.

For the eight economies selected, the share of employment from digitally enabled sectors in 2015 was highest in Denmark, at 35% in 2015 (Figure 25). Denmark was followed closely by Germany at 33% and the US at 31.6%. In level terms, employment in digitally enabled sectors was largest in the US at 1.9 million (1.5 million from the media content sector and 0.4 million from the retail sales sector), followed by Germany's digitally enabled sectors, which employed close to 500,000 people (347,000 from the media content sector and 150,000 from the retail sales sector). It must be noted that, since the definition of digitally enabled sectors employed in the PREDICT dataset is narrow, it is likely that the estimates do not capture the total employment in the digitally dependent economy as defined in earlier chapters of this report. Rather, values calculated can be considered as a lower bound of employment within the digitally dependent economies of the individual economies in Figure 25.

Overall, improvements in technology appear to have positively affected labor demand in the digital economy. However, studies on the distributional implications of such increases should be nuanced by the levels of skill. While such disaggregation is beyond the scope of this chapter, the rise of disruptive technologies such as artificial intelligence and automation in manufacturing has been associated with the increased demand for high-skilled labor, while simultaneously reducing the demand for low-skilled labor (ILO 2020; Graetz and Michaels 2018). In addition, the effect of technology improvements on labor decisions is difficult to isolate from other factors affecting employment, such as changes in sector composition of production tasks (Bertulfo et al. 2018).

Decomposing Employment in the Economies Studied

The trends in employment in the previous section reflect changes in total employment, net of the impact of job losses and interindustry human capital movements. To describe changes in total employment, the remainder of this chapter leans to the structural decomposition analysis (SDA) framework by Reijnders and de Vries (2018) as discussed in Box 8. Using this methodology, changes in total employment may be attributed to changes within sectors, changes between sectors, and changes in consumption levels. This is applied to the NIOTs of five economies: the US, Canada, Germany, Japan, and India. These economies were selected based on the size of their digital economies as determined in the earlier chapters.

United States

For the US, employment in core digital sectors experienced net losses from 2007 to 2012, except for the following sectors: custom computer programming services, wireless telecommunications carriers (except satellite), and computer systems design services (Figure 26).[45] Changes in production recipe, represented by the green bars in Figure 26, comprised the largest source of change in labor demand for most of the digital sectors in the US. This implies that the labor requirements of the core digital sectors in general, relative to other sectors in the economy, largely determined the change in its overall employment during the 2007–2012 period. The change in labor requirements resulting in job losses may have been adversely affected by the GFC from 2008 to 2009, in addition to changes in sector-specific production structure.

Except computer storage device manufacturing, digital sectors in manufacturing (e.g., electronic computer manufacturing, manufacturing and reproducing magnetic and optical media, and computer terminals and other computer peripheral equipment manufacturing) experienced a net decline in labor demand relative to other sectors in the economy, primarily due to changes in efficiency within these sectors. This means that productivity of factors (capital and labor) within these sectors had likely increased over time, thus causing a decline in labor requirements. Computer storage device manufacturing was also met with losses due to changes in efficiency within the sector; however, its net change in employment from 2007 to 2012 was positive, as gains coming from changes in production recipe, sector technology, and consumption

---

45   It is also shown in Figure 24 that the US registered net losses in employment in the digital economy from 2008 to 2012 (CAGR of –0.01%).

Box 8: Decomposing Change in Total Employment Using Structural Decomposition Analysis

Reijnders and de Vries (2018) applied structural decomposition analysis (SDA) to multiregional input-output tables (MRIOTs) in determining how changes in technology affect labor demand in global value chains (GVCs) across different economies (Bertulfo et al. 2018). Their framework assumes that labor inputs are determined by demand and applies a one-to-one mapping between occupations and tasks. In addition, Reijnders and de Vries assumed that tasks along a GVC are perfect complements and that proportions of production functions are fixed. Overall, they decomposed changes in employment into changes within GVCs, between GVCs, and changes in consumption levels.

The analysis by Reijnders and de Vries (2018) is replicated using national input-output tables (NIOTs). The use of NIOTs takes into consideration that disaggregation of digital sectors is not available in the Asian Development Bank's Multiregional Input-Output Tables and that cross-economy data on employment in digital sectors are limited. The basic structure of a standard NIOT is provided in Appendix 1 of this report. Overall, this approach decomposes changes in total employment into changes within sectors, changes between sectors, and changes in consumption levels.

Assuming that there are N industries and K occupations, let x_k denote the employment in occupation k. The vector x_k can be expressed as

$$x_k = \hat{\pi}^{-1} R_k \widehat{l_k^*} [T^* \circ (S^* \cdot c)] u \tag{1}$$

In Equation 1, c is a scalar indicating the total final demand for economy i. The matrix S^* is an $N \times 1$ vector describing the relative distribution of final demand use across the domestic industries. In the NIOT framework, this corresponds to the vector of final demand f. The matrix T^* is an $N \times 1$ vector of ones, while u is a scalar equal to one.

The vector $\widehat{l_k^*}$ denotes the labor of occupation k in efficiency units and is computed as $\widehat{l_k^*} = (\pi \circ l_k)'\mathbf{B}$ where $\mathbf{B}$ is the local Leontief inverse (i.e., based on NIOTs) and π is a vector containing sector-level multifactor productivity in economy i. Meanwhile, l_k is a vector whose ith element, l_{ki} pertains to the number of employed in occupation k per unit of output in sector i. Thus, $\widehat{l_k^*}$ captures the relative use of labor across sectors. Meanwhile, matrix $\mathbf{R}$ captures the share of sector i to the total employment in occupation k or a unit of final demand produced. It is calculated as $\mathbf{R} = (\widehat{\pi l_k}B)\widehat{l_k^*}^{-1}$.

To determine the intertemporal changes in employment, employment vectors in time 0 and time 1 are denoted as x_k^0 and x_k^1, respectively. The change in occupational labor between time 0 and time 1 is decomposed as:

$$x_k^1 - x_k^0 = \frac{1}{2}\{(\hat{\pi}_1^{-1} - \hat{\pi}_0^{-1})R_{k1}\widehat{l_{k1}^*}[T_1^* \circ (S_1^* \cdot \hat{c}_1)]u + (\hat{\pi}_1^{-1} - \hat{\pi}_0^{-1})R_{k0}\widehat{l_{k0}^*}[T_0^* \circ (S_0^* \cdot \hat{c}_0)]u\} + \tag{2a}$$

$$\frac{1}{2}\{\hat{\pi}_0^{-1}(R_{k1} - R_{k0})\widehat{l_{k1}^*}[T_1^* \circ (S_1^* \cdot \hat{c}_1)]u + \hat{\pi}_1^{-1}(R_{k1} - R_{k0})\widehat{l_{k0}^*}[T_0^* \circ (S_0^* \cdot \hat{c}_0)]u\} + \tag{2b}$$

$$\frac{1}{2}\{\hat{\pi}_0^{-1}R_{k0}(\widehat{l_{k1}^*} - \widehat{l_{k0}^*})[T_1^* \circ (S_1^* \cdot \hat{c}_1)]u + \hat{\pi}_1^{-1}R_{k1}(\widehat{l_{k1}^*} - \widehat{l_{k0}^*})[T_0^* \circ (S_0^* \cdot \hat{c}_0)]u\} + \tag{2c}$$

$$\frac{1}{2}\{\hat{\pi}_0^{-1}R_{k0}\widehat{l_{k0}^*}[(T_1^* - T_0^*) \circ (S_1^* \cdot \hat{c}_1)]u + \hat{\pi}_1^{-1}R_{k1}\widehat{l_{k1}^*}[T_1^* \circ ((S_1^* - S_0^*) \cdot \hat{c}_0)]u\} + \tag{2d}$$

$$\frac{1}{2}\{\hat{\pi}_0^{-1}R_{k0}\widehat{l_{k0}^*}[T_0^* \circ (S_0^* \cdot (\hat{c}_1 - \hat{c}_0))]u + \hat{\pi}_1^{-1}R_{k1}\widehat{l_{k1}^*}[T_1^* \circ (S_1^* \cdot (\hat{c}_1 - \hat{c}_0))]u\} \tag{2e}$$

Changes in occupational demand at the national level are comprised of five effects. The term 2a represents the changes in domestic demand for labor in occupation k that is attributed to changes in productivity per sector (changes in efficiency or Total Factor Productivity). The term 2b isolates the changes in labor demand due to changes in intermediate demand shares of sector i (change in production recipe). Meanwhile, term 2c indicates changes in labor demand assuming that the only source of change is the technological change within the sector (change in sector technology). The three terms comprise the change in employment due to changes within sectors.

Term 2d denotes the changes in labor demand due to changes in consumption patterns across sectors (change in consumption composition) and comprises changes between sectors. Lastly, term 2e isolates the effect of the overall change in total consumption in economy I to labor demand (changes in consumption levels).

In addition to the structural decomposition analysis, employment multipliers based on standard input-output analysis are derived to determine the effect of changes in final demand in digital sectors to employment in other sectors (Miller and Blair 2009). Employment multipliers are calculated as

$$e = EBY$$

continued on next page.

Box 8 *continued.*

where E is an $N \times 1$ vector containing the labor per unit of output for all sectors in the NIOTs, B is the Leontief inverse, and Y is an $N \times 1$ vector of sector-level final demand. Employment multipliers can also be calculated by estimating forward linkages and multiplying it to labor per unit of output. This approach changes the specification to $e = EGY$, where G is the Ghosh inverse. The multipliers generated by both approaches are very similar. For consistency in the existing literature, the estimates using the first approach are reported in this section (Miller and Blair 2009; ten Raa 2006).

This section uses constant NIOTs for selected economies to conduct the decomposition analysis. The level of disaggregation of sectors differs across economies because of the level of granularity available in different NIOT structures. Data on employed persons by industry are sourced from multiple labor force surveys, while sector-level measures of total factor productivity are sourced from national accounts. A summary of data sources is provided below.

Data Sources for Measuring Employment in the Digital Economy

Economy	Year	Data	Source
United States	2007; 2012	• Constant-price NIOTs • Employed persons by detailed industry • Multifactor productivity by detailed industry	United States National Accounts, Bureau of Labor Statistics
Canada	2012; 2016		Statistics Canada
Germany	2010; 2016		Statistisches Bundesamt OECD Multifactor Productivity
Japan	2011; 2015		Statistics Bureau of Japan OECD Multifactor Productivity
India	2010; 2014		MOSPI, CEIC OECD Multifactor Productivity

MOSPI = Ministry of Statistics and Programme Implementation, NIOT = national input-output table, OECD = Organisation for Economic Co-operation and Development.
Note: For unavailable data, constant-price NIOTs are derived using published current-price NIOTs deflated using applicable price indices.

It must be noted that sector classification for employment does not match sector classification provided in economy level-NIOTs. Whenever a sector disaggregation is not available, employment per sector is mapped to the sectors in the NIOTs by using the value-added of the sector to distribute employment. Meanwhile, sector-level data on multifactor productivity are mapped to the sectors in the NIOTs.[a] Moreover, digitally enabled sectors are expanded to include 10 sectors considered increasingly digitally disrupted by the Advisory Expert Group on National Accounts (2019). A list of subsectors is provided in Table 3 of this report.

---

[a]   Multifactor productivity (MFP) measures the efficiency by which factors of production are used in the production process. The US and Canada produce their own measure of MFP, while Germany uses the MFP definition of the OECD.

References:
Advisory Expert Group on National Accounts (AEG). 2019. *13th Meeting of the Advisory Expert Group on National Accounts: Framework for a Satellite Account on the Digital Economy*. Washington, D.C. https://unstats.un.org/unsd/nationalaccount/aeg/2019/M13.asp
D. J. Bertulfo, E. Gentile, and G. de Vries. 2019. The Employment Effects of Technological Innovation, Consumption, and Participation in Global Value Chains: Evidence from Developing Asia. *Asian Development Bank Economics Working Paper Series*. No. 572. Manila: Asian Development Bank.
R. Miller and P. Blair. 2009. *Input-Output Analysis Foundations and Extensions* (2nd ed.). Cambridge: Cambridge University Press.
L. Reijnders and G. de Vries. 2018. Trade, Technology, and the Rise of Non-Routine Jobs. Journal of Development Economics. 135. pp. 412–32.
T. ten Raa. 2006. *The Economics of Input-Output Analysis*. Cambridge: Cambridge University Press. doi:10.1017/CBO9780511610783.

level were enough to offset these employment losses. Computer storage devices had drastically evolved through the 2000s in terms of variety and accessibility – from the thumb drives of 2000 that could only store 8 megabytes of data and was priced at $28, down to the hard disk drives of 2013 with storage capacity of 4 terabytes at a cost of $190 (Chowdhury 2013).[46] This has influenced labor demand in the sector in ways which were favorable to boosting net employment.

---

[46]   1 terabyte has $1 \times e^6$ megabytes.

Figure 26: Change in Employment in Core Digital Sectors of the United States, 2007 and 2012
('000 persons)

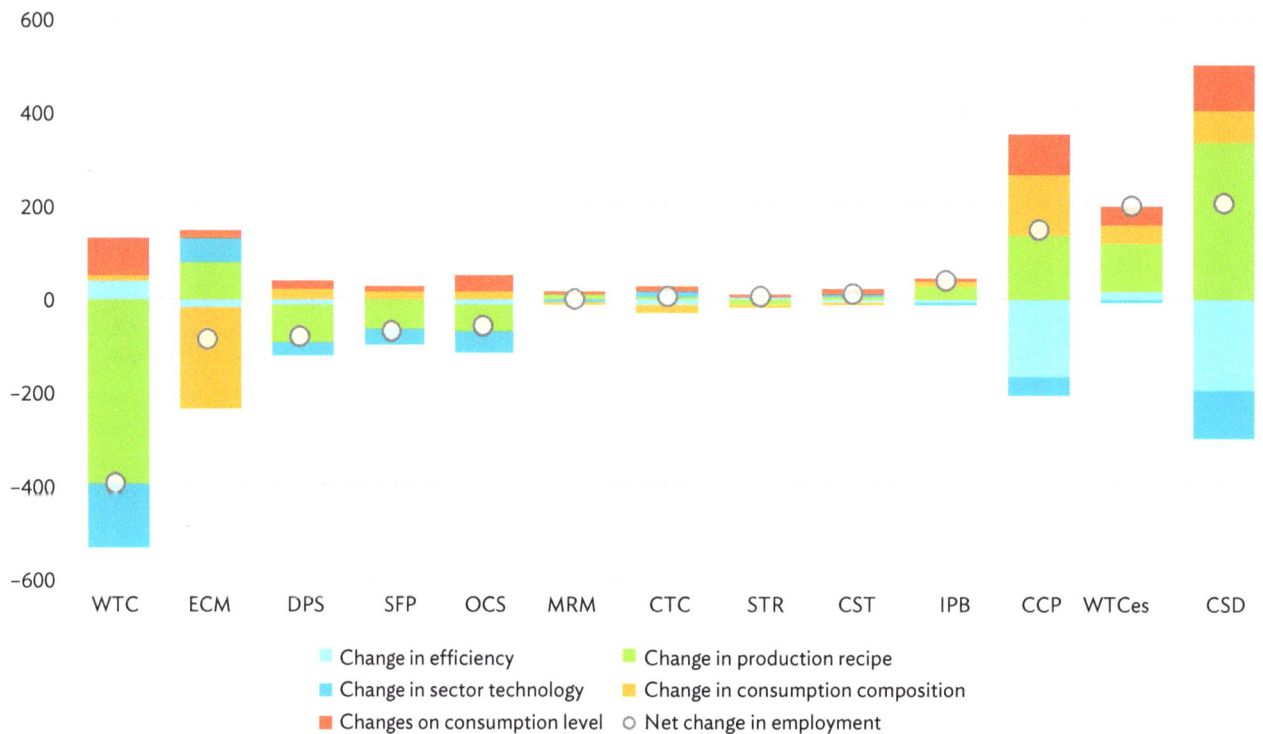

CCP = custom computer programming services; CSD = computer systems design services; CST = computer storage device manufacturing; CTC = computer terminals and other computer peripheral equipment manufacturing; DPS = data processing, hosting, and related services; ECM = electronic computer manufacturing; IPB = internet publishing and broadcasting, and web search portals; MRM = manufacturing and reproducing magnetic and optical media; OCS = other computer related services, including facilities management; SFP = software publishers; STR = satellite, telecommunications resellers, and all other telecommunications; WTC = wired telecommunications carriers; WTCes = wireless telecommunications carriers (except satellite).
Source: Calculations of the Digital Economy Measurement Framework study team, using data from United States National Accounts, Bureau of Labor Statistics.

Meanwhile, labor was generally more in demand in digital services sectors [internet publishing and broadcasting and web search portals, custom computer programming services, wireless telecommunications carriers (except satellite), and computer systems design services] relative to other sectors in the economy, such that the change in employment reflected net gains. The largest gains were derived from changes in production recipe and consumption composition. Other digital services sectors such as wired telecommunication carriers, data processing, hosting, and related services, software publishers, and other computer related services, including facilities management suffered from net losses in employment because of the large negative impact of changes in production recipe in these sectors.

Changes in sector technology capture the changes in labor demand due to technological improvements in the digital sectors. While it was not the biggest contributor to the change in employment across digital sectors, it generally led to a reduction in labor demand in most of the digital sectors, consistent with the results in the literature

(ILO 2020; OECD and IDB 2016). However, the effect of technological improvements on labor demand was offset in other aspects, such as changes in composition of consumption and changes in consumption level. This implies that, for the US, improvements in technology in the digital sector does not automatically result in an overall reduction in employment in these sectors.

For digitally enabled sectors, improvements in sector technology had a larger negative effect in overall employment compared to core digital sectors (Figure 27), providing evidence of the potentially disruptive impact digital technologies such as Industry 4.0 technologies have on employment. As with the digital sectors, the effect of technological improvements on employment was offset by an increase in demand for the products of these sectors (changes in composition of consumption) or an overall increase in consumption: such was the case for education services and for food and beverages services. Despite these gains, the large losses coming from changes in sector technology within digitally enabled sectors cannot be overlooked. It highlights the policy urgency of reskilling the labor force such that existing skills will not be made redundant by existing and budding Industry 4.0 technologies, and larger gains can be earned from changes in consumption patterns.

Figure 27: Change in Employment in Digitally Enabled Sectors of the United States, 2007 and 2012
('000 persons)

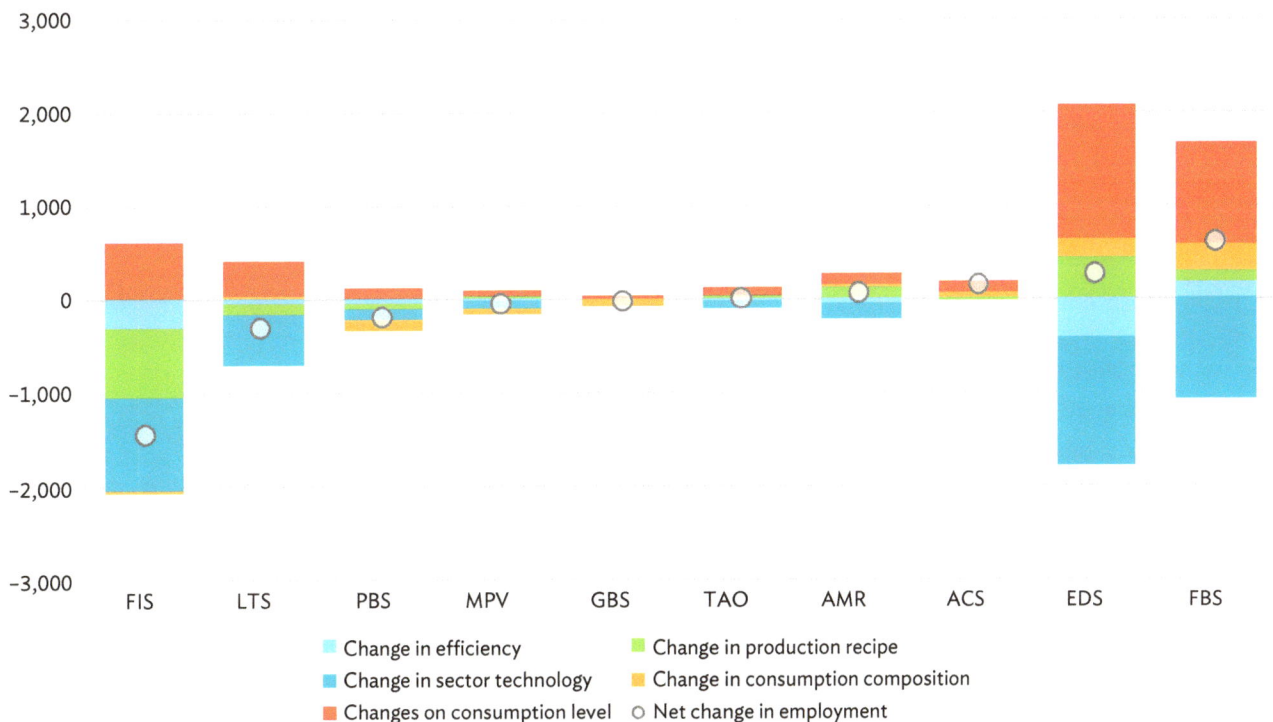

ACS = accommodation services; AMR = advertising and market research services; EDS = education services; FBS = food and beverage serving services; FIS = financial and insurance services; GBS = gambling and betting services; LTS = land transport services and transport services via pipelines; MPV = motion picture, video and television program production services, sound recording, and music publishing; PBS = publishing services; TAO = travel agency, tour operator, and other reservation services.
Source: Calculations of the Digital Economy Measurement Framework study team, using data from United States National Accounts, Bureau of Labor Statistics.

Germany

In contrast with the employment in 2007–2012 US, changes in consumption level and changes in efficiency were the main contributors to job changes in 2010–2016 Germany (Figure 28). The former mainly resulted in job increases, and the latter, in job losses. An increase in jobs due to changes in consumption level is caused by the growth of final demand for digital products from 2010 to 2016 in Germany. Meanwhile, decline in jobs due to changes in efficiency represents the decline in labor requirements due to improvements in multifactor productivity in digital sectors. Changes in production recipe were only significant for the data processing, hosting and related activities; web portals etc. sector, indicating that changes in labor requirements within the core digital sector of Germany did not significantly affect employment, relative to other sectors in the economy.

In the computers and peripheral equipment sector, job losses from changes in efficiency were marginally offset by gains from changes in consumption level and composition. Meanwhile, in the data processing, hosting and related activities; web portals etc. sector, job increases from changes in production recipe and consumption level overwhelmingly overturned the job losses. In telecommunication services sector and software publishing, publishing of computer games, and other software publishing sector, additional jobs from changes in consumption level and composition were not high enough to offset the job losses from changes in efficiency, production recipe, and sector technology.

As with the 2007–2012 US and consistent with the literature, changes in sector technology resulted in decreased labor demand not just for the core digital sector, but also and primarily for digitally enabled sectors in 2010–2016 Germany. The unfavorable impact of technological improvement to employment was greatest for motion picture, video and television program production services, sound recording, and music publishing; publishing services; and education services (Figure 29). Unlike the US, changes in sector technology were not as disruptive to employment in Germany. In half of the digitally enabled sectors, additional jobs from changes in consumption level and

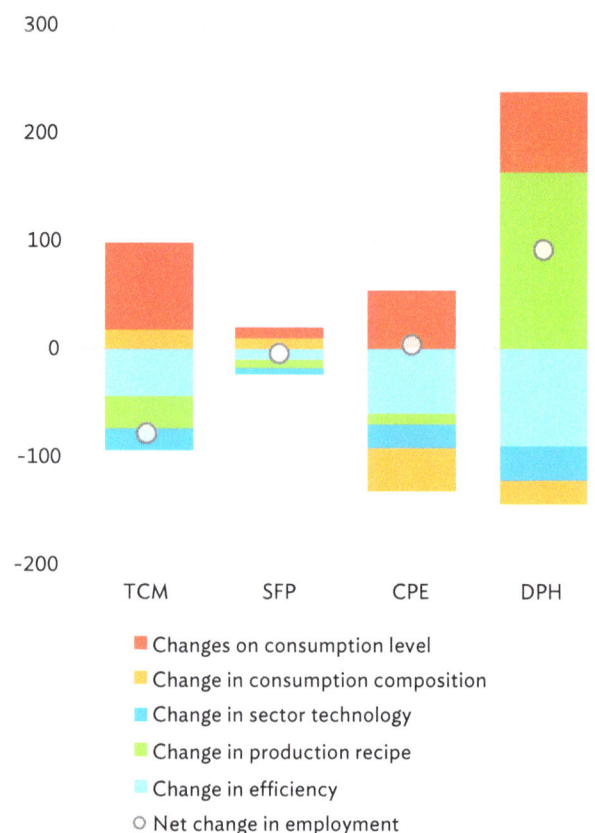

Figure 28: Change in Employment in Core Digital Sectors of Germany, 2010 and 2016
('000 persons)

- Changes on consumption level
- Change in consumption composition
- Change in sector technology
- Change in production recipe
- Change in efficiency
- Net change in employment

CPE = computers and peripheral equipment; DPH = data processing, hosting and related activities; web portals etc.; SFP = software publishing, publishing of computer games, other software publishing; TCM = telecommunication services.
Source: Calculations of the Digital Economy Measurement Framework study team, using data from Statistisches Bundesamt and the Organisation for Economic Co-operation and Development Multifactor Productivity.

composition were able to offset the losses. Meanwhile, the other half suffered minimal net job losses. A likely factor contributing to this phenomenon is the unique labor environment in Germany at the 2010–2016 period. Germany during the 2010s had been recognized for its relatively resilient labor market amid the recession caused by the GFC, and this had been linked to the economy's labor market reforms before and during the crisis, as part of its "Agenda 2010" (Rinne and Zimmermann 2012).

Figure 29: Change in Employment in Digitally Enabled Sectors of Germany, 2010 and 2016
('000 persons)

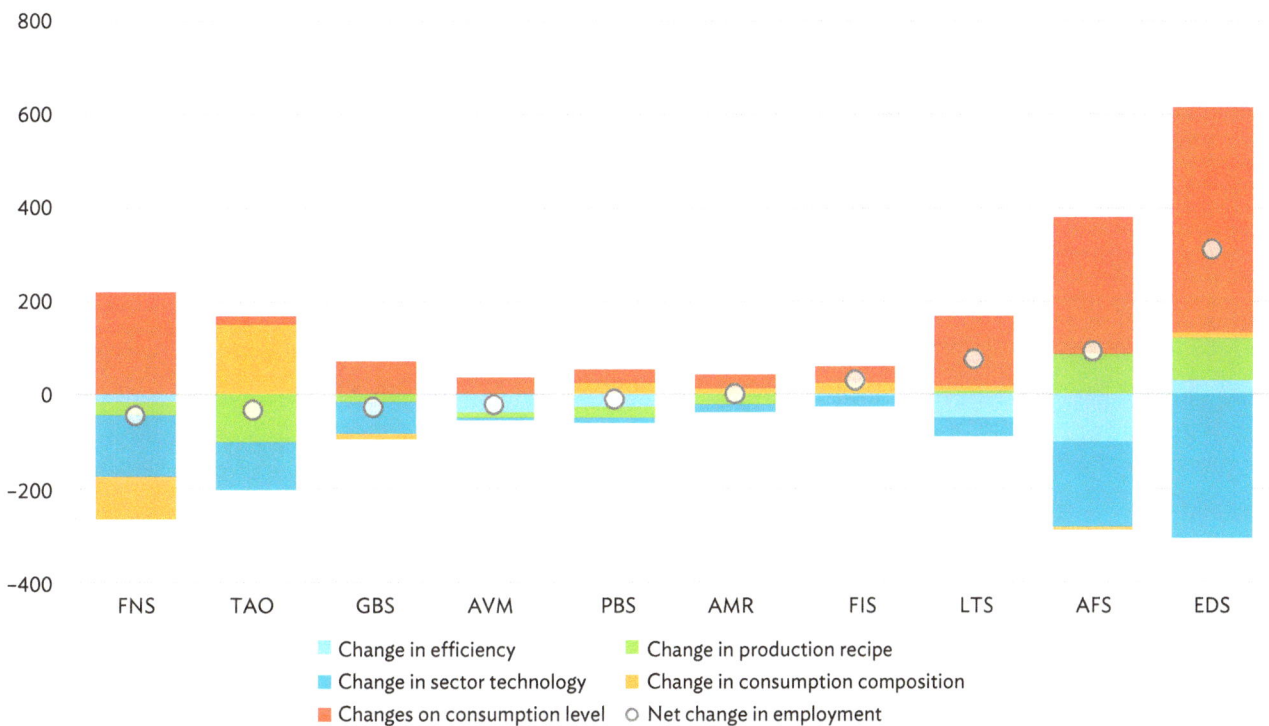

AFS = accommodation and food services; AMR = advertising and market research services; AVM = audio-visual media, music publishing, broadcasting; EDS = education services; FIS = services related to financial and insurance services; FNS = financial services; GBS = arts, culture, and gambling services; LTS = land transport services and transport services via pipelines; PBS = publishing services (nondigital); TAO = travel agency, tour operator, other reservation services.
Source: Calculations of the Digital Economy Measurement Framework study team, using data from Statistisches Bundesamt and the Organisation for Economic Co-operation and Development Multifactor Productivity.

Canada

The structure of the change in employment in Canada from 2012 to 2016 was closely similar to that of the US from 2007 to 2012 (Figure 30). Change in production recipe was also the largest contributor to changes in employment in Canada's digital sectors. The same largely contributed to the net decline in jobs in the telecommunications sector. Conversely, in the rest of the digital services sectors—namely internet publishing and broadcasting, web search portals; data processing, hosting, and related services; software publishers; and computer systems design and related services—changes in production recipe contributed positively to employment such that these sectors met job gains from 2012 to 2016. In the sole digital manufacturing sector (computer and peripheral equipment manufacturing) change in employment was minimal and is mainly driven by changes in the pattern of final consumption expenditure across sectors (yellow bar), and this resulted in a marginal decline in labor demanded by the sector.

Consistent with the results from the US and Germany, improvements in sector technology also resulted in decreased employment for all of Canada's core digital sectors over the 2012–2016 period. However, the overall increase in consumption level (red bars) for Canada from 2012 to 2016 offset much of the decline in employment across all digital sectors in general. In fact, if all employment changes were aggregated into one core digital sector—that is, summing across the net employment changes in telecommunications, computer and peripheral equipment manufacturing, computer systems design and related services, data processing, hosting, and related services, internet publishing and broadcasting, web search portals, and software publishers— it yields in an overall increase in jobs within Canada's digital sector.

Similarly, improvements in sector technology of Canada's digitally enabled sectors reduced labor demand in these sectors. The impact of changes in sector technology was largest for food and beverage services, followed by accommodation services (Figure 31). In the former, increase in employment due to changes in consumption composition, level, and production recipe were enough to offset the significant decline in jobs due to changes in sector technology. Meanwhile, in the latter, the positive impact of changes in consumption level was not sufficient, such that the accommodation services sector was met with net job losses from 2012 to 2016.

Figure 30: Change in Employment in Core Digital Sectors of Canada, 2012 and 2016
('000 persons)

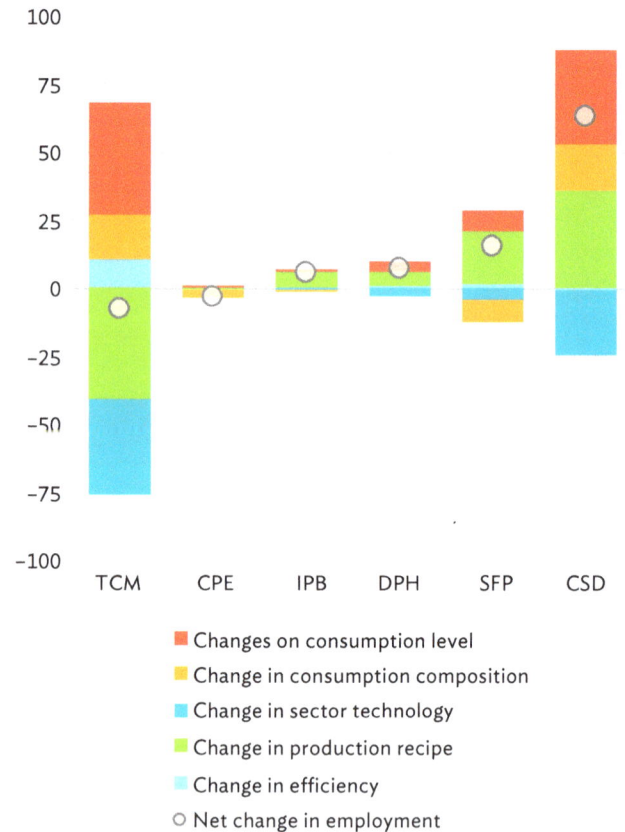

CPE = computer and peripheral equipment manufacturing; CSD = computer systems design and related services; DPH = data processing, hosting, and related services; IPB = internet publishing and broadcasting, web search portals; SFP = software publishers; TCM = telecommunications.
Source: Calculations of the Digital Economy Measurement Framework study team, using data from Statistics Canada.

Figure 31: Change in Employment in Digitally Enabled Sectors of Canada, 2012 and 2016
('000 persons)

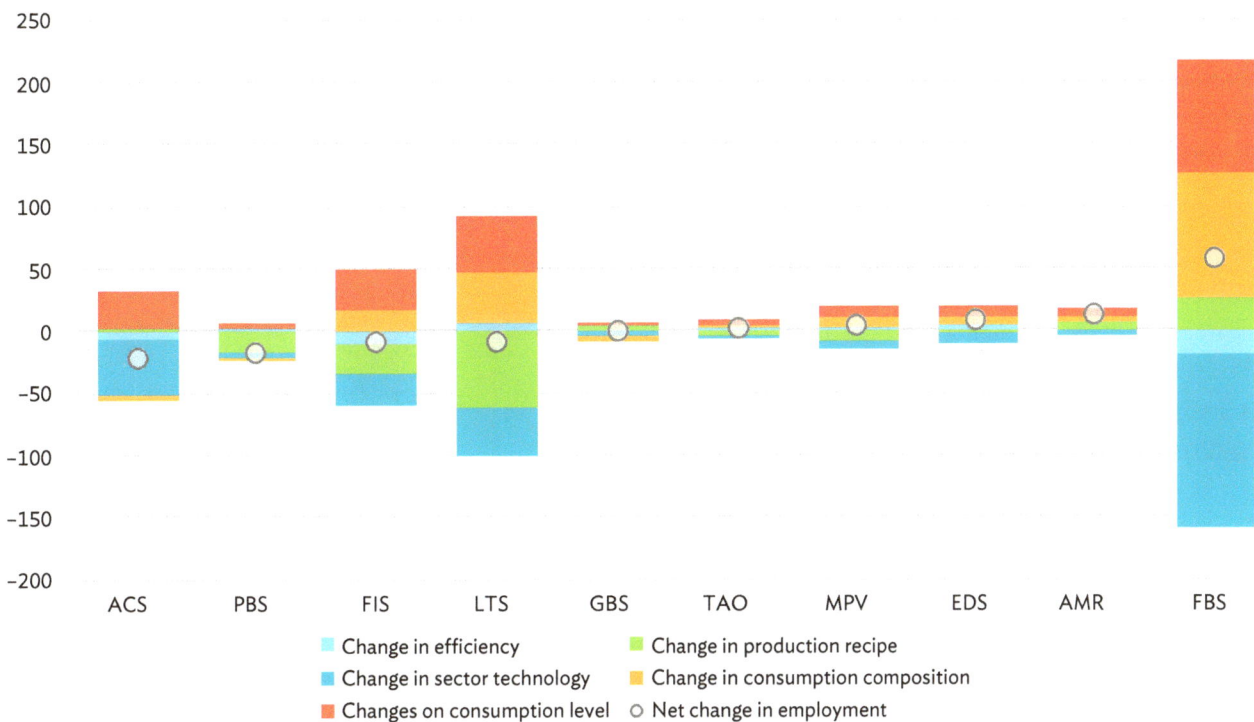

Change in efficiency
Change in production recipe
Change in sector technology
Change in consumption composition
Changes on consumption level ○ Net change in employment

ACS = accommodation services; AMR = advertising and market research services; EDS = education services; FBS = food and beverage serving services; FIS = financial and insurance services; GBS = gambling and betting services; LTS = land transport services and transport services via pipelines; MPV = motion picture, video and television programme production services, sound recording, and music publishing; PBS = publishing services; TAO = travel agency, tour operator, and other reservation services.
Source: Calculations of the Digital Economy Measurement Framework study team, using data from Statistics Canada.

Japan

Interestingly, all of Japan's core digital sectors registered net gains in employment over the period of 2011 to 2015, albeit only minimal (Figure 32). Change in production recipe and consumption levels were the main drivers of change in employment of Japan's digital sectors. For electronic computing equipment and accessory equipment manufacturing, the change in labor requirements across sectors, measured by change in production recipe, was the greatest positive contributor to the net change in employment from 2011 to 2015. Meanwhile, net employment in digital services sectors— namely, internet-based services, communications, and information services— was significantly and positively affected by changes in consumption level. Moreover, these digital services sectors posted higher gains in employment compared to the sole digital manufacturing sector, which registered least gains over the four-year period.

As with the core digital sectors, changes in employment in digitally enabled sectors of Japan from 2011 to 2015 (Figure 33) were also not as drastic compared to the United States from 2007 to 2012, Germany from 2010 to 2016, and Canada from 2012 to 2016.

This suggests that employment in both the core digital sectors and digitally enabled sectors is not immune from the general rigidity of the Japanese labor market, which is a result of common labor practices of Japanese firms that include long-term job security, seniority-based wages, and company-based labor unions (Yashiro 2011). The strong negative impact of improvements in sector technology on employment also puts Japan's digital and digitally enabled economy at greater risk of experiencing job losses, because of the economy's declining labor supply from its ageing population (OECD 2021). During the 2011–2015 period, however, the decline in jobs due to changes in sector technology were completely compensated by changes in consumption level, efficiency, and production recipe in the following digitally enabled sectors: financial and insurance services, publishing services, accommodation services, education services, advertising and market research services, food and beverage serving services, and motion picture, video and television programme etc. However, the interaction of technological progress and population ageing is continuously transforming the labor supply and demand in Japan, whereby it is becoming increasingly difficult for employers to find workers with the correct skills, and for workers to find jobs that match their expertise (OECD 2021).

Figure 32: Change in Employment in Core Digital Sectors of Japan, 2011 and 2015
('000 persons)

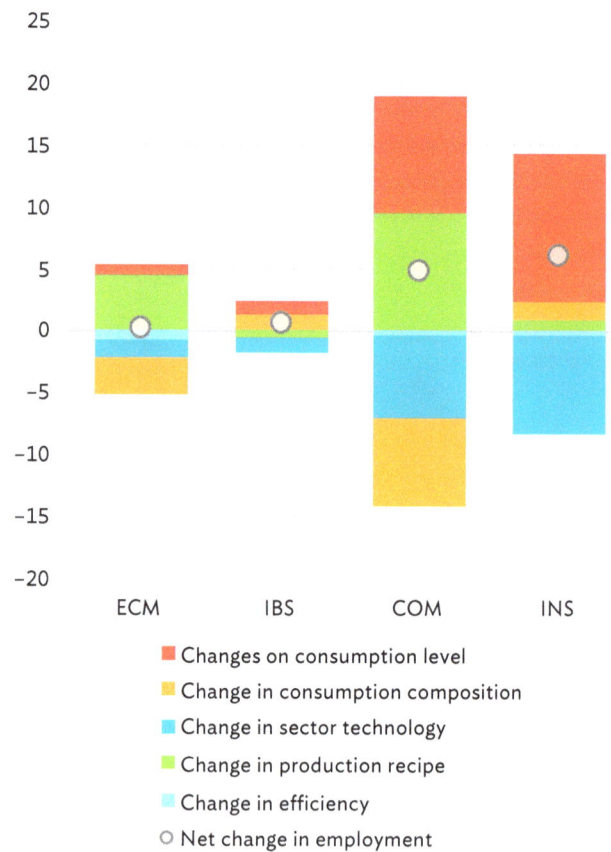

- Changes on consumption level
- Change in consumption composition
- Change in sector technology
- Change in production recipe
- Change in efficiency
- Net change in employment

CPE = computer and peripheral equipment manufacturing; CSD = computer systems design and related services; DPH = data processing, hosting, and related services; IPB = internet publishing and broadcasting, web search portals; SFP = software publishers; TCM = telecommunications.
Source: Calculations of the Digital Economy Measurement Framework study team, using data from Statistics Canada.

Figure 33: Change in Employment in Digitally Enabled Sectors of Japan, 2011 and 2015
('000 persons)

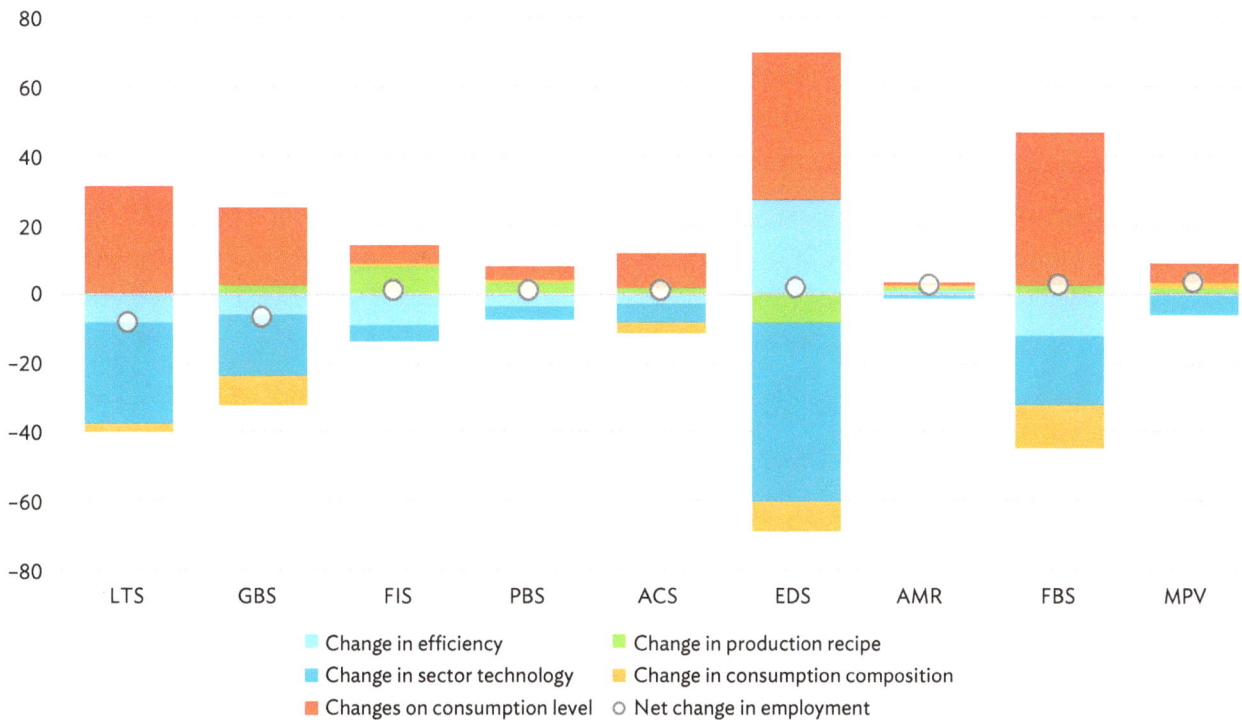

ACS = accommodation services; AMR = advertising and market research services; EDS = education services; FBS = food and beverage serving services; FIS = financial and insurance services; GBS = gambling and betting services; LTS = land transport services and transport services via pipelines; MPV = motion picture, video and television program, etc.; PBS = publishing services.
Source: Calculations of the Digital Economy Measurement Framework study team, using data the Statistics Bureau of Japan and the Organisation for Economic Co-operation and Development Multifactor Productivity.

India

Employment in India increased at a macro level from 2010 to 2014, and the same trend can be seen in India's core digital sectors (Figure 34). Similar with the US, Germany, Canada, and Japan, changes in production recipe contributed significantly to the change in employment in India from 2010 to 2014. Additionally, changes in sector technology also played a large and positive role in employment generation in India. This is in contrast to the US, Germany, Canada, and Japan, where changes in sector technology primarily contributed to job losses over time.

Employment increased from 2010 to 2014 for all core digital sectors: computer consultancy and related activities, manufacture of computers and peripheral equipment, and telecommunications. However, only the latter two were met with huge boosts in employment, while the former was almost unchanged from 2010 to 2014. In the digital services sectors (computer consultancy and related activities and telecommunications), only improvements in total factor productivity (light blue bars) resulted in job losses. Meanwhile, in the manufacture of computers and peripheral equipment, change in consumption patterns across sectors (yellow bar) also contributed to employment decline.

India's digitally enabled sectors likewise exhibited increases in labor demand from 2010 to 2014. Education and land transport services generated the largest increase in labor demand among the digitally enabled sectors. Changes in sector technology also contributed significantly and positively to employment in all digitally enabled sectors, except in accommodation services where change in the sector's technology contributed marginally to employment and the change in the sector's labor requirements (green bar) contributed the most to additional employment. As with the core digital sectors, improvements in total factor productivity, embodied in changes in efficiency, contributed to a decline in labor demanded in all digitally enabled sectors (Figure 35).

Noticeably, improvement in sector technology was an important factor affecting employment in core digital and digitally enabled sectors in India from 2010 to 2014. However, in contrast with more developed economies such as the US, Germany, Canada, and Japan, technological improvements contributed positively to labor demand in these sectors in India. This result puts into question existing literature that posit how technological improvements in developing economies reduce a sector's ability to absorb additional labor, thus reducing labor demanded (ILO 2020). With limited data, the results suggest that more investigation needs to be done to determine how improvements in technology in digital and digitally enabled sectors will affect employment, especially in the context of developing economies. Future research may be done to assess how the interactions of technological improvement and labor force upgrade affect the demand and supply of labor in the core digital and digitally enabled sectors in equilibrium.

For the five economies studied, improvements in technology as well as increased productivity of factors have been generally associated with a decrease in labor demand in the core digital and digitally enabled sectors. However, the disruption brought

Figure 34: Change in Employment in Core Digital Sectors of India, 2010 and 2014
('000 persons)

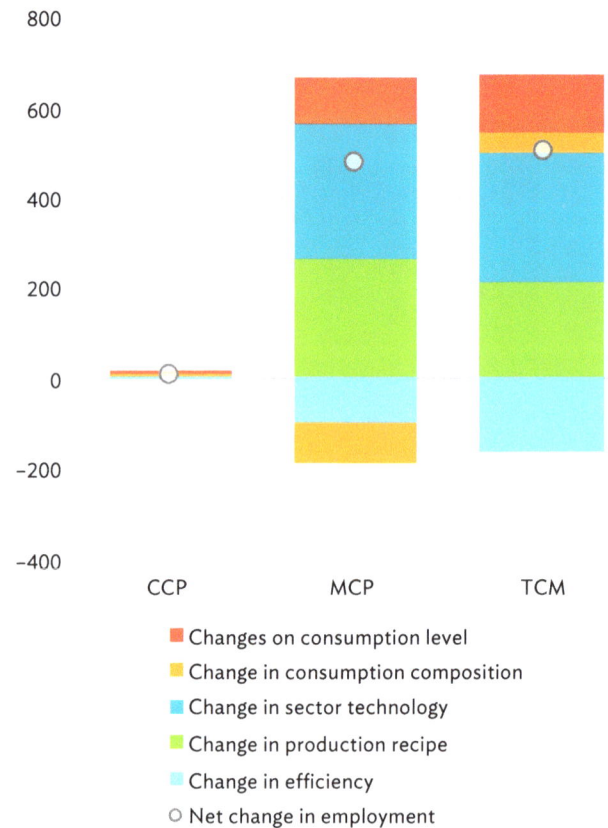

CCP = computer consultancy and related activities; information service activities. MCP = manufacture of computers and peripheral equipment; TCM = telecommunications.
Source: Calculations of the Digital Economy Measurement Framework study team, using data from the Ministry of Statistics and Programme Implementation, CEIC database, and Organisation for Economic Co-operation and Development Multifactor Productivity.

about by these changes may be potentially offset by employment gains from other channels. These channels include (1) the increased consumption of products of core digital and digitally enabled sectors, (2) the increased overall consumption in the economy, and (3) the increased labor requirements in the core digital and digitally enabled sectors. As previously noted, technological improvements in digital and digitally enabled sectors have been associated with increases in labor demand in India. Whether this is true for other developing economies requires further study, especially given concerns about how automation and other technological improvements can replace low-skilled labor.

Employment Multipliers

The concept of employment in the digital economy can be extended to other nondigital sectors, through backward and forward linkages that digital and digitally enabled sectors have with other sectors in an economy. Employment multipliers capture how many additional jobs the digital economy can generate through its interlinkages with other sectors.

To determine how much employment is generated by the digital economy, given changes in final demand, employment multipliers are estimated for each economy. This section simulates how much employment is generated by a $1 million increase in final demand for the following aggregated sectors: core digital sectors, digitally enabled sectors, and nondigital sectors (Figure 36). To construct the jobs created by a final demand increase, a final demand increase of $1 million is distributed within sectors to generate a new final demand vector. This is multiplied by the employment multipliers to estimate the jobs generated by the final demand increase. Because a $1 million increase in final demand is small for economies with large GDP and digital GDP, the magnitude of additional jobs generated by a final demand increase of $1 million is expected to be small. For the more developed economies studied, new jobs generated reach as high as 20. Meanwhile, the converse is true for India, where a final demand increase of $1 million is large, relative to the size and income of the economy, and, thus, produces as high as 200 additional jobs.

Figure 35: Change in Employment in Digitally Enabled Sectors of India, 2010 and 2014
('000 persons)

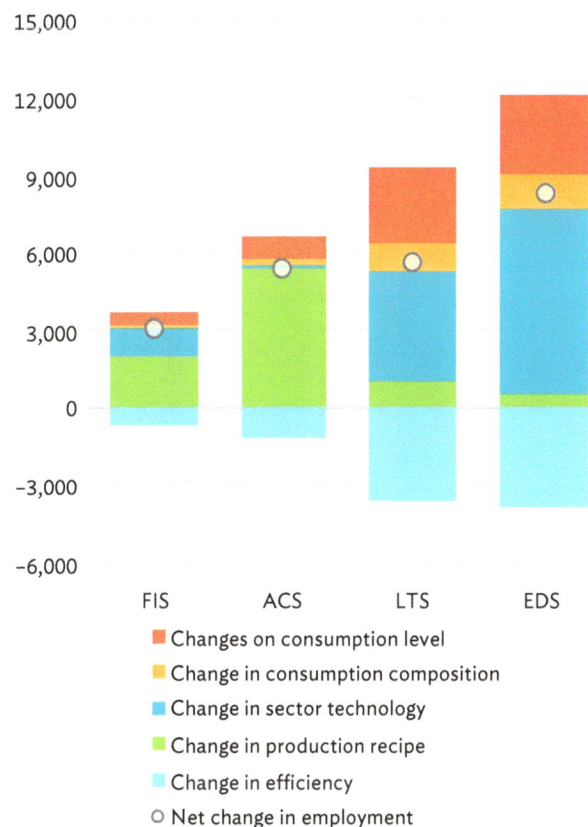

Changes on consumption level
Change in consumption composition
Change in sector technology
Change in production recipe
Change in efficiency
Net change in employment

ACS = accommodation services; EDS = education services; FIS = financial and insurance services; LTS = land transport services and transport services via pipelines.
Source: Calculations of the Digital Economy Measurement Framework study team, using data from the Ministry of Statistics and Programme Implementation, CEIC database, and Organisation for Economic Co-operation and Development Multifactor Productivity.

Figure 36: Employment Generated per $1 Million Increase in Final Demand of Digital, Digitally Enabled, and Nondigital Sectors
(number of jobs added)

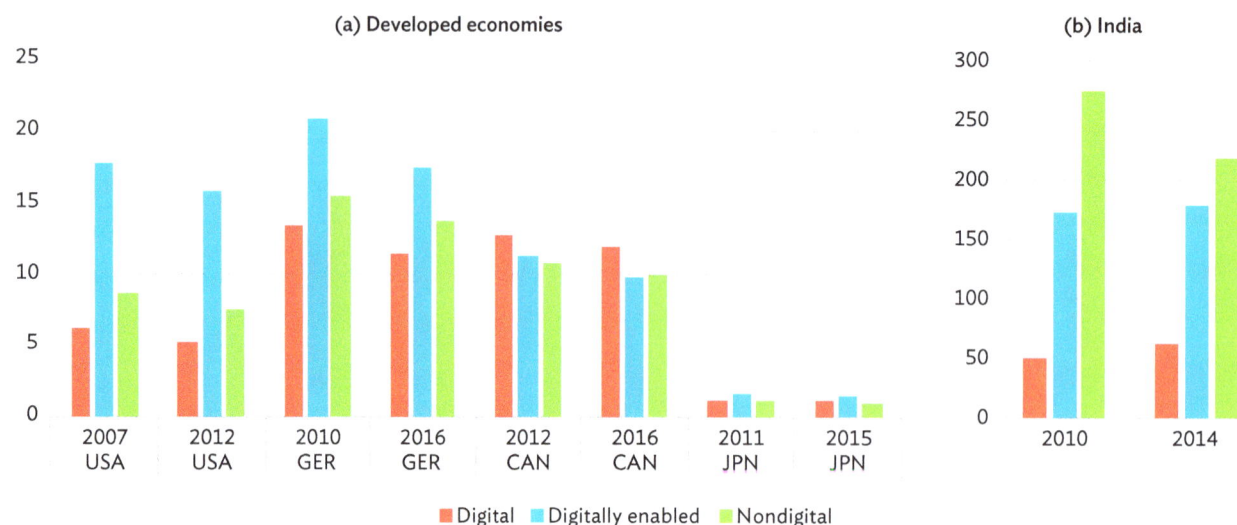

CAN = Canada; GER = Germany; JPN = Japan; USA = United States.
Source: Estimates of the Digital Economy Measurement Framework study team, using data from national input-output tables published on national statistics office websites for Canada, Germany, Japan, and India.

The digital services sectors generate more employment for a final demand increase in the core digital sectors of Canada, India, Japan, and the US. For the US, custom computer programming services, wired telecommunications carriers, and wireless telecommunications carriers (except satellite) create more jobs, given an increase in final demand of core digital sectors. Meanwhile, the telecommunications subsector generates more jobs in Canada, India, and Japan. Germany's biggest contributor to new jobs is computer manufacturing, followed closely by telecommunications.

Meanwhile, education, food services and accommodation, and transport are the top contributors to additional jobs for a final demand increase in digitally enabled sectors. In the US, more jobs are created in education and food services, relative to other digitally enabled sectors for a given final demand increase. For Germany, education and accommodation are the top contributors, as is the case for Canada, where the accommodation subsector generates more additional jobs, relative to other digitally enabled sectors. In Japan, transport and education have the highest employment generated, while the analogous sectors for India are transport and education.

Overall, employment generated by digitally enabled sectors is larger relative to that of core digital sectors in developed economies. Both the core digital sectors and digitally enabled sectors generate employment that is comparable in magnitude to nondigital sectors, suggesting that the digital economy exhibited strong potential for employment generation. In the case of India, final demand increases in core digital sectors and digitally enabled sectors generate a significant amount of employment. Core digital sectors produce 61 additional jobs, while digitally enabled sectors produce 179 jobs for a $1 million increase in final demand. This highlights the role of these sectors in overall employment, especially for developing economies.

Employment in the digital economy has changed significantly beyond 2010. The drastic technological change in digital sectors has resulted in creation of jobs and transformation of skills required for laborers across the globe (OECD and IDB 2016). However, these technological improvements have raised concerns about job losses as production becomes increasingly automated (ILO 2020).

While this section provides information on the sector changes in employment, it does not provide insights into how labor demands across economies and across occupational types will change as improvements in technology are made. Will technological improvements reduce demand for low-skilled workers, consequently reducing the comparative advantage of developing economies (ILO 2020)? Further research to assess these impacts is needed. However, a lack of cross-country data on outputs of the digital economy and occupation in related sectors poses challenges in determining these impacts. Nevertheless, the currently available data allow some detailed analyses on the inter-economy linkages of digital sectors, which may be a starting point to studying the effect of digital GVCs on employment, among other factors.

Digital Sectors in Global Value Chains

In this chapter, the latest World Input-Output Database (WIOD) tables, which cover 44 economies, including an aggregated economy for "the rest of the world," and 56 sectors from 2000 to 2014, are used (Timmer et. al. 2015). The 56 sectors in the WIOD tables provide a disaggregation level that meets the requirements of the definition specified in the section "Defining the Core of the Digital Economy" (p. 4).[47] In addition, ADB's 38-sector MRIOT for 2017 to 2019 is used to augment the analysis of digital GVCs.

Global Value Chain Participation of Digital Sectors

Applying the methodology by Wang et al. (2017), forward GVC participation of digital economy-sectors describes the exporting of intermediate products for a foreign economy-sector's production, while backward GVC participation of digital economy-sectors describes the importing of intermediate products for its own production. Using the digital economy-sector's relative participation in forward and backward linkages, one can deduce its relative position in the value chains. On the one hand, digital economy-sectors that have higher backward than forward GVC participation rates (below the 45-degree line in Figure 37) are economy-sectors that are more engaged in downstream activities. On the other hand, digital economy-sectors that have higher forward than backward GVC participation rates (above the 45-degree line in Figure 37) are sectors that are more engaged in upstream activities.

Figure 37 presents the evolution of forward and backward GVC participation rates of three digital sectors in 44 WIOD economies across 2000, 2007, 2014, and 2019.[48] From this figure, it can be observed that points scatter following a general outward movement (i.e., movement away from the origin) from 2000 to 2007. The same outward movement is observed from 2007 to 2014 and from 2014 to 2019. This movement implies a growing participation of digital economy-sectors in GVCs from a backward and forward perspective from 2000 to 2019, notwithstanding the 2008-2009 GFC and the following period which had been marked by an era of sluggishness in international trade or "slowbalization" (The Economist 2019b).

---

[47] The disaggregation level in the WIOD tables meet the definition, except for a possible portion of software publishing, and possible nondigital components under "manufacture of computer, electronic, and optical products," which have been maintained, both for purposes of convenience.

[48] The 44 economies covered in the WIOD are Australia; Austria; Belgium; Bulgaria; Brazil; Canada; Croatia; Cyprus; the Czech Republic; Denmark; Estonia; Finland; France; Germany; Greece; Hungary; India; Indonesia; Ireland; Italy; Japan; Latvia; Lithuania; Luxembourg; Malta; Mexico; the Netherlands; Norway; Poland; Portugal; the PRC; the ROK; Romania; Russia; the Slovak Republic; Slovenia; Spain; Sweden; Switzerland; Taipei,China; Turkey; the United Kingdom, the US, and "the rest of the world."

Figure 37: Global Value Chain Participation Rates by Digital Sector, World Input-Output Database

(44 economies)

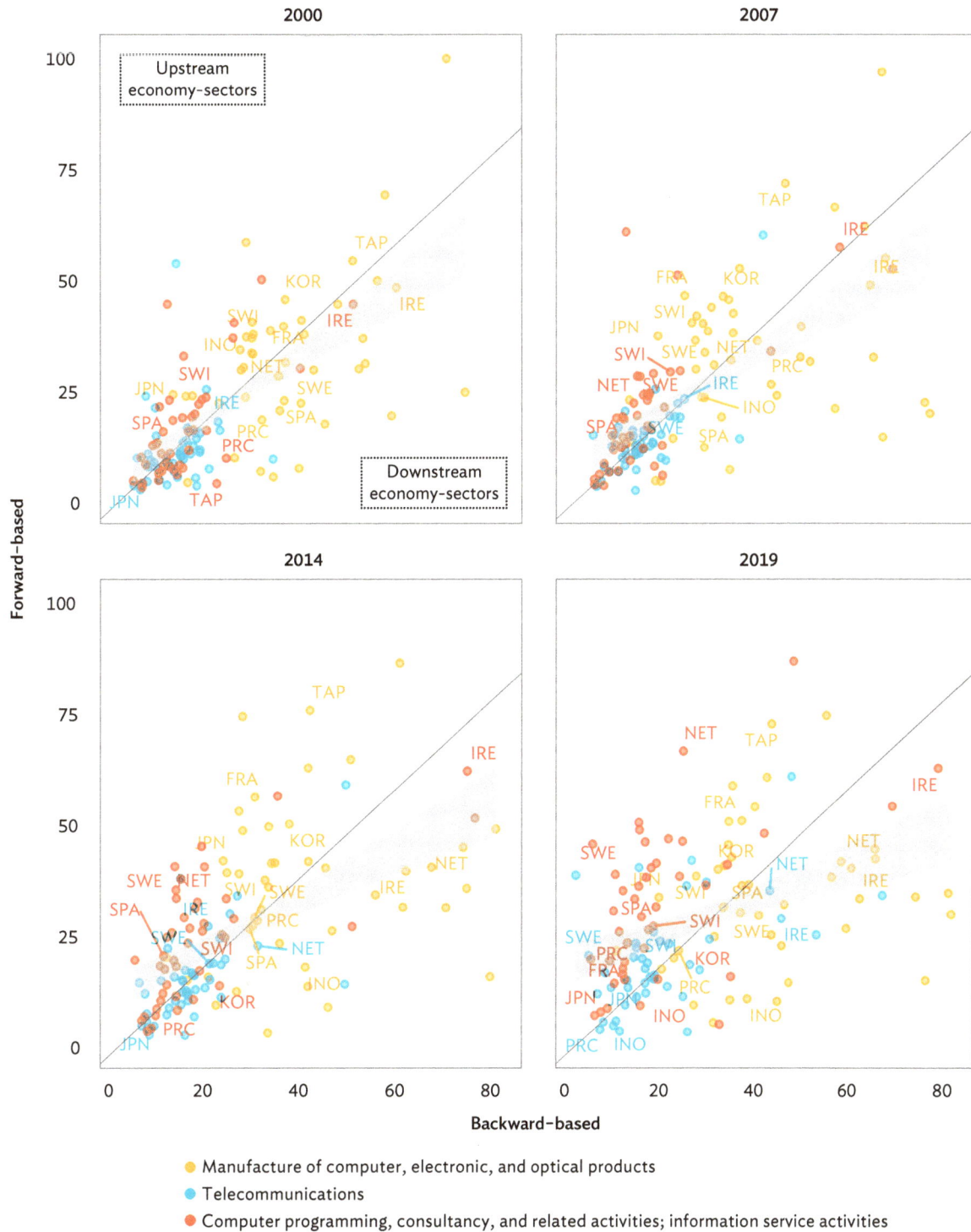

FRA = France; INO = Indonesia; IRE = Ireland; JPN = Japan; KOR = Republic of Korea; NET = Netherlands; PRC = People's Republic of China; SPA = Spain; SWE = Sweden; SWI = Switzerland.

Notes: Digital sector = manufacture of computer, electronic, and optical products; telecommunications; and computer programming, consultancy, and related activities, and information service activities. The scatterplot shows 44 economies, including "the Rest of the World." Asian Development Bank estimates are based on the methodology of Wang, Wei, Yu, and Zhu (2017).

Sources: World Input–Output Database Tables, 2000, 2007, and 2014; and the Asian Development Bank's 38-sector Multiregional Input-Output Table 2019.

Global Value Chain Participation of Digital Sectors Threatened by International Trade Tensions

To examine how the GVC participation of digital sectors evolved from 2000 to 2019, relative to nondigital sectors, Figure 38 shows the evolution of the world average of total GVC participation of digital and nondigital sectors.[49] Four distinct phases for the total GVC participation of digital sectors are evident in the figure. First is the period from 2000 to 2003, when the gap between total GVC participation of nondigital sectors (blue line) and digital sectors (red line) is minimal. Over this period, the total GVC participation of digital sectors declined as a result of the bursting of the dot-com bubble, while that of nondigital sectors marginally increased.

Second is the 2003–2008 period, which is the period leading to the GFC (pre-GFC). During this period, total GVC participation of both digital and nondigital sectors increased as inter-economy production fragmentation proliferated. However, the total GVC participation of digital sectors never caught up with that of nondigital sectors. Furthermore, the gap between the red and blue lines widened from 2003 to 2008, indicating that total GVC participation of nondigital sectors grew at a more rapid pace compared to digital sectors. This is possibly because GVCs during the early 2000s had been primarily shaped by trading in automotive parts, electronics, fuel, plastics, and synthetic rubber, most of which are generally nondigital in nature (UNCTAD 2013).

Third is the 2008–2009 period (GFC), where total GVC participation rates plunged for both digital and nondigital sectors. Observably, however, total GVC participation rates fell more sharply for nondigital sectors (by –5%) than for digital sectors (by –2.6%). This signals more resilient demand and supply linkages for digital sectors, in the midst of crises such as the GFC, possibly because digital sectors were not as globally integrated as nondigital sectors during the GFC.

Last is the period from 2009 to 2019 (post-GFC). In 2010, immediately following the GFC, total GVC participation rates for both digital and nondigital

Figure 38: Total Global Value Chain Participation Rates of Digital and Nondigital Sectors
(world average)

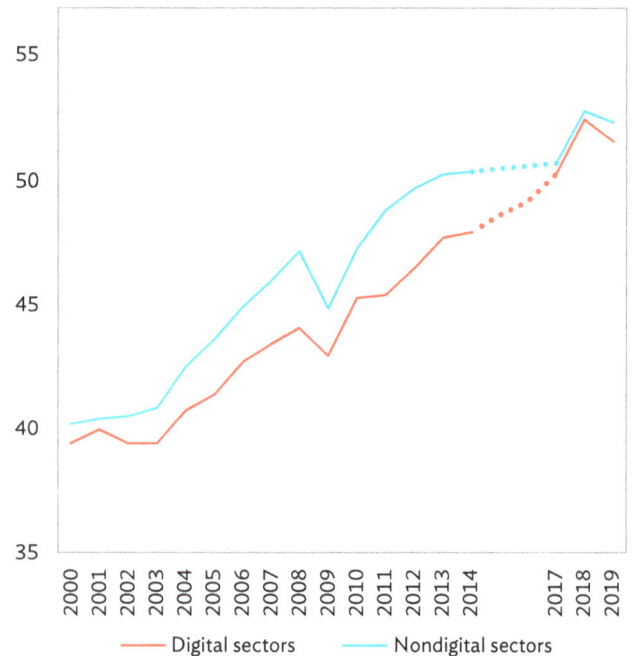

Legend: —— Digital sectors   —— Nondigital sectors

Notes: Digital sector = manufacture of computer, electronic and optical products; telecommunications; and computer programming, consultancy, and related activities, and information service activities. Asian Development Bank estimates are based on the methodology of Wang, Wei, Yu, and Zhu (2017). The world average of total global value chain (GVC) participation is calculated by taking the sum of the world average of forward GVC participation and backward GVC participation. Certain economy-sectors were excluded in calculating for the world average because of mathematical inconsistencies.
Sources: World Input–Output Database Tables, 2000–2014; and the Asian Development Bank's 38-sector Multiregional Input-Output Table 2017–2019.

---

49   The world average of total GVC participation is calculated by taking the sum of the world average of forward GVC participation and backward GVC participation based on the methodology by Wang et al. (2017).

sectors rebounded at nearly the same rate (by 5.4%). Thereafter, until 2018, the total GVC participation of digital sectors grew at an average annual rate of 2.9%, which is 0.5 percentage points higher than that of nondigital sectors.[50] This indicates rapid trading in intermediate inputs, with digital sectors as the supplier and user of such. The emergence of novel technologies beyond the 2010s supports this narrative. These technologies include the Internet of Things (IoT); new end-user devices such as smartphones, tablets, notebooks, laptops, and 3D printers; new offerings such as cloud computing, digital platforms, and digital services; and other Industry 4.0 technologies such as automation and robotics (Bukht and Heeks 2017).

In 2019, total GVC participation of digital and nondigital sectors declined, which is attributable to international trade tensions, beginning 2018. The total GVC participation of digital sectors contracted by a greater rate (–1.6%) than nondigital sectors (–0.7%), indicative of the disproportionate impact of the trade tensions against the total GVC participation of digital sectors. Digital sectors are more GVC-oriented during this period, which is one reason why the impact of international trade tensions to digital sector GVCs is greater compared to that of the GFC. In addition, the sharper decline in digital sector GVCs also happened amid restrictions imposed by the US on exports of vital chips and technologies to the PRC's tech giants in 2019 (Shapardson and Freifield 2019). By late 2020, the trade tension had gradually transformed into a tech cold conflict, as localization and onshoring sentiments in both the US and the PRC's semiconductor industry arose (Ioannou 2020). This could further threaten the expansion of digital sectors' GVCs beyond 2021.

Figure 39 presents the total GVC participation rates of digital sectors, disaggregated across five major economic regions: (i) advanced Asian economies, (ii) the Eurozone, (iii) the PRC, (iv) the US, and (v) the rest of the world. In three of these five economic regions, a decline in total

Figure 39: Total Global Value Chain Participation Rates of the Digital Sector by Major Economic Region

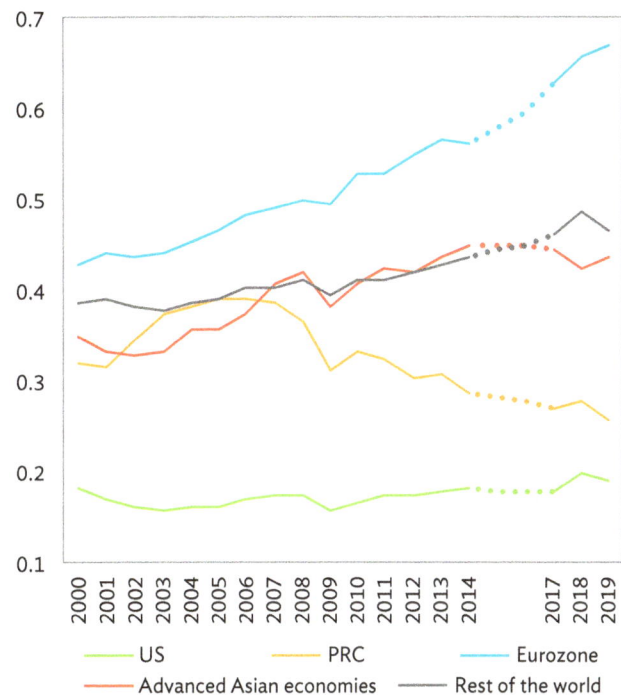

PRC = People's Republic of China; US = United States.
Notes: The Eurozone = Austria, Belgium, Cyprus, Estonia, Finland, France, Germany, Greece, Ireland, Italy, Latvia, Lithuania, Luxembuorg, Malta, the Netherlands, Portugal, Slovakia, Slovenia, and Spain. Advanced Asian economies = Japan; Republic of Korea; and Taipei,China. Digital sector = manufacture of computer, electronic and optical products; telecommunications; and computer programming, consultancy, and related activities, and information service activities. Asian Development Bank estimates are based on the methodology of Wang, Wei, Yu, and Zhu (2017). Total global value chain (GVC) participation is calculated by taking the sum of the forward GVC participation and backward GVC participation.
Sources: World Input–Output Database Tables, 2000–2014; and the Asian Development Bank's 38-sector Multiregional Input-Output Table 2017–2019.

---

[50] Note that total GVC participation estimates for both digital and nondigital firms were calculated using two different databases: the WIOD for 2000 to 2014 and the MRIOT for 2017 to 2019. Weaving data points estimated using the WIOD and the MRIOT may cause the 2014–2019 slope to be higher than when just one database is used. Therefore, the level of total GVC participation rates for 2019 may be slightly lower for both digital and nondigital sectors. Nonetheless, the paths of total GVC participation rates should follow the same direction.

GVC participation of digital sectors was observed from 2018 to 2019. The decline was most pronounced in the PRC (–7%) followed by the US (–5%) and the rest of the world (–4%). Meanwhile, the digital sectors in the Eurozone and in advanced Asian economies (comprised of Japan; the ROK; and Taipei,China in the database used) expanded their total GVC participation from 2018 to 2019 by 2% and 3%, respectively. This is indicative of digital sectors' trade diversion from the US and the PRC to the Eurozone and other advanced Asian economies. In particular, Taipei,China is considered to have gained the most additional exports due to the tech cold conflict, partly owing to its communication equipment exports. While some productive activities were merely diverted between economies, others were completely lost or absorbed by domestic production (UNCTAD 2019c). This potentially exposes the global economy to losses of gains from trade. Therefore, should 2018–2019 trade conditions persist, international trade tensions could threaten GVC expansion of digital sectors, and any gains that would have been derived from it, may be threatened beyond 2021.

The Increasing Role of Digital Services in Global Value Chain Expansion

The digital sectors of the world economy, except those of the PRC, expanded their GVC participation from 2000 to 2019, albeit at varying speeds per region. Figure 39 shows that the GVC participation of digital sectors in the Eurozone expanded the fastest (slope of 1.3), followed by advanced Asian economies (slope of 0.7), the rest of the world (slope of 0.5), and the US (slope of 0.1).

To further examine which particular activity contributed the most to the expansion of the digital sector between 2000 and 2019, Figure 37 provides a disaggregation of the digital sector into three subsectors: the manufacture of computer, electronic, and optical products ("manufacture of computers"); telecommunications ("telecom"); and computer programming, consultancy, and related activities, and information service activities ("information services"). Additionally, Figure 40 provides the same level of disaggregation of digital subsectors, but instead shows the evolution of digital sectors of the 62 ADB member economies and "the rest of the world" included in the MRIOTs for 2017 to 2019. The figure particularly highlights the GVC participation of select Southeast Asian economies, Malaysia, the Philippines, Thailand, Viet Nam, and Singapore.

From 2000 to 2014, the expansion of GVC participation among digital subsectors is significant in the manufacture of computers (yellow points), as indicated by the spread of yellow points between the two periods (Figure 37). In this subsector, Ireland and the Netherlands became increasingly more downstream in 2014 compared to 2000. Indonesia's manufacture of computers, meanwhile, shifted from being a relatively more upstream sector in 2000 to relatively more downstream by 2014. This is indicative of the subsector's greater participation in assembly tasks as well as its focus on consumer electronics, which are closer to final use. In 2020, Indonesia imposed an export ban on

Figure 40: Global Value Chain Participation Rates by Digital Sector, ADB Multiregional Input-Output Tables

(63 economies)

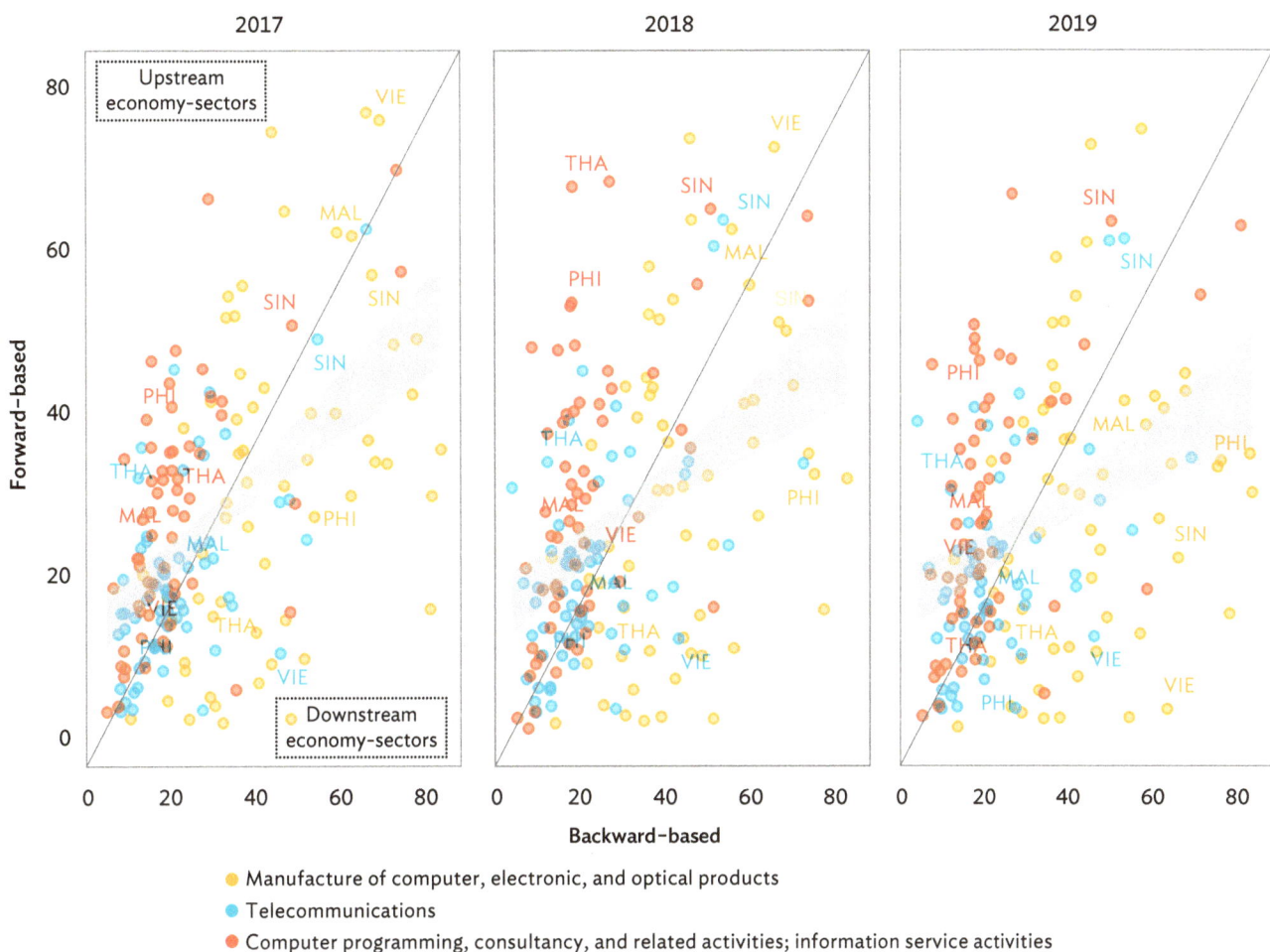

ADB = Asian Development Bank; MAL = Malaysia; PHI = Philippines; SIN = Singapore; THA = Thailand; VIE = Viet Nam.
Notes: Digital sector = manufacture of computer, electronic, and optical products; telecommunications; and computer programming, consultancy, and related activities, and information service activities. The scatterplot shows the 62 ADB member economies and the "rest of the world" economy included in the Multiregional Input-Output Table 2017–2019. ADB estimates are based on the methodology of Wang, Wei, Yu, and Zhu (2017).
Source: Asian Development Bank Multiregional Input-Output Table 2017–2019.

nickel, as part of its plan to wholly localize battery production. While its effect on the GVCs of Indonesia's manufacture of computers is yet to be realized, one may expect its relative position in the value chains to move relatively more upstream beyond 2020 because of possible increased reliance on domestic markets and reduced dependence on imports of intermediate products, as was the case for the PRC from 2000 to 2014. The PRC's manufacture of computers moved from being relatively more downstream in 2000 to more upstream in 2014 (and even more upstream by 2019), which is consistent with the PRC's economic rebalancing strategy that increased reliance on its domestic markets and reduced dependence on imports. This resulted in a stronger localization of production and consumption in the PRC over the 2010s, as shown by the increasing domestic value-added component of its final products (Alvarez et al. 2021).

The dynamics are different for digital subsectors from 2014 to 2019. In Figure 37, it can be observed that the expansion of GVC participation was more intense in the two digital services subsectors: telecom (blue points) and information services (red points), than in the digital products subsector: manufacture of computers. The said expansion is seen from the more scattered blue and red points in 2019 than in 2014 compared to that of yellow points.

In general, economies' information services became relatively more upstream by 2019 (Figure 37). The PRC, for instance, moved from being relatively downstream in 2014 to more upstream by 2019. Likewise, several economies in the Eurozone—France, the Netherlands, Spain, Sweden, and Switzerland—moved farther upstream in 2019 compared to their 2014 positions. From the advanced Asian economies, the ROK and Taipei,China also expanded their forward GVC participation, but not enough to put them in a relatively upstream position by 2019. Figure 40 also shows relatively more upstream information services in select Southeast Asian economies for 2017 to 2019. By 2019, information services in Malaysia, the Philippines, Singapore, and Viet Nam were all in an upstream position.

In the telecom subsector, Figure 37 shows that economies expanded to varying positions from 2014 to 2019. Economies such as Indonesia, Ireland, and Japan moved more downstream, while Sweden and Switzerland were more upstream in 2019. Among Southeast Asian economies, Figure 40 shows large expansions from 2017 to 2019. The telecom subsectors of Singapore and Thailand moved farther upstream, while Malaysia, the Philippines, and Viet Nam were more downstream in 2019 compared to 2017.

Figure 41 summarizes how each digital subsector's GVC participation, on average, expanded in 2000–2014 and 2014–2019. On average, from 2000 to 2014, all three digital subsectors expanded both their forward and backward participation. For the manufacture of computers in 2000–2014, the average forward participation rate increased by 4 percentage points, while the backward participation rate increased by 3 percentage points. This resulted in a forward participation rate of 36% and backward participation rate of 39% in manufacture of computers; the highest participation rates among the three digital subsectors in 2014. By 2019, the manufacture of computers receded in its average forward participation rate, down to 34%.

An expansion was likewise observed from 2000 to 2014 in both digital services subsectors. Within telecom, forward and backward GVC participation rates each increased by 4 percentage points. Meanwhile, within information services, the average expansion was even greater at 7 percentage points for forward participation rates, and 3 percentage points for backward participation rates. Unlike the manufacture of computers, which receded in its forward participation in 2019, both digital services subsectors further increased their participation from 2014 to 2019, confirming preliminary observations. To highlight the point, the forward participation rate of information services increased by 8 percentage points from 2014 to 2019, resulting in a forward participation rate of 32% in 2019, which is close to the 34% forward participation rate of manufacture of computers.[51] This is indicative of more rapid trading in services compared to goods within the digital economy over 2014–2019.

The slowing of goods trading, replaced by rapid exchange in digital services and cross-border data flows, is considered the new "face" of globalization (Choudary 2018). As such, these trends show that, while localization initiatives are underway for digital goods production due to international trade tensions (causing GVC participation rates to recede), trading in digital services is not as threatened by onshoring sentiments. This is possibly because trading in digital services is not subject to import or export tariffs, and only by way of taxation and data localization initiatives are the integration of digital services GVCs hampered.

Digital Sectors as a Supplier of Value-Added that Enables Production

The $\hat{v}B\hat{y}$ matrix described in the section "Measurement Framework" (p. 14) can be applied to multiregional tables such as the WIOD tables and ADB's MRIOTs. Doing so is intended to extend the analysis of backward and forward linkages to determine the foreign users of value-added—that is, whether value-added imported or exported ends up being consumed directly by final users or further processed as intermediate input abroad. Wang et al. (2017) developed an organized framework that disaggregates internationally traded value-added between traditional trade and GVC activity. Value-added traded traditionally reaches an economy's borders as finished goods and is consumed directly by final users (traditional trade). Meanwhile, value-added traded via GVCs reaches an economy's borders as intermediate inputs for further processing, before it enters the markets as final products (GVC activity).

Figure 41: Global Value Chain Participation Rates by Broad Sector
(world average)

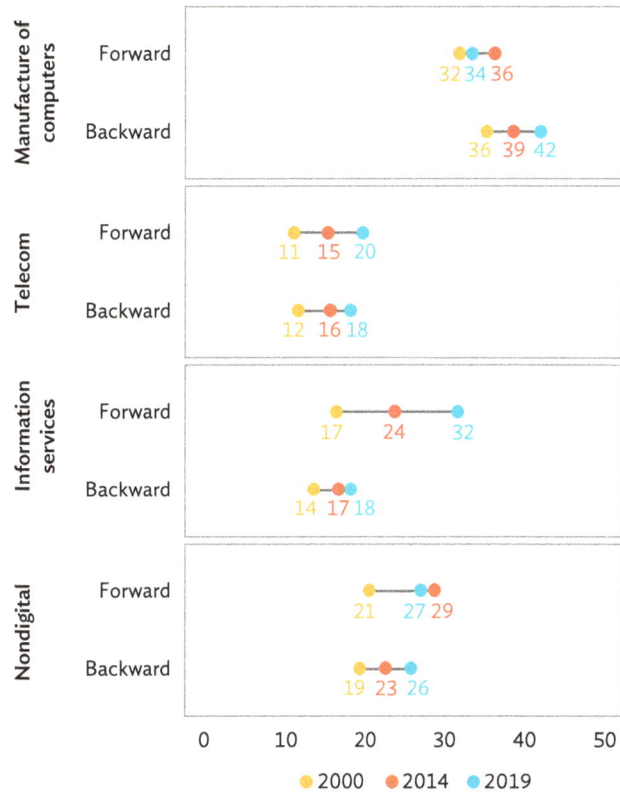

Notes: "Information services" = computer programming, consultancy, and related activities, and information service activities; "Manufacture of computers" = manufacture of computer, electronic, and optical products; "Telecom" = telecommunications sector. Digital sector = manufacture of computer, electronic, and optical products; telecommunications; and computer programming, consultancy, and related activities, and information service activities. Nondigital sector = all other sectors in the Asian Development Bank (ADB)'s Multiregional Input-Output Table 2019 that are not part of the digital sector. ADB estimates are based on the methodology of Wang, Wei, Yu, and Zhu (2017).
Sources: World Input–Output Database Tables, 2000 and 2014; and ADB's 38-sector Multiregional Input-Output Table 2019.

---

51 Footnote 50, p. 93.

Traditional trade and GVC activity of the digital sector can be analyzed in two perspectives: backward and forward. From a backward perspective, international trade in value-added (TiVA) measures how much of the digital sector's final products are derived from foreign sources. Meanwhile, from a forward perspective, international TiVA measures how much of any given economy's digital sector value-added is embedded in the production of commodities finally consumed abroad.

In Figure 42, TiVA from the backward perspective (left panel) and the forward perspective (right panel), aggregated across all digital economy-sectors, is shown. From a backward perspective, it can be observed that the level of TiVA via traditional trade was consistently higher than the level of TiVA via GVCs from 2000 to 2014 and from 2017 to 2019. This means that, on aggregate, products imported by the digital sector were comprised of more goods immediately sold to consumer markets than goods used by the digital sector as inputs to its own production.

From a forward perspective, the complete opposite is observed, as the level of TiVA via traditional trade was consistently lower than the level of TiVA via GVCs from 2000 to 2014 and from 2017 to 2019. This means that, on aggregate, digital sectors exported more of their output to the production of goods and services of foreign economy-sectors (digital or nondigital) than they exported to foreign final users. In addition, the digital sector's TiVA via GVCs from a forward perspective

Figure 42: Trade in Value-Added via Traditional Trade and Global Value Chains

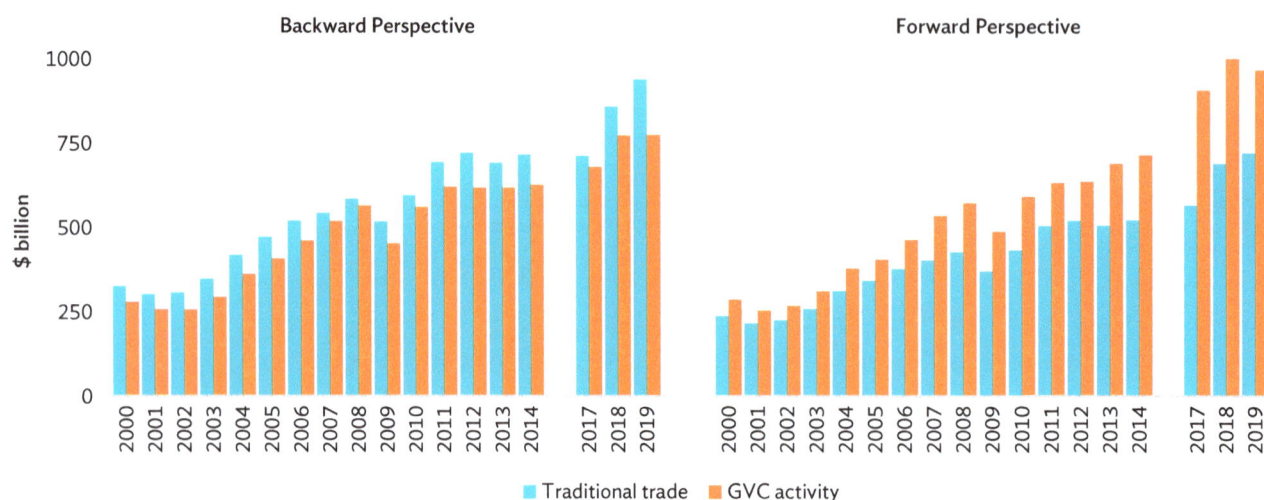

$ = United States dollars, GVC = global value chain.
Notes: Digital sector = manufacture of computer, electronic, and optical products; telecommunications; and computer programming, consultancy, and related activities, and information service activities. Asian Development Bank estimates are based on the methodology of Wang, Wei, Yu, and Zhu (2017). Bars refer to the sum of trade in value-added of all digital economy-sectors via traditional channels (i.e., export or import of finished products) and via GVCs (i.e., export or import of intermediates).
Sources: World Input–Output Database Tables, 2000–2014; and the Asian Development Bank's 38-sector Multiregional Input-Output Table 2017–2019.

increased at an exponential rate, notwithstanding the GFC. This highlights the increasing role of the digital sector as a supplier of value-added to enable final goods production of other domestic and foreign sectors, including itself.

Additionally, when the levels of value-added traded via GVCs from a backward and forward perspective are compared, one can observe that the digital sector's GVC activity via forward linkages exceeds GVC activity via backward linkages in all years assessed, except 2001 and 2005. This further signifies how digital sectors generally take more of an upstream position in the GVCs, highlighting the digital sector's prominent role not just as a supplier of value-added to various foreign sectors but also the increasing efforts of nondigital firms to incorporate digital technologies into their products and processes.

Figure 42 likewise shows the slowing of GVC trade between 2018 and 2019 as a result of international trade tensions; and because of the COVID-19 pandemic, prospects for GVCs after 2019 is under speculation—but only with respect to the depth of the negative impact and the period of expected recovery. The pandemic left stark images of dozens of grounded airplanes, docked ships, and empty roads and railways, which is the reason why the phenomena has been called "the Great Cessation" (Zweig 2020). However, despite traditional logistics channels coming to a halt, novel digital technologies paved the way for some GVC activity—and, in some cases, any economic activity—to continue. This is likely to mitigate some of the unfavorable effects of the pandemic on both trade and income. The next chapter provides more insights on this, by presenting some statistics on the digital economy in the time of the COVID-19 pandemic.

Digital in the Time of COVID-19

The world in 2020 was a picture of economic distress. In response to the highly contagious novel coronavirus SARS-CoV-2, governments have been forced to impose unprecedented restrictions on human movement, crippling trade and travel and causing economic activity to plummet to historic lows. Most economies plunged into recession in 2020, even as many had positive pre-pandemic growth projections for the year. These drastic measures employed to contain COVID-19's spread compelled economies to use available digital technologies to enable market transactions, shift to remote work and learning, and access online entertainment services, among others.

Common among the salient observations during the pandemic is the demand-oriented nature of digital activities as means to cope with restrictions. However, while there is an anticipated increase in the use of digital technologies, there are also constraining factors in play. For hardware, demand is likely influenced by work-from-home arrangements, adjustments in business processes, and shifts to the online medium for students. Even so, new purchases of, say, personal computers might be tempered by factors related to cash flow or a generally lower propensity to spend. For software, despite the surge in online activity and use of communication platforms, the ability to accommodate increased data flows is also constrained by the quality of, and access to, internet infrastructure. Lastly, while e-commerce has seen an uptrend, adoption by households and businesses is still at nascent levels in many economies (UNCTAD 2021).

It is important to measure the net impacts of these contrasting trends at the aggregate-level of digital economies. To do so, this section uses ADB's MRIOTs to estimate the overall changes in the digital economy from 2019 to 2020. The same methodology for the core digital framework is used, but applying the changes in final demand observed from 2019 to 2020 while holding technical coefficients constant (Equation 10). These changes in final demand for all economies and products refer to the difference of final demand matrices of all economies from 2019 to 2020. To estimate the final demand for 2020, detailed national accounts and external trade data from 62 economies, plus an aggregate for "the rest of the world," were compiled and harmonized with the MRIOT sector detail. Box 9 details how the final demand was disaggregated to measure the impact of the pandemic on the digital sectors. Note that figures are in current United States dollar prices.

Box 9: Estimating the Impact of COVID-19 on the Digital Economy

Prior to applying the final demand changes for 2020 to the core digital economy methodology (Equation 10 in this study), an intermediate procedure is taken in order to isolate the changes related to e-commerce activity (hereafter "digitally ordered"). For each economy's final demand, the proportion of business-to-consumer sales ordered online was estimated from various sources and applied to relevant products. Data on digitally ordered shares were obtained for both 2019 and 2020 and were applied to respective final-demand matrices. Where data are not available, it is assumed that the same proportion applies for both domestic and international sales via computer networks. Resulting matrices yield digitally ordered final demand for all economies in the multiregional input-output tables.

Aside from digitally ordered demand, also of interest in the digital economy during the pandemic is the demand for hardware, such as personal computers and other data-processing units, and software services, such as telecommunication services and information technology (IT) services. As such, changes in demand for digital products were introduced in the model separately. This distinction is applied to both digitally and nondigitally ordered final demand matrices.

Finally, demand for nondigital goods and services has also been affected by the COVID-19 pandemic. As a running theme throughout this report, the linkages of these sectors to the digital economy are necessary in understanding the full impact of the pandemic. For instance, the continuity measures in education forced many institutions to adopt online teaching platforms. Travel and booking agencies, a digitally dependent sector, have also been affected by containment measures, travel bubbles, and restrictions. Hence, changes in nondigital goods and services, such as education, travel services, and accommodation (among others), are also isolated from other types of demand in order to distinguish their impact from the rest of the trends discussed.

In all, eight final demand matrices are estimated per year which, by definition, should sum to the total final demand for all economies. These demand matrices are (i) digitally ordered digital goods, (ii) digitally ordered nondigital goods, (iii) digitally ordered digital services, (iv) digitally ordered nondigital services, (v) nondigitally ordered digital goods, (vi) nondigitally ordered nondigital goods, (vii) nondigitally ordered digital services, and (viii) nondigitally ordered nondigital services, as illustrated below. While impacts of goods were isolated from services (Level 4), for ease of presentation, results are shown at Level 3.

Final Demand Matrices by Nature of Transaction and Product

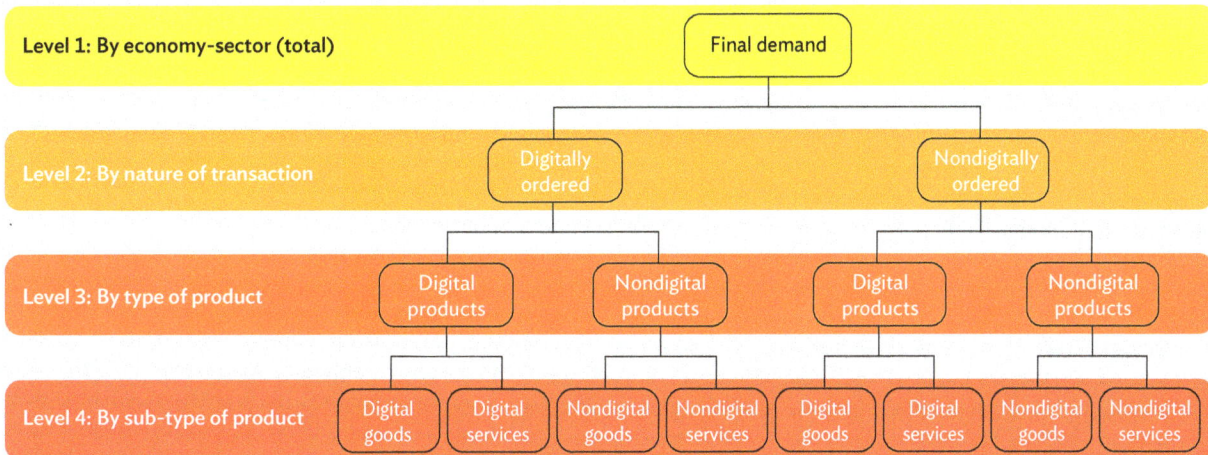

Level 1: By economy-sector (total)	Final demand
Level 2: By nature of transaction	Digitally ordered — Nondigitally ordered
Level 3: By type of product	Digital products / Nondigital products / Digital products / Nondigital products
Level 4: By sub-type of product	Digital goods / Digital services / Nondigital goods / Nondigital services / Digital goods / Digital services / Nondigital goods / Nondigital services

In matrix terms,

$$\mathbf{y}_{i,k}^{r} = \mathbf{y}_{(i,k)}^{r}[\hat{\alpha}_{r}\otimes\mathbf{I}_{i}] + \mathbf{y}_{i,k}^{r}[\widehat{(\iota-\alpha_{r})}\otimes\mathbf{I}_{i}]$$

$$\mathbf{y}_{i,k}^{r} = \underbrace{\hat{\boldsymbol{\varepsilon}}_{i(d)}^{r}\mathbf{y}_{(i,k)}^{r}[\hat{\alpha}_{r}\otimes\mathbf{I}_{i}]}_{\substack{\text{Digitally ordered} \\ \text{Digital products}}} + \underbrace{\hat{\boldsymbol{\varepsilon}}_{i(-d)}^{r}\mathbf{y}_{(i,k)}^{r}[\hat{\alpha}_{r}\otimes\mathbf{I}_{i}]}_{\substack{\text{Digitally ordered} \\ \text{Nondigital products}}} + \underbrace{\hat{\boldsymbol{\varepsilon}}_{i(d)}^{r}\mathbf{y}_{i,k}^{r}[\widehat{(\iota-\alpha_{r})}\otimes\mathbf{I}_{i}]}_{\substack{\text{Nondigitally ordered} \\ \text{Digital products}}} + \underbrace{\hat{\boldsymbol{\varepsilon}}_{i(-d)}^{r}\mathbf{y}_{i,k}^{r}[\widehat{(\iota-\alpha_{r})}\otimes\mathbf{I}_{i}]}_{\substack{\text{Nondigitally ordered} \\ \text{Nondigital products}}}$$

where $\mathbf{y}_{i,k}^{r}$ is the final demand matrix with i sectors (products) with k categories of final demand for economy r. $\hat{a}_{r}$ is the diagonalized vector of economy-level shares of products sold online (digitally ordered). $\mathbf{I}_{i,i}$ is a unit matrix with dimensions corresponding to the number of sectors per economy. $\hat{\boldsymbol{\varepsilon}}_{i(d)}^{r}$ is the diagonalized matrix of elimination vector where corresponding rows of digital sectors $i^{(d)}$ take the number of 1, and 0 if otherwise. In the same manner, $\hat{\boldsymbol{\varepsilon}}_{i(d)}^{r}$ is the diagonalized elimination vector for nondigital products $i^{(-d)}$. Note that '$\otimes$' refers to Kronecker product operation.

continued on next page.

Box 9 *continued.*

After isolating final demand estimates as above, the core digital equation (Equation 10) is used to estimate the first three terms: (i) economy-wide value-added contribution to core digital products (backward linkage), (ii) core digital sectors' value-added contribution to economy-wide demand (forward linkage), and (iii) core digital sectors' value-added contribution to its own final products. The fourth term of the equation (i.e., value-added attributed to digital sectors' nondigital fixed investments) is ignored in current estimates due to data constraints but will be included in future studies. Note that the same limitations of the core digital framework apply here as well.

Source: Methodology of the Digital Economy Measurement Framework study team.

Results of the analysis indicate a decline in the digital economy in 2020 as a share of 2019 GDP across the 16 economies, except for Denmark; Malaysia; the PRC; and Taipei,China (Figure 43). Nevertheless, when compared with the declines in overall GDP growth of the economies in 2020, the changes in the digital sector of these economies were relatively muted, ranging from -0.5% to 1% share of GDP.[52] At 0.7%, Malaysia had the highest increase in the share of GDP, with final demand for its digital sectors increasing despite the decrease in its overall GDP growth for 2020 at -5.6%. The PRC, which experienced a rapid economic recovery in 2020, had a 0.67% increase in its digital sector share, followed by Taipei,China at 0.03% and Denmark at 0.02%. These results are aligned with the estimates of the International Data Corporation (IDC) for 2020, which reported flat growth for global digital spending.

Figure 43-A decomposes the changes according to the three major terms defined in the core digital economy framework (Equation 10). For Malaysia, the digital sector's backward linkages as well as its own contribution to its final products spurred the growth of the digital economy in 2020. This is fueled by the observed increases in the demand for digital orders (Figure 43-B) and the demand increases for computer, electronics, and optical products and for telecommunications services (Figure 43-C). The PRC showed increases in both the backward and forward linkages of the digital sector, as well as its own contribution to its final products. These increases in the PRC's value-added were spurred by online sales and demand across all digital products. For Taipei,China, the digital sector's value-added contribution to economy-wide demand or forward linkage kept the digital economy afloat in 2020. Demand for digitally ordered products likewise carried the positive changes seen in Taipei,China's digital economy in 2020.

Across economies, Figure 43-B suggests growth in digitally ordered digital and nondigital products. The pandemic accelerated the pace of e-commerce adoption in 2020. Given mobility restrictions, consumers have resorted to shopping online, prompting retailers to quickly adjust or risk obsolescence. Figure 44 and Figure 45 further depict the trend in e-commerce sales relative to total retail sales for Singapore and the US. Data suggest spikes in the early months of the lockdown period have since subsided, but online sales

---

[52] In its April 2021 World Economic Outlook, the International Monetary Fund estimated that the 2020 global economy declined by 3.3%, with emerging markets falling by 2.2%.

Figure 43: Changes in the Digital Economy, 2020
(% of 2019 gross domestic product)

(A) By Value-Added Contribution

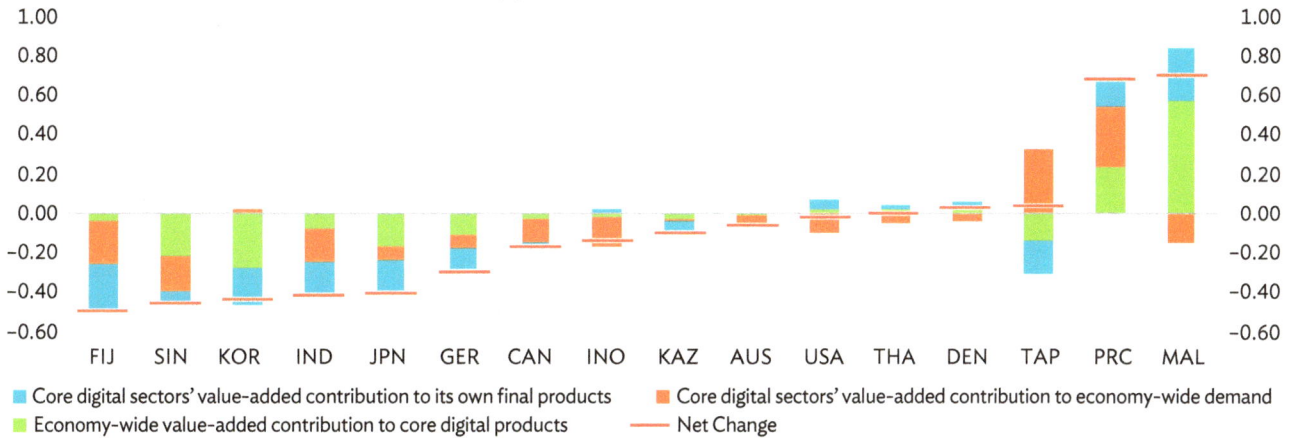

- ■ Core digital sectors' value-added contribution to its own final products
- ■ Core digital sectors' value-added contribution to economy-wide demand
- ■ Economy-wide value-added contribution to core digital products
- — Net Change

(B) By Type of Demand

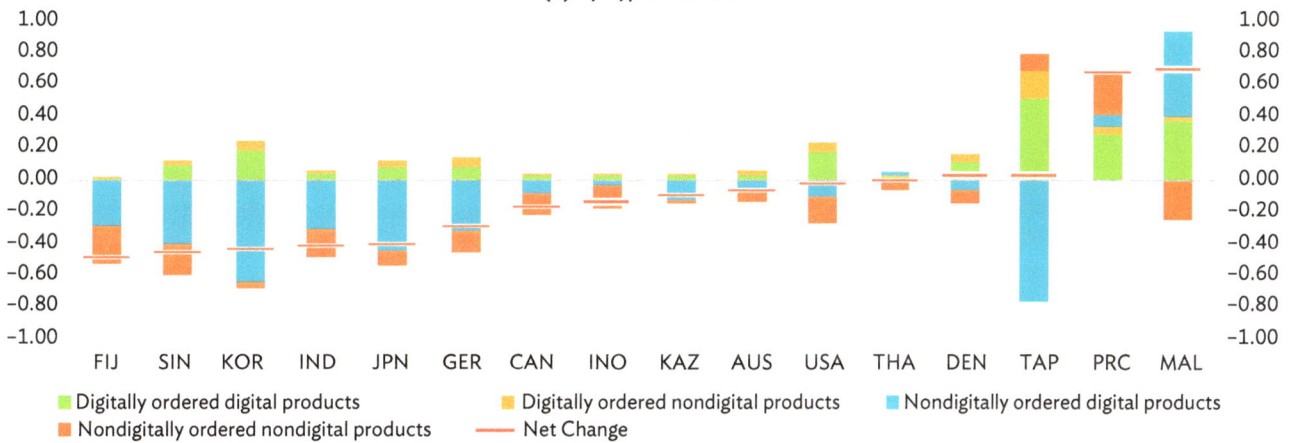

- ■ Digitally ordered digital products
- ■ Digitally ordered nondigital products
- ■ Nondigitally ordered digital products
- ■ Nondigitally ordered nondigital products
- — Net Change

(C) By Digital Product

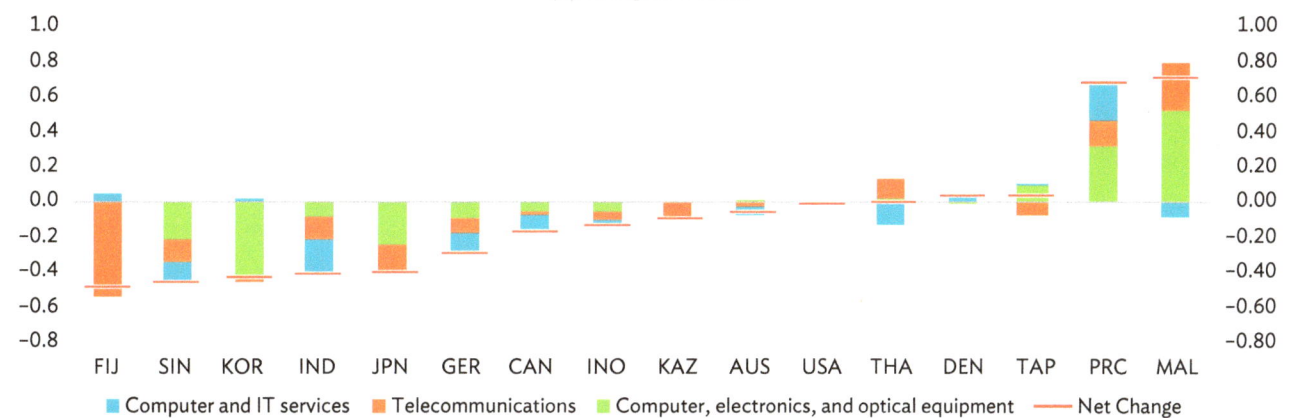

- ■ Computer and IT services
- ■ Telecommunications
- ■ Computer, electronics, and optical equipment
- — Net Change

AUS = Australia; CAN = Canada; DEN = Denmark; FIJ = Fiji; GER = Germany; IND = India; INO = Indonesia; IT = information technology; JPN = Japan; KAZ = Kazakhstan; KOR = Republic of Korea; MAL = Malaysia; PRC = People's Republic of China; SIN = Singapore; TAP = Taipei,China; THA = Thailand; USA = United States.

Source: Calculations of the Digital Economy Measurement Framework study team, based on the Asian Development Bank's 38-sector Multiregional Input-Output Table 2019, national accounts, and various sources of digitally ordered business-to-consumer shares to total sales.

Figure 44: E-Commerce Sales as a Proportion of Total Sales in the United States and Singapore
(%)

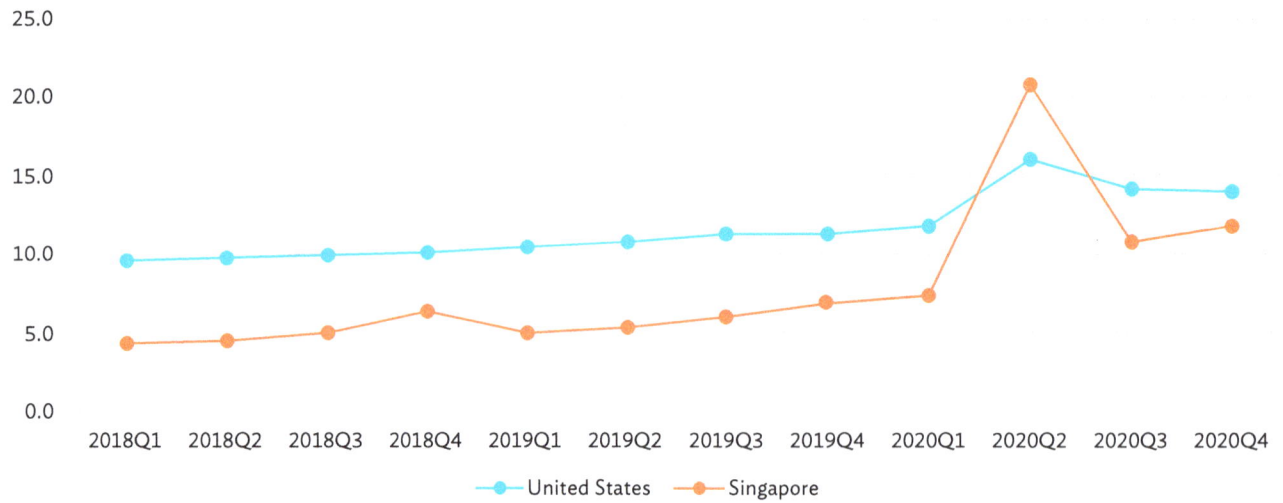

Q = quarter.
Note: Singapore quarterly data points are averages of published monthly data.
Sources: Federal Reserve Bank of St. Louis (United States). E-commerce Retail Sales as Percent of Total Sales. https://fred.stlouisfed.org/series/ECOMPCTSA (accessed March 2021); SingStat (Singapore). Online Retail Sales Proportion Out of Respective Industry's Total Sales. https://www.singstat.gov.sg/find-data/search-by-theme/industry/services/latest-data (accessed March 2021).

Figure 45: Singapore's E-Commerce Sales as a Proportion of Total Sales, by Industry
(%)

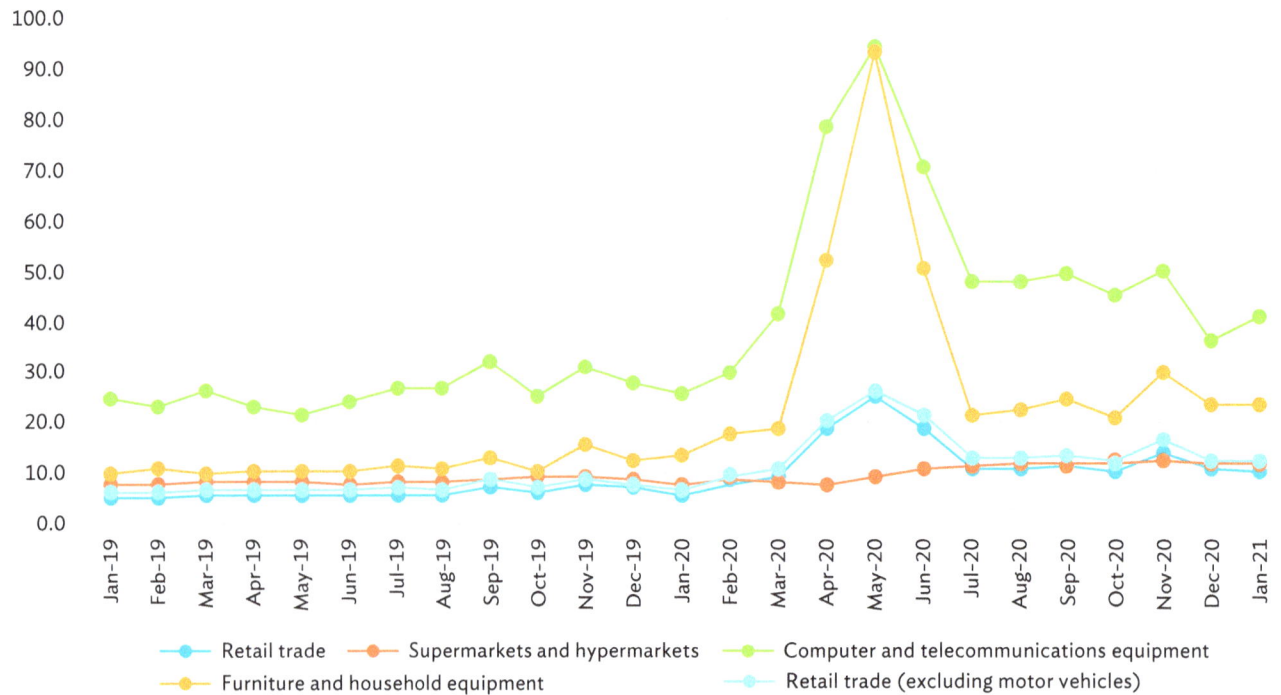

Source: SingStat (Singapore). Online Retail Sales Proportion Out of Respective Industry's Total Sales.
https://www.singstat.gov.sg/find-data/search-by-theme/industry/services/latest-data (accessed March 2021).

are still at a higher proportion in relation to total retail sales. Figure 45 shows Singapore's online purchases as a proportion of total sales by industry. The highest online sales spikes are seen for communications and telecommunications equipment and for furniture and household equipment, presumably the impact of the surge in remote work and as a substitute for physical stores that had to close due to lockdown policies (as opposed to grocery stores, which were mostly allowed to remain open).

These indicators suggest an uncertainty as to whether e-commerce activity will be sustained or revert to pre-covid levels. Broadly speaking, three post-pandemic scenarios are possible. The first scenario focuses on how the pandemic has accelerated the digitalization of industries, potentially starting an altogether new phase of globalization. Consumers have grown accustomed to shopping online, prompting retailers to adopt. Amazon and Alibaba may define this new era the way the previous era was defined by Apple and Boeing (The Economist 2019). The second scenario is that the pandemic is a temporary shock, and the world will revert to pre-pandemic trends in the coming years. The third is the middle path, which anticipates more "hybrid" remote work models (Lund et al. 2020) and growing e-commerce and digital service sectors, albeit not as robust as during the pandemic.

European economies reported considerable increases in individuals using the internet, as a percentage of the total population, for telephoning and video calls (Figure 46). Association of Southeast Asian Nations (ASEAN)-6 economies, moreover, saw increases in the daily average hours spent online for personal use due to the pandemic, according to a survey by Bain & Company, Google, and Temasek in 2020.[53] Indonesia and Viet Nam saw the highest growth rates in usage: Indonesia from 3.6 on average before the pandemic to 4.7 during the pandemic, and Viet Nam from 3.1 hours to 4.2 hours (Bain & Company, Google, and Temasek 2020). In the same survey, the Philippines had the highest average internet usage at 5.2 hours per day during the pandemic, increasing from the pre-pandemic baseline of 4.0 hours.

Consequently, digital communications platforms reported increases in traffic and subscriptions. Zoom Video Communications Inc., in its financial results for the 2021 fiscal year, reported an estimated 467,100 paying customers at end of the fourth quarter of 2020, increasing by 470% year on year (Zoom Video Communications 2021). Microsoft Teams' daily active users jumped from 20 million users in November 2019 to 115 million in October 2020. Delivery Hero processed a total of 1.3 billion orders in 2020, increasing by 98% year on year, according to its 2020 financial results (Delivery Hero 2021).[54] Large firms that operate video conferencing, business processes, social media, streaming, e-commerce, delivery, and other digital services platforms have recorded revenue growth during the pandemic – Zoom (+325.8%),

---

[53] ASEAN-6 is composed of Indonesia, Malaysia, the Philippines, Singapore, Thailand, and Viet Nam.

[54] Delivery Hero owns Foodpanda.

Figure 46: Individuals Accessing the Internet, by Reason for Usage
(% of total population)

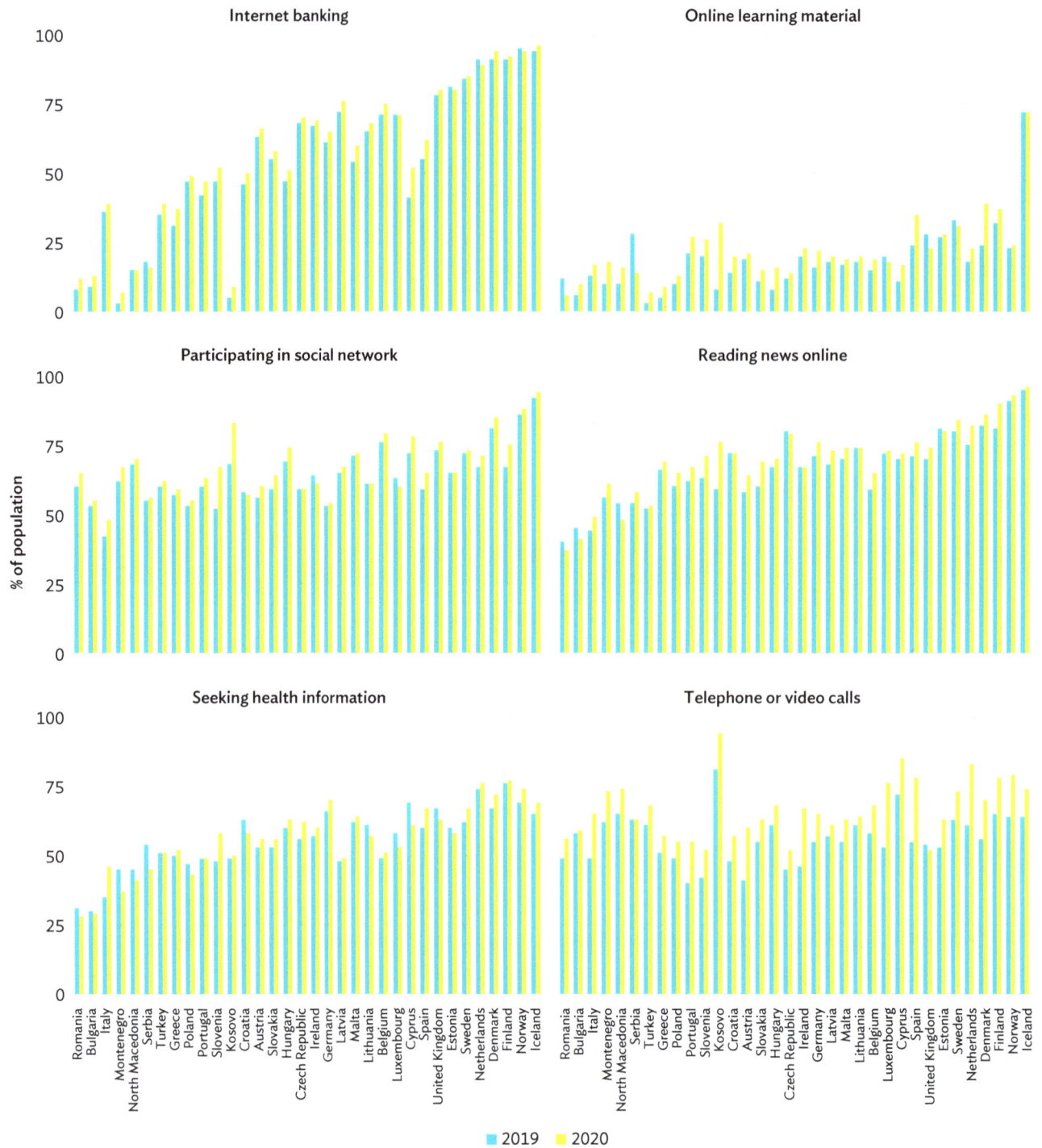

Data source: Eurostat. Digital Economy and Society Database. https://ec.europa.eu/eurostat/web/digital-economy-and-society/data/database (accessed April 2021).

Netflix (+24%), Sea Limited (+101.1%), Delivery Hero (+98%), Facebook (+21.6%), and Microsoft (+13.6%) – as reported in individual press releases on 2020 financial results accessed via each company's website.[55]

The demand for personal computers likewise increased in 2020 due to the shift to remote work and distance learning. According to IDC, the demand for computers surged in 2020, with an annual increase of 13.1% to 302.6 million units shipped in 2020. Companies such as Apple and Acer exhibited double-digit growth in their personal computer shipments in 2020, with increases of 29.1% and 22.9%, respectively, as opposed to the decreases experienced by these companies in 2019, at –2.2% for Apple and –4.6% for Acer. Tablets also had a robust year, with sales growing by 19.5% in 2020, according to the preliminary data from the IDC.

This spike in the demand for personal computers and tablets, as well as other digital products, fueled the already growing shortage in the supply of semiconductors, which are used to make computer chips, even before the pandemic. The lag time between orders and delivery for computer chips increased to an average of 15 weeks in February 2021, surpassing the demand peak seen in 2018 (Bloomberg 2021). Early in the new year, the US President signed an executive order to review the computer chips supply chain and address the shortage (Feinier 2021). Plans to revive the computer chip industry in the US, with Intel already pledging $20 billion in investments, could prove to be another bone of contention that compounds international trade tensions (The Economist 2021).

Despite the increases in the use of digital platforms and the demand for certain digital products, value-added of hardware, software, telecommunications, and IT services mostly netted a decline in 2020 across economies. This indicates that the recession in 2020 also affected the demand for digital products. While the restrictive measures during the pandemic forced many individuals to shift to digital platforms, many households and businesses are not in a cash-ready position to purchase computer equipment or internet services. In addition, accommodating the demand for digital products and platforms is also constrained by the quality of, and access to, appropriate infrastructure and capacity. Infrastructure investments take time before becoming operational, with economies having to make do with available ICT infrastructure in 2020.

Particularly, aggregate ICT indicators show no abrupt increases in investment in 2020 (Figure 47). The International Telecommunication Union (2020) observed the acceleration of capital expenditure (CAPEX) by telecom service providers for operations and maintenance of services in light of the surge in network traffic. Consequently, CAPEX for network modernization, e.g., investments in fifth generation

---

[55] Sea Limited operates (i) Shopee, an e-commerce platform; (ii) SeaMoney, a digital payments and financial services platform; and (iii) Garena, an online games developer and publisher.

(5G) expansion, were postponed and channeled to "maintenance" category of CAPEX. The union also noted that internet platforms or "over the top" providers would perform better than network operators due to the former's lower dependence on CAPEX.

Lund et al. (2020) also observed that remote work is more efficient in advanced economies with sufficient digital infrastructure, which is often lacking in emerging economies. The remote work potential is uneven for sectors in the economy: finance, management, professional services, and information sectors have the highest potential for remote work; while agriculture, accommodation and food services, and construction sectors have the lowest potential. Further, firms that have existing Industry 4.0 technologies fared better during the crisis. A McKinsey survey of 400 companies showed that early adopters of Industry 4.0 technologies adapted better to the pandemic (Agrawal et. al. 2021). The survey suggests that 96% of those with more mature Industry 4.0 implementation had stronger ability to respond to the pandemic, while 56% of those without Industry 4.0 implementation were inhibited in their pandemic response.

Figure 47: Select Indicators for Information and Communication Technology

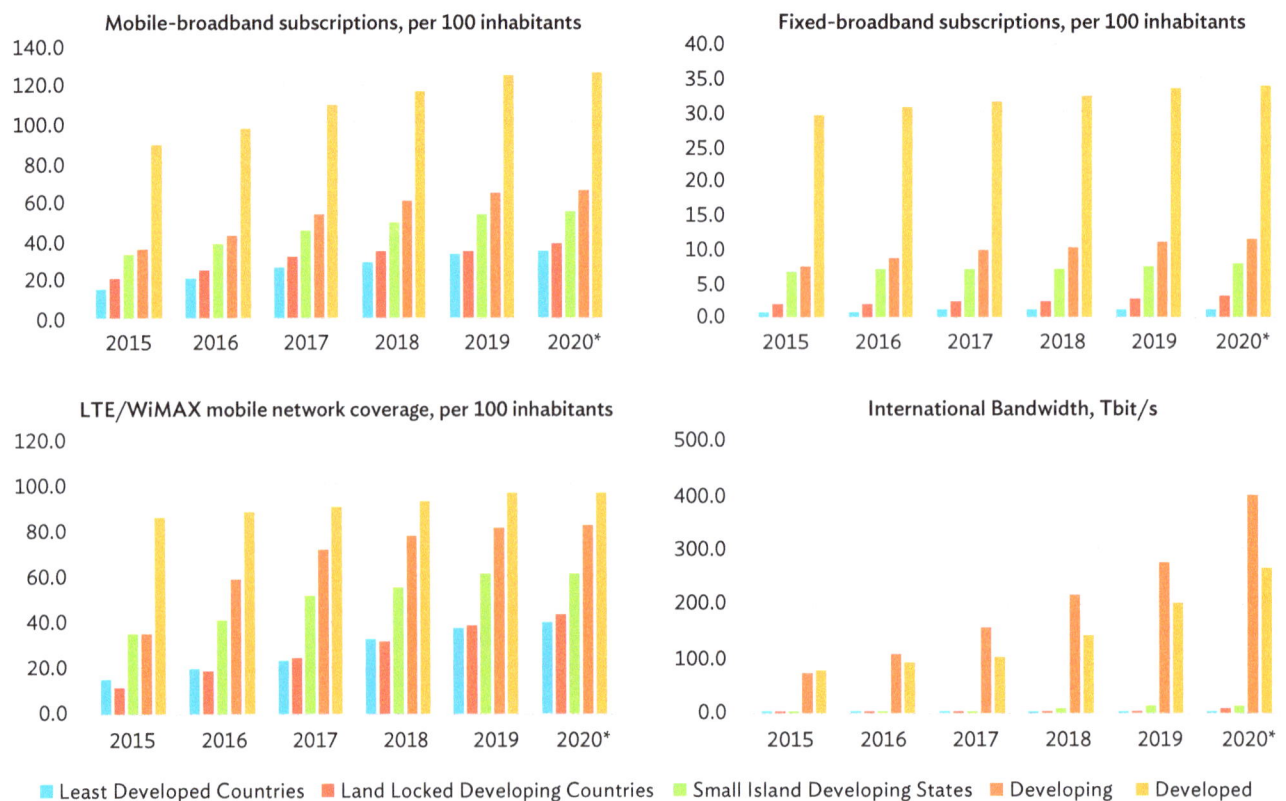

LTE = Long-Term Evolution, Tbit = terabit, WiMAX = Worldwide Interoperability for Microwave Access.
Note: Preliminary data as of November 2020.
Source: International Telecommunication Union. World Telecommunication/ICT Indicators Database. https://www.itu.int/pub/D-IND-WTID.OL-2019 (accessed November 2020).

As the world continues to reel from the economic impacts of the COVID-19 pandemic, transformative effects in economies' process of digitalization have been positive but uneven. This section has shown that the surge in e-commerce and communication technologies has helped cushion the impact of the pandemic. However, gains from digitalization are constrained by dampened demand, cash flow disruptions, income losses, and infrastructure gaps. This has significantly widened the gap between early and late adopters of digital technologies, with the former being able to respond better to the crisis while the latter found themselves in a more difficult position to roll out and expand digital projects.

Economic forecasters are cautiously hopeful that, with vaccination programs in progress, the world is on track for a sharp economic recovery in 2021 (ADB 2021).[56] Whether this recovery is accompanied by digitalization is uncertain but will likely be uneven, as evidenced by the economic performance of several sectors in 2020. What is clear is that the pandemic has changed the way businesses view investment in digital technologies. For example, there is an indication that, since the onset of the pandemic, more companies now value Industry 4.0 technologies more, not only from the perspective of cost and efficiency but that of ability to respond to future shocks (Agrawal et. al. 2021). How these emerging technologies are shaping the current state of play in certain industries is explored further in the next chapter.

---

[56] The *Asian Development Outlook 2021*, in particular, was projecting a rebound of 7.3% growth for developing Asia as of April 2021. For global digital spending, the IDC expects at least 5% growth annually through to 2023.

Industry 4.0 and the Future of the Digital Economy

The first three industrial revolutions were marked by the stimulation of production through steam and water power, electric power, and electronics and information technology, respectively (Vollmer 2018). As the digital economy evolves, emerging technologies centered around smarter and autonomous solutions are gaining prominence across a multitude of industries. These technologies are at the heart of the fourth industrial revolution, or Industry 4.0: frontier innovations that encompass automation and digitalization in manufacturing, the Internet of Things (IoT), artificial intelligence, big data, analytics and cloud computing, additive manufacturing or three-dimensional (3D) printing, and robotics (UNCTAD 2019).

Computer systems design has been utilized in this regard by integrating software and technologies specific to certain product components. Such practices include computer-aided design (CAD) to create virtual illustrations and 3D models; computer-aided engineering to validate, analyze, and optimize designs; and computer-aided manufacturing to automate manufacturing processes through machine instruction (Michigan State University 2020).

IoT is the interconnectivity of computing devices over a network, allowing their communication, data transfer, and processing without the need for human interaction (Ahmadi 2019), based on a set of commands (i.e., software) programmed by the user. Examples of this are various smart appliances used in home automation, such as thermostat and lighting systems programmed to monitor physical conditions and human activity, then automatically change temperature and brightness, respectively. The use of 5G networks greatly supports IoT systems, boasting higher efficiency, higher speed, larger bandwidth, and lower latency than network predecessors (Thales 2021).

Artificial intelligence is the adaptation of machines to perform human cognitive abilities, such as decision-making based on past occurrences, self-improving algorithms, and continuous learning, independent of human command, using techniques such as machine learning (Heath 2020). The most visible demonstrations of artificial intelligence are the rise of virtual assistants (e.g., Amazon Alexa, Apple Siri, Google Assistant) and website and social media features (e.g., Facebook's face recognition, friend recommendations, targeted advertising based on page engagement, demographics, and many other factors). A more radical implementation of machine learning is embodied in the development of self-driving cars.

Perhaps the ultimate manifestation of automation is the use of robots. Amazon utilizes robotic arms and drive units in its warehouses to accomplish more tedious tasks, such as heavy lifting and moving inventory (Amazon n.d.). The first robot lawyer, DoNotPay, which provides access to legal advice with a chatbot using artificial intelligence technology, for a minimal fee, has gained widespread success in the US (Bosilkovski 2020).

Businesses are able to leverage Industry 4.0 technologies to optimize supply chains and operations, increasing efficiency, productivity, and cost-effectiveness. Consumers are offered better-quality products and more convenient solutions. The effects of these technologies on global trade are expected to be complex, as these technologies are likely to reduce transaction costs, influence production processes, and create or transform goods and services (Lund et al. 2019), which could reshape comparative advantage and redistribute income based on the adaptive capacity of firms (Alvarez et al. 2021).

Estimated Size and Trends of Industry 4.0

Data limitations in national accounts pose challenges for the exact measurement of Industry 4.0 technologies. These are difficult to pinpoint strictly in one sector and lack a detailed subclassification within current product or industry classification systems. However, the North American Industry Classification System provides some detail related to Industry 4.0 (Table 5). Industry 4.0 technologies are either considered digital products or require an overlap of nearly all the identified digital products in the framework, and are therefore captured in the resulting digital economy estimates. Although additive manufacturing and robotics products are not considered main digital products, based on the framework definition of the core, the production of these would require both software (or custom computer programming) and computing machinery components. For example, CAD modelling is the primary process from which 3D printable models in additive manufacturing are produced.

Table 5: Industry 4.0 Technologies, North American Industry Classification System 2012

Industry 4.0 Technology	Code	Description
Artificial Intelligence Cloud Platforms	511210/541511	Software Publishers / Custom Computer Programming Services
Internet of Things (devices)	334111/334112	Electronic Computer Manufacturing / Computer Storage Device Manufacturing
Internet of Things (software)	511210/541511	Software Publishers / Custom Computer Programming Services
Robotics	333999	Miscellaneous General Purpose Machinery Manufacturing
3D Printers	333249	Other Industrial Machinery Manufacturing

3D = three-dimensional.
Note: The North American Industry Classification System 2012 was used as it appears to have the most available details with regard to Industry 4.0 technologies among classification systems. The technologies listed here are not necessarily exhaustive of Industry 4.0 technologies.
Source: North American Industry Classification System 2012. https://www.naics.com/.

In order to identify the firms that primarily specialize in artificial intelligence, for example, a more granular approach to the disaggregation methods cited under the "Methodological Requirements" section (p. 23) must be taken. However, doing so requires access to detailed microdata on the software sector and the resources to conduct thorough examination. Nevertheless, some organizations have generated preliminary data that could illustrate the current and forthcoming state of the industry. Fragmentary revenue and unit sales information have been estimated for varying years per industry. For simplicity, Industry 4.0 can be segmented into four major technologies: artificial intelligence, additive manufacturing, IoT, and robotics.

A time series of the industry sizes of service robots (for professional and domestic uses), additive manufacturing, and artificial intelligence for enterprise applications using revenues shows steady growth overall (Figure 48). Total robot installations actually declined by 12% in 2019 (IFR 2020a), which can be attributed to a significant decrease in industrial robots despite the progress of service robots. The International Federation of Robotics (2020b) theorizes that the decline is largely the effect of falling demand of the automotive and electrical-electronics sectors and uncertainty caused by international trade tensions.

Figure 48: Global Industry 4.0 Revenues by Technology

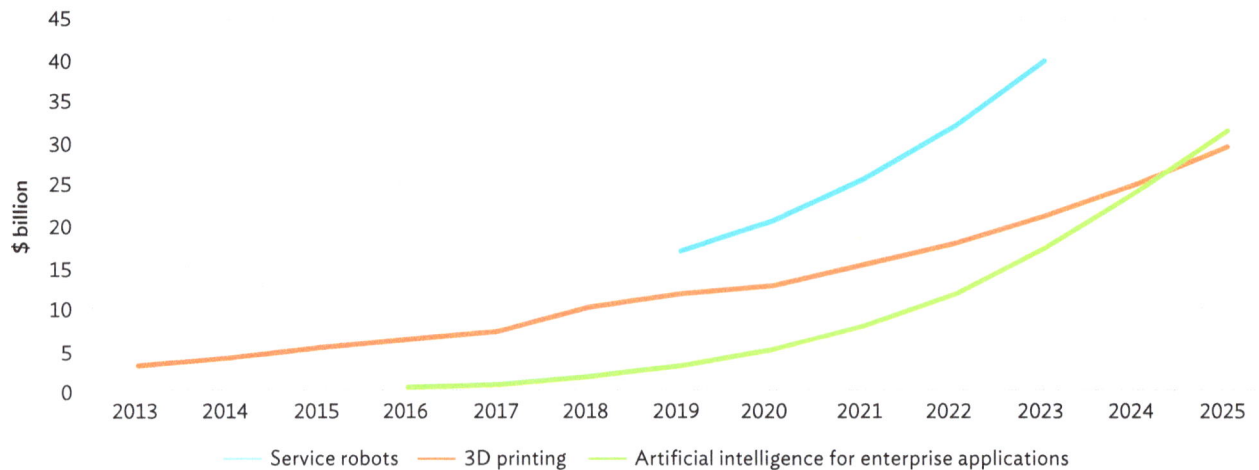

$ = United States dollars, 3D = three-dimensional.
Note: Estimated compound annual growth rate was used to compute values for 2021–2022 of service robots, 2021–2025 of 3D printing, and 2020–2025 of artificial intelligence for enterprise applications.
Sources: International Federation of Robotics (IFR). 2020. "IFR Press Conference." https://ifr.org/downloads/press2018/Presentation_WR_2020.pdf (accessed September 2020); Autonomous Manufacturing. 2020. "40+ 3D Printing Industry Stats You Should Know." https://amfg.ai/2020/01/14/40-3d-printing-industry-stats-you-should-know-2020-redirect/; Wohler's Associates, Inc. 2021. "New Wohlers Report 2021 Finds 7.5% Growth in Additive Manufacturing Industry Despite Pandemic." Press Release, March 16, 2021. http://wohlersassociates.com/press83.html; Statista. 2018. "Enterprise Artificial Intelligence Market Revenue Worldwide 2016–2025." https://blogs-images.forbes.com/louiscolumbus/files/2018/01/AI-for-enterprise-Apps.jpg (accessed September 2020); Global Industry Analysts, Inc. (GIA). 2021. "Global Artificial Intelligence (AI) Market to Reach $228.3 Billion by 2026." Cision PR Newswire, 18 May 2021. https://www.prnewswire.com/news-releases/global-artificial-intelligence-ai-market-to-reach-228-3-billion-by-2026--301293951.html (accessed May 2021).

For additive manufacturing, a conservative compound annual growth rate (CAGR) of 18.2% was used to project values from 2021 onwards, but other research cites forecasts as high as 27.2% (Autonomous Manufacturing 2020).[57] Artificial intelligence revenues after 2019 were projected using Global Industry Analysts (GIA) Inc.'s CAGR estimates (GIA 2021) and historical data from Statista (2018). Due to its significantly higher revenues, the IoT industry's size and the number of connections across a series of years are shown separately in Figure 49. While the revenue sales projections by IoT Analytics were made pre-pandemic (Lueth 2018), they accord closely to their November 2020 projections of CAGR and increasing connections.

Geographically, consumption and market share of Industry 4.0 technologies are concentrated in highly developed economies as well as the PRC. More than half of global additive manufacturing revenues are produced by France, Germany, Italy, the PRC, the United Kingdom, and the US (Sher 2020). Almost three-quarters of installations of industrial robots worldwide take place in Germany, Japan, the PRC, the ROK, and the US (IFR 2020a). Currently, North America and Europe lead the additive manufacturing market (Autonomous Manufacturing 2019), but it is projected that, by 2030, the PRC will have the largest share at 26% (Transforma Insights 2020). Interestingly, the PRC currently accounts for 75% of IoT cellular connections worldwide, up from just 27% in 2015 (Lueth 2020). Similarly, the US dominates today's artificial intelligence market, although major advances in Canada, Germany, Japan, and the PRC are expected by 2026 (GIA 2021).

Figure 49: Connections and Revenues for the Global Internet of Things

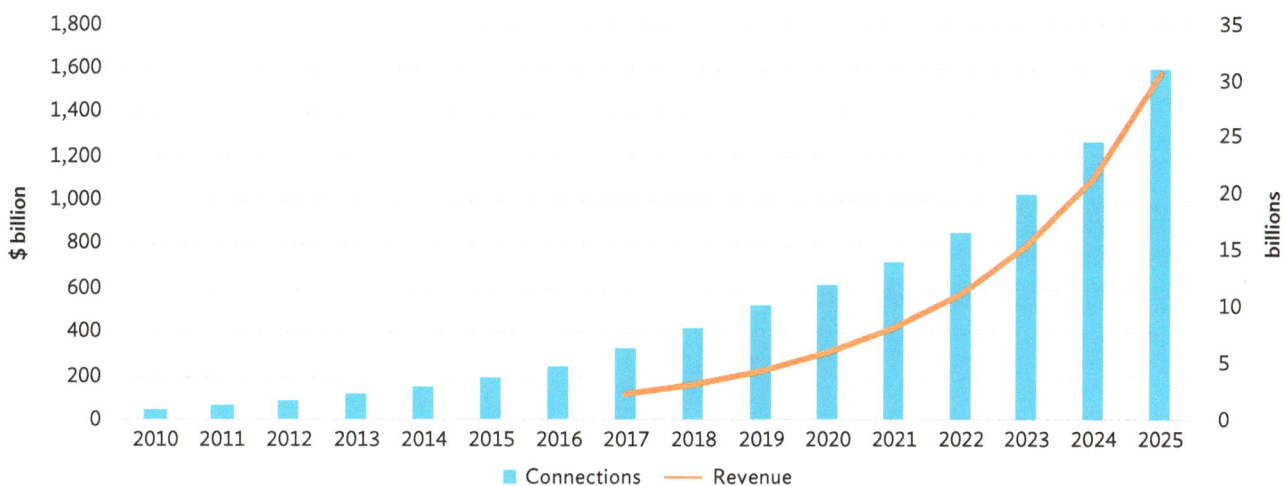

$ = United States dollars.
Sources: K. Lueth. 2018. "State of the IoT 2018: Number of IoT Devices Now at 7B— – Market Aaccelerating." IoT Analytics, 8 August 2018. https://iot-analytics.com/state-of-the-iot-update-q1-q2-2018-number-of-iot-devices-now-7b/ (accessed May 2021); K. Lueth. 2020. "State of the IoT 2020: 12 Billion IoT Connections, Surpassing Non-IoT for the First Time." IOT Analytics, 19 November 2020. https://iot-analytics.com/state-of-the-iot-2020-12-billion-iot-connections-surpassing-non-iot-for-the-first-time/ (accessed May 2021).

[57] The reference article was published in January 2020, before the full onset of the COVID-19 pandemic, which is why the lower bound CAGR was used for the additive manufacturing projections.

With the outbreak of COVID-19, 2020 became an inflection point for many industries, including digital operations. While e-commerce and certain digital indicators posted significant growth during the affected years, deployment of Industry 4.0 technologies may not be as advantaged considering their high-technology and capital-intensive nature. Insufficient funding was cited as companies' top hindrance from adopting Industry 4.0 technologies, with at least one-third of survey respondents foreseeing at least a year required in recovery from the pandemic's impacts (Agrawal et al. 2021). Nonetheless, other responses reflect that such technologies are becoming more vital for most companies. For instance, additive manufacturing would allow the acceleration of supply chains, and inclination toward automation may be fast-tracked due to employee lockdown (de Nicola et al. 2020). Fortune Business Insights (2021) projects Industry 4.0's CAGR to reach 16.4% from 2021 to 2028, up from 14% in 2020. In general, Industry 4.0 is expected to grow in the next decade, but much speculation surrounds the pace at which it develops, especially given the varying trends of its specific subsectors amidst COVID-19 ramifications.

The decline in the industrial robot industry is expected to continue in the short-term, but industry experts theorize that technological advancements and imminent demand pose growth opportunities in the long-term (IFR 2020a). Sales of service robots related to logistics and disinfectants, however, have increased (IFR 2020c). The additive manufacturing industry's annual growth remains positive at 7.5% for 2020, albeit this is a significantly lower rate than the average growth of 27.4% recorded in 2010 through 2019 (Wohlers Associates 2021). In contrast, the outlook for IoT markets appears increasingly bullish despite the pandemic, with higher CAGR estimations and forecasts (13% and 10%, respectively) post-2019 than in previous years, fueled by accelerated use of personal devices and global cellular IoT connections (Lueth 2020). The growth prospects of artificial intelligence are excellent, estimated at 32.7% from 2020 to 2026, mainly due to the rise of cloud-based solutions (GIA 2021). In fact, artificial intelligence may play a critical part in COVID-19 eradication initiatives, as it has historically with medical sciences (Al-Hashimi and Hamdan 2021). These trends align with findings in the World Economic Forum's Future of Jobs Report 2020 that, by 2025, more than 80% of companies are likely to adopt IoT and artificial intelligence technologies, while less than 40% are likely to adopt robots.

Prospects for Industry 5.0

Industry 4.0 technologies characterize the future general direction of the digital economy and may have staggering implications on different facets of society, especially as a strong contributor to the "new normal." Consequently, discussions of the succeeding industrial revolution, Industry 5.0, are already underway.

A common concern in discussions around Industry 4.0 is the threat that robots and artificial intelligence are displacing manual repetitive labor. As concluded in the chapter "Jobs in the Digital Economy" (p. 72), improvements in the digital sectors' technology can indeed reduce labor demand, but this may be offset by increased labor requirements. According to the World Economic Forum (2020) report, due to the adoption of automation technologies, 43% of surveyed businesses intended to reduce their labor force, while 34% intended to expand theirs. Despite the likelihood that such technologies will increasingly substitute low-skilled labor, there is also potential for even higher job generation through reallocation of roles (WEF 2020), which makes the reskilling of the labor force a primary policy concern.

This strategic harmonization between humans and machine intelligence is a developing interest, if not an imminent necessity, which is the foundation behind Industry 5.0 (Vollmer 2018). While Industry 4.0 provides the smart tools, Industry 5.0 integrates innovation with social as well as environmental needs (Müller 2020), fostering a collaborative relationship that may benefit economies more holistically. While still an immature concept, the early attempt to mitigate ongoing and potential risks, such as those faced by labor and productivity, may lead to more prosperous development of the digital economy and affected industries in the long run.

Like Industry 4.0, the economic contribution of Industry 5.0 can be captured in the proposed framework through the value of its digital products and its nondigital products' linkages with digital products. It would complement Industry 4.0, prioritizing societal interests through innovations in artificial intelligence (e.g., skills matching), cloud computing (e.g., cybersafe infrastructure), robotics (e.g., collaborative robots), and energy-efficient technologies, among others (Müller 2020). Considering the projected growth of Industry 4.0, the extended and advanced use of these products by Industry 5.0 would likely contribute positively to the global digital economy. The digitally dependent economy may likewise benefit from the integration of these newer technologies, especially for firms and industries adopting practices in corporate social responsibility.

Summary and Conclusion

At this stage, the proposed framework for measuring the digital economy seeks to put into focus the evolving products and industries of the digital era, by teasing out their economic contribution within the bounds of national accounts. The framework measures the share of GDP attributable to the digital economy from economy-wide GDP, which is captured by taking the value-added contributions to and from a defined set of core digital products, corresponding respectively to the digital economy's backward and forward linkages.

Using a core equation (Equation 10) centered on the conventional input-output model, the digital economy can be broken down into the following main elements: contributions of digitally enabling industries, contributions to digitally enabled industries, and digital sectors' purchases of nondigital capital. Data requirements are generally straightforward and adjustments to comply with the framework, if necessary, prove to be feasible for any domestic or multiregional input-output table (IOT). Employing national accounts data from 16 economies across different regions of the world has provided insightful results. Despite the narrow definition adopted in the framework, the digital economy yields a significant portion (about 2% to 9%) of every selected economy's GDP. However, characterization of the role of the digital economy varies across economies—some act more as a supplier of value-added in the economy, while others act as a user.

As digital technologies take distinctive roles in nondigital products, measuring the digitally dependent economy allows for a more comprehensive understanding of the digital economy in general. Indicators of nondigital industries' digital dependence reveal that service sectors tend more toward digitalization, with the estimated overall digitally dependent economies ranging from 17% to 35% of GDP. Given the estimates of the digital and digitally enabled economies, the established interindustry and interregional linkages of the core digital sectors, as indicated by digital multipliers, reveal a strong potential for the digital sectors in output propagation in the economy.

Over time, growth in the digital economy appears to slow down for most economies when observing CAGRs of IOTs in current prices. However, analysis using certain economies' constant-price IOTs suggests growth in volume terms. Moreover, as the digital economies grow in volume over time, it is imperative to understand their impact on jobs. Data suggest that, while effects of technology improvements observably reduce labor demand as a result of substitution, positive job impacts coming from consumption and new labor requirements may compensate. Prospectively, however, the adoption of Industry 4.0 technologies and the emergence of Industry 5.0 technologies require reskilling of the labor force, such that job losses from changes in sector technology are mitigated.

From a multiregional perspective, GVC participation of digital sectors grew from 2009 to 2019, driven by rapid trading in services. However, international trade tensions disproportionately disrupted the integration of digital GVCs from 2018 to 2019. The COVID-19 pandemic is expected to exacerbate such disruption, although the depth of the impact is still subject to speculation. The e-commerce sector, which is a digitally enabled industry, was observed to counter the negative effects of the pandemic, albeit from the perspective of the national economy.

To further the discourse in previous chapters, disaggregation of national accounts may be extended to the level of small and medium-sized enterprises, to establish how technological adoption is impacting their profitability, productivity, and ability to reach markets. Moreover, the framework may be applied to analyze the link between the productivity of sectors and their use of digital technologies. Moving forward, the study's authors seek to explore other key issues within the subject of the digital economy, including taxation, the effects of trade and technology on employment in digital and digitally enabled sectors from a multi-economy perspective, and the post-pandemic impacts of COVID-19 on the digital economy.[58]

Digital technologies are continuously evolving or adapting to present-day conditions, and studying their role may be more important than ever before. While existing macroeconomic frameworks remain relevant, improvements in the quality of traditional statistics and the generation of new statistics are becoming more necessary. Thus far, the endeavors by various institutions and the continually growing body of knowledge are informative and encouraging. International statistical cooperation will be crucial in standardizing approaches and providing guidance on existing and emerging issues brought about by digitalization. As the authors of this study move forward in this initiative, they hope to produce more evidence and insight to contribute to a universal, standard system for measuring the digital economy.

---

[58] Initial analysis by the study's authors found that digital services sectors in low- to no-tax jurisdictions exhibited relatively higher forward links to foreign sectors, compared to those in high-tax jurisdictions. This provides preliminary evidence of base erosion and profit shifting, as well as its increasing relevance to digital firms that can easily derive profits from high-tax locations, while being taxed at a lower rate based on its physical location.

Appendix 1: A Standard Input-Output Table

A standard input-output table (IOT) is generally comprised of three quadrants. The first quadrant contains the $\mathbf{Z} = [\mathbf{z_{ij}}]$ matrix, which is a matrix of interindustry flows of output from industry i (row) to industry j (column). The second quadrant contains the $\mathbf{y} = [\mathbf{y_i}]$ vector, which is a column vector of the final consumption of output from industry i. The vector of final demand is comprised of the aggregated final consumption of households, nonprofit institutions serving households, and government; and gross capital formation. The third quadrant contains the $\mathbf{gva'} = [\mathrm{gva}_j]$ vector, which is a row vector of the gross value-added of industry j.

One of the important features of a standard IOT is its symmetry. Put simply, in an IOT, total output of industries (i.e., summing columns under intermediate consumption along the rows or $\mathbf{x'}$) is equal to the total output used by industries and by final users (i.e., summing rows along columns or $\mathbf{x}$). Table A1.1 shows the structure of a standard n-industry IOT.

Table A1.1: Standard Industry Input-Output Table

	Intermediate consumption				Final demand	Gross output
	Industry 1	Industry 2	...	Industry n		
Industry 1						
Industry 2		Quadrant I: $\mathbf{Z}$			Quadrant II: $\mathbf{y}$	$\mathbf{x}$
⋮						
Industry n						
Value-added		Quadrant III: $\mathbf{gva'}$				
Gross output		$\mathbf{x'}$				

	Intermediate consumption				Final demand	Gross output
	Industry 1	Industry 2	...	Industry n		
Industry 1	z_{11}	z_{12}	...	z_{1n}	y_1	x_1
Industry 2	z_{21}	z_{22}	...	z_{2n}	y_2	x_2
⋮	⋮	⋮	⋱	⋮	⋮	⋮
Industry n	z_{n1}	z_{n2}	...	z_{nn}	y_n	x_n
Value-added	gva_1	gva_2	...	gva_n		
Gross output	x_1	x_2	...	x_n		

Source: Construction of the Digital Economy Measurement Framework study team.

The symmetry of the IOT provides an organized visual model of the circular flow resources in any economy. We show below how this can be approached in a similarly organized but more concise manner from a mathematical perspective.

Consider an economy with n industries, as in the IOT in Table A1.1. Each industry i produces its own output, x_i, where $i = 1, 2, .., n$. Each x_i can either be used as inputs to industrial production or finally consumed by households, government, nonprofit institutions serving households, and even other industries (the interactions within an IOT are discussed in detail under "Methodological Requirements" on p. 23 of the main text). Let z_{ij} represent the monetary value of industry j's purchases of industry i output for intermediate use, and y_i be the total amount of purchases from industry i intended for final consumption. As is customary in traditional input-output analysis, we will assume that interindustry flows from i to j contemporaneously depend entirely on sector 's total output (Miller and Blair 2009), which implies that final demand is exogenous. Given this information, in Equation (1), we describe the gross output of each industry i to be broken down across its intermediate users and final users.

$$x_i = z_{i1} + z_{i2} + \cdots + z_{in} + y_i, \quad i = 1, 2, ..., n \tag{1}$$

Given that Equation (1) is a system of n equations, we express it in matrix notation in Equation (2).

$$\begin{pmatrix} x_1 \\ x_2 \\ \vdots \\ x_n \end{pmatrix} = \begin{bmatrix} z_{11} & z_{12} & \cdots & z_{1n} \\ z_{21} & z_{22} & \cdots & z_{2n} \\ \vdots & \vdots & \ddots & \vdots \\ z_{n1} & z_{n2} & \cdots & z_{nn} \end{bmatrix} \begin{pmatrix} 1 \\ 1 \\ \vdots \\ 1 \end{pmatrix} + \begin{pmatrix} y_1 \\ y_2 \\ \vdots \\ y_n \end{pmatrix}$$

$$\mathbf{x = Zi + y} \tag{2}$$

We derive a technical coefficient, a_{ij}, to describe the ratio between the amount of industry i's output used by j and the amount of industry j's output; that is, $a_{ij} = z_{ij}/x_j$. Following the Leontief insight, each a_{ij} is assumed to be unchanging over the course of an accounting period. Stating z_{ij} in terms of a_{ij}, the gross output in Equation (1) becomes

$$x_i = a_{i1}x_1 + a_{i2}x_2 + \cdots + a_{in}x_n + y_i, \quad i = 1, 2, ..., n$$

which may be re-expressed as

$$\begin{pmatrix} x_1 \\ x_2 \\ \vdots \\ x_n \end{pmatrix} = \begin{bmatrix} z_{11} & z_{12} & \cdots & z_{1n} \\ z_{21} & z_{22} & \cdots & z_{2n} \\ \vdots & \vdots & \ddots & \vdots \\ z_{n1} & z_{n2} & \cdots & z_{nn} \end{bmatrix} \begin{bmatrix} x_1 & 0 & \cdots & 0 \\ 0 & x_2 & \cdots & 0 \\ \vdots & \vdots & \ddots & \vdots \\ 0 & 0 & \cdots & x_n \end{bmatrix}^{-1} \begin{pmatrix} x_1 \\ x_2 \\ \vdots \\ x_n \end{pmatrix} + \begin{pmatrix} y_1 \\ y_2 \\ \vdots \\ y_n \end{pmatrix}$$

$$= \begin{bmatrix} a_{11} & a_{12} & \cdots & a_{1n} \\ a_{21} & a_{22} & \cdots & a_{2n} \\ \vdots & \vdots & \ddots & \vdots \\ a_{n1} & a_{n2} & \cdots & a_{nn} \end{bmatrix} \begin{pmatrix} x_1 \\ x_2 \\ \vdots \\ x_n \end{pmatrix} + \begin{pmatrix} y_1 \\ y_2 \\ \vdots \\ y_n \end{pmatrix}$$

$$\mathbf{x = Ax + y} \tag{3}$$

Rearranging Equation (3):

$$\mathbf{x} = \mathbf{Ax} + \mathbf{y} \rightarrow \mathbf{x} - \mathbf{Ax} = \mathbf{y} \rightarrow (\mathbf{I} - \mathbf{A})\mathbf{x} = \mathbf{y}$$

Assuming that $\mathbf{I} - \mathbf{A}$ is nonsingular, we have the fundamental Leontief identity:

$$\mathbf{x} = (\mathbf{I} - \mathbf{A})^{-1}\mathbf{y} \qquad (4)$$

We refer to $(\mathbf{I} - \mathbf{A})^{-1}$ as the Leontief inverse, which gives the total output requirements from each industry in order to meet final demand for a specific time period. Note that $\mathbf{x}$ from Equation (4) would yield the exact same vector of gross output $\mathbf{x}$ in a standard n-industry IOT. Therefore, we could mathematically represent Table A1.1 through Equation (4).

Reference:

R. Miller and P. Blair. 2009. *Input-Output Analysis: Foundations and Extensions.* Cambridge: Cambridge University Press.

Appendix 2: Aggregating Matrices

Suppose one has a 4 × 4 input matrix, **Z**:

$$\mathbf{Z} = \begin{bmatrix} z_{11} & z_{12} & z_{13} & z_{14} \\ z_{21} & z_{22} & z_{23} & z_{24} \\ z_{31} & z_{32} & z_{33} & z_{34} \\ z_{41} & z_{42} & z_{43} & z_{44} \end{bmatrix}$$

The dimensions of the aggregator matrix are [n-(q-1)] × n, where n is the original number of industries and q is the number of industries to be aggregated into one sector. Thus, to aggregate two industries, one needs a (4 – 2 +1) × 4 or a 3 × 4 aggregator matrix. To aggregate column vectors, one only needs to pre-multiply the aggregator matrix to them, while matrices (**Z** in this case) have to be pre- and post-multiplied with the aggregator matrix and its transpose, respectively. Letting **Q** denote the aggregator matrix, these steps are given by the equations:

$$\mathbf{x}_{agg} = \mathbf{Qx}$$

$$\mathbf{f}_{agg} = \mathbf{Qf}$$

$$\mathbf{gva}_{agg} = \mathbf{Qgva}$$

$$\mathbf{Z}_{agg} = \mathbf{QZQ}^T$$

The logic behind aggregator matrices is discussed with the aid of some examples. To aggregate Industries 1 and 2, the following aggregator matrix is needed:

$$\mathbf{Q} = \begin{bmatrix} 1 & 1 & 0 & 0 \\ 0 & 0 & 1 & 0 \\ 0 & 0 & 0 & 1 \end{bmatrix}$$

For Industries 1 and 3:

$$\mathbf{Q} = \begin{bmatrix} 1 & 0 & 1 & 0 \\ 0 & 1 & 0 & 0 \\ 0 & 0 & 0 & 1 \end{bmatrix}$$

For Industries 1 and 4:

$$\mathbf{Q} = \begin{bmatrix} 1 & 0 & 0 & 1 \\ 0 & 1 & 0 & 0 \\ 0 & 0 & 1 & 0 \end{bmatrix}$$

For Industries 2 and 3:

$$\mathbf{Q} = \begin{bmatrix} 1 & 0 & 0 & 0 \\ 0 & 1 & 1 & 0 \\ 0 & 0 & 0 & 1 \end{bmatrix}$$

And for Industries 2 and 4:

$$\mathbf{Q} = \begin{bmatrix} 1 & 0 & 0 & 0 \\ 0 & 1 & 0 & 1 \\ 0 & 0 & 1 & 0 \end{bmatrix}$$

In aggregating Industries 1 and 2, the contents of the first row of $\mathbf{Q}$ depend on whether the first industry should be aggregated with any other industry. Since 1 and 2 will be aggregated, the entries of the first and second columns take the value of 1. Entries for the third and fourth columns are set to zero since Industry 1 will not be grouped with any of those industries. In the second row, only the entry in the third column corresponding to Industry 3 is set to 1, since Industry 3 will not be grouped with any other industry. Lastly, after accounting for the first three industries, the third row of $\mathbf{Q}$ should be altered depending on whether Industry 4 will be grouped with any other industry. Since this is not the case, only the entry in the fourth column is set to 1, with everything else being zero.

In aggregating Industries 1 and 3, the entries in the first row of $\mathbf{Q}$ depend on whether the first industry will be aggregated with any other industry. Since 1 and 3 will be grouped together, the entries in the first and third columns are set to 1 and zero to the second and fourth columns. Since Industry 2 is not yet accounted for, the second row should consider if Industry 2 will be grouped with any other industry. Since this is not the case, the second column is set to 1, with all other entries set to zero. Finally, since Industries 1, 2, and 3 have already been accounted for, the third row of $\mathbf{Q}$ should consider if Industry 4 will be grouped with any other industry. Since this is not the case, the fourth column is set to 1 and all others to zero.

Thus, the sequence of industries in an input-output table (IOT) is crucial when it comes to the use of aggregator matrices. Columns still correspond to the exact order of industries in an IOT, but rows will be adjusted whenever industries are grouped together. However, inputting values to rows of $\mathbf{Q}$ is still based on the sequence of industries in an IOT, with skips occurring when an industry has already been lumped with another that appeared prior to it.

Appendix 3: Stating Current-Price National Input-Output Tables in Volume Terms

Given a current-price national input-output table (NIOT) of economy i in year t ("current-NIOT") and price indices at year t and base year b, a corresponding NIOT stated at year b prices can be generated. The latter is considered the year t NIOT of economy i in volume terms ("volume-NIOT").

Suppose the NIOT system is described by $\mathbf{Zi} + \mathbf{Yi} = \mathbf{x}$ and $\mathbf{i'} \mathbf{Z} + \mathbf{gva'} = \mathbf{x'}$, where $\mathbf{Z}$ is a matrix of intermediate consumption, $\mathbf{Y}$ is a matrix of final demand, $\mathbf{gva}$ is a vector of gross value-added (GVA), and $\mathbf{x}$ is a vector of gross output. Further, let $\mathbf{p^x}$ denote a vector of price indices of sector gross output, $\widehat{\mathbf{p^x}}$ be a matrix with $\mathbf{p^x}$ in its diagonal and zeros in its off-diagonals, and p^{gdp} be the GDP deflator. Five general steps are followed to convert a current-NIOT into a volume-NIOT.

First, sector gross output at current prices is deflated using the corresponding sector's gross output price index. Gross output in volume terms is described by $\bar{\mathbf{x}} = \widehat{\mathbf{p^x}}^{-1}\mathbf{x}$.[1] The derived $\bar{\mathbf{x}}$ and $\bar{\mathbf{x}}'$ will serve as row and column control totals, respectively, of the volume-NIOT. Second, the changes in inventory (**CII**) component of $\mathbf{Y}$ is deflated using p^{gdp}, $\overline{\mathbf{CII}} = \mathbf{CII} \cdot p^{gdp^{-1}}$.[2] Third, each element of the vector difference $\bar{\mathbf{x}} - \overline{\mathbf{CII}}$ is allocated row-wise, to populate the $\overline{\mathbf{Z}}$ and the $\overline{\mathbf{Y}}$ matrices.[3] These represent the intermediate consumption matrix and final demand matrix in volume terms, respectively. The allocation basis is in proportion to the values in the corresponding current-price NIOT. Fourth, once the $\overline{\mathbf{Z}}$ matrix is fully populated, a vector of total intermediate consumption by sector ($\overline{\mathbf{IC}}$) is derived, $\overline{\mathbf{IC}}' = \mathbf{i'}\overline{\mathbf{Z}}$. Last, the difference $\bar{\mathbf{x}}' - \overline{\mathbf{IC}}'$ is equal the sector's GVA in volume terms, $\overline{\mathbf{gva}}'$. Following the five-step process, the system of the volume-NIOT would be described by $\overline{\mathbf{Z}}\mathbf{i} + \overline{\mathbf{Y}}\mathbf{i} = \bar{\mathbf{x}}$ and $\mathbf{i'}\overline{\mathbf{Z}} + \overline{\mathbf{gva}}' = \bar{\mathbf{x}}'$.[4]

While the most desired methodology in deriving a volume-NIOT is by deflating the underlying supply and use tables (SUTs) and then transforming the constant-price SUTs to a volume-NIOT, the five-step approach employed in this study is slightly akin to the double-deflation method that is desired in stating SUTs in volume terms. On the one hand, under the double-deflation method, price indices are collected

---

[1] Let values in volume terms be accented with a bar.

[2] Let **CII** denote the vector of changes in inventory by product. Changes in inventory (**CII**) is deflated independently using the GDP deflator p^{gdp} because **CII**, when negative, may distort the deflation process.

[3] The $\overline{\mathbf{CII}}$ component of $\overline{\mathbf{Y}}$ need not be populated in the third step since $\overline{\mathbf{CII}}$ was already derived in the second step.

[4] Immediately following the five-step process, consistency checks are employed. If, in the process of these consistency checks, imbalances arise, adjustments to rebalance the volume-NIOT are done using an iterative process.

for both gross output and intermediate consumption items.[5] On the other hand, although the five-step approach in this study only employs a deflator for gross output $\mathbf{p^x}$, the implicit deflator for intermediate consumption, $\mathbf{p^{ic}} = \mathbf{IC} \circ \overline{1/\mathbf{ic}}$, would be mathematically different from $\mathbf{p^x}$. Thus, $p^x_j \neq p^{ic}_j$.

---

[5]   Current-price gross output and intermediate consumption are both deflated by the appropriate price indices; and then constant-price GVA is derived by subtraction (Eurostat. 2008. The Eurostat Manual of Supply, Use and Input-Output Tables. Luxembourg: Office for Official Publications of the European Communities).

Appendix 4: Source Tables

Table A4.1: A Comparison of Estimation Methods for the Digital Economy

Authors	Definition	Estimation method	Data requirements	Advantages	Limitations
ADB Digital Economy Measurement Framework study team	Digital products generate, process or store digitized data; identified using the CPC 2 and differentiated from analog. The primary producers of such products are the digital industries with their backward and forward linkages defined as digitally enabling and digitally enabled, respectively.	Input-output analysis framework	National SUTs or IOTs Disaggregation of products and industries in the IOTs by isolating the digital out of the aggregated product and industry groupings.	Produces a finer estimation vis-a-vis other methods and can capture sector interdependencies and indirect digital contributions to the economy.	Data availability dependent on the frequency of NSO data releases; assumes fixed technical coefficients within the given data period; national accounts limitations.
Mitchell (2018)	Digital transactions are either digitally ordered, digitally delivered, or platform enabled. Digital goods and services are aligned with the ICT classification in CPC 2.1. Digital industries are either digitally enabling, digital intermediary platforms, firms dependent on intermediary platforms, e-sellers, or other digital businesses.	Supply-use framework	National SUTs Disaggregation of products and industries in the SUTs by isolating the digital out of the aggregated product and industry groupings.	No need to transform SUTs to IOTs	Data availability dependent on the frequency of NSO data releases; does not fully capture sector interdependencies and indirect digital contributions to economy; national accounts limitations.
Barefoot et al. (2018)	Digital economy is composed of digital-enabling infrastructure, e-commerce, and digital media; classified using NAICS. Digital-enabling infrastructure include computer hardware, software, telecommunications, IoT, and support services. Digital commodities are identified using six-digit NAICS code.	Supply-use framework	National SUTs Disaggregation of products and industries in the SUTs by isolating the digital out of the aggregated product and industry groupings.	No need to transform SUTs to IOTs	Data availability dependent on the frequency of NSO data releases; does not fully capture sector interdependencies and indirect digital contributions to economy; national accounts limitations.
Brynjolfsson et al. (2019)	"Free" digital goods and services such as Wikipedia, Facebook, and Google	Extending GDP to GDP-B to capture digital benefits	Survey to measure how much the consumers are willing to pay to give up digital products and services.	Captures economic well-being or welfare and supplements the GDP.	Challenge of conducting a representative survey for various products on a national scale and on a regular basis
Huawei and Oxford Economics (2017)	The definition of digital assets is extended to include digital goods depreciable within one year but with the same contribution to production processes as capital, as well as all kinds of capital used by the digital sector including services imported through digital assets abroad.	Total economic returns to accumulated digital investment value including productivity gains and indirect spillover effects	Growth of services from ICT capital stock and contribution of ICT capital stock to GDP growth IOTs to determine shares of digital intermediate inputs considered digital assets	Captures the value generated by the use of digital assets rather than cost of purchasing and/or producing them	Intermediate consumption by other industries of digital products that do not have the same characteristics of capital (i.e., are used as components in production processes) are excluded

ADB = Asian Development Bank, CPC = Central Product Classification, ERCD-SDIU = Economic Research and Regional Cooperation Department - Statistics and Data Innovation Unit, GDP = gross domestic product, ICT = information and communication technology, IMF = International Monetary Fund, IoT = internet of things, IOT = input-output table, NAICS = North American Industry Classification System, NSO = national statistics office, OECD = Organisation for Economic Co-operation and Development; SUT = supply and use table, US BEA = United States Bureau of Economic Analysis.

Note: Input-output analysis was initially developed by the economist Wassily Leontief.

Source: Construction of the Digital Economy Measurement Framework study team based on the works of: K. Barefoot, C. Dave, W. Jolliff, J. Nicholson, and R. Omohundro. 2018. *Defining and Measuring the Digital Economy.* United States Department of Commerce, Bureau of Economic Analysis; E. Brynjolfsson, A. Collis, W. E. Diewert, F. Eggers, and K. J. Fox. 2019. GDP-B: Accounting for the Value of New and Free Goods in the Digital Economy. *National Bureau of Economic Research Working Paper.* No. 25695. National Bureau of Economic Research; Huawei and Oxford Economics. 2017. *Digital Spillover: Measuring the True Impact of the Digital Economy.* https://www.huawei.com/minisite/gci/en/digital-spillover/index.html; and J. Mitchell. 2018. *A Proposed Framework for Digital Supply-Use Tables.* OECD. https://www.oecd.org/officialdocuments/publicdisplaydocumentpdf/?cote=SDD/CSSP/WPNA(2018)3&docLanguage=En.

Table A4.2: Main Digital Industries by International Standard Industrial Classification of All Economic Activities Revision 4

Main Activity Group	Code	Industry
Hardware	2620	Manufacture of computers and peripheral equipment
	2680	Manufacture of magnetic and optical media
Software publishing	5820	Software publishing
Web publishing	6312	Web portals
Telecommunications services	61	Telecommunications services
Specialized and support services	62	Computer programming services, consulting, and other related services
	6311	Data processing, hosting and related activities

Source: United Nations. 2008. *International Standard Industrial Classification of All Economic Activities (ISIC), Rev. 4.* New York: United Nations.

Table A4.3: ADB Multiregional Input–Output 35-Sector Classification

Code	Sector	Code	Sector
c1	Agriculture, hunting, forestry, and fishing	c19	Sale, maintenance, and repair of motor vehicles and motorcycles; retail sale of fuel
c2	Mining and quarrying	c20	Wholesale trade and commission trade, except of motor vehicles and motorcycles
c3	Food, beverages, and tobacco	c21	Retail trade, except of motor vehicles and motorcycles; repair of household goods
c4	Textiles and textile products	c22	Hotels and restaurants
c5	Leather, leather products and footwear	c23	Inland transport
c6	Wood and products of wood and cork	c24	Water transport
c7	Pulp, paper, paper products, printing, and publishing	c25	Air transport
c8	Coke, refined petroleum, and nuclear fuel	c26	Other supporting and auxiliary transport activities; activities of travel agencies
c9	Chemicals and chemical products	c27	Post and telecommunications
c10	Rubber and plastics	c28	Financial intermediation
c11	Other nonmetallic minerals	c29	Real estate activities
c12	Basic metals and fabricated metal	c30	Renting of M&Eq and other business activities
c13	Machinery, n.e.c.	c31	Public administration and defense; compulsory social security
c14	Electrical and optical equipment	c32	Education
c15	Transport equipment	c33	Health and social work
c16	Manufacturing, n.e.c.; recycling	c34	Other community, social, and personal services
c17	Electricity, gas and water supply	c35	Private households with employed persons
c18	Construction		

M&Eq= machinery and equipment, n.e.c.= not elsewhere classified.
Source: Asian Development Bank Multiregional Input-Output Database.

Table A4.4: Data Used for Digital Economy Estimations per Economy

Economy	Year(s) Used for Estimation	Source(s) of IOT, SUT and/or Related Data	Disaggregation Data Source(s)	No. of Industries	No. of Digital Industries Identified (Total or disaggregated from total)
Australia	2010, 2018	Australian Bureau of Statistics	Orbis, OECD	114	4
Canada	2012, 2016	Statistics Canada	Statistics Canada	236 (2012), 240 (2016)	7
Denmark	2010, 2016	Statistics Denmark	Orbis, Statistics Denmark	117	5
Fiji	2011	Fiji Bureau of Statistics	Orbis, Fiji Bureau of Statistics	50	4
Germany	2010, 2016	Federal Statistical Office of Germany	Orbis	72	4
India	2010, 2014	World Input-Output Database	Orbis, Ministry of Statistics & Programme Implementation (Government of India)	56	4
Indonesia	2010, 2014	World Input-Output Database	Orbis, Thailand data, SUT	56	4
Japan	2000, 2005, 2011, 2015	e-Stat – Statistics Bureau, Ministry of Internal Affairs and Communications	None	104 (2000), 108 (2005 and 2011), 107 (2015)	4 (2000), 5 (2005-2015)
Kazakhstan	2001, 2010, 2018	Committee on Statistics of the Republic of Kazakhstan	Bureau of National Statistics of the Agency for Strategic Planning and Reforms of the Republic of Kazakhstan	72	3
Malaysia	2010, 2015	Department of Statistics Malaysia	SUT, Thailand data	86 (2010), 124 (2015)	5 (2010), 5 (2015)
People's Republic of China	2012	National Bureau of Statistics of China	Orbis, National Bureau of Statistics of China	64	5
Republic of Korea	2010, 2018	Economics Statistics System – Bank of Korea	Statistics Korea	161 (2010), 165 (2018)	5 (2010), 5 (2018)
Singapore	2000, 2016	Singapore Department of Statistics	Orbis, SUT	152 (2000), 105 (2016)	3 (2000), 5 (2016)
Taipei,China	2016	Directorate-General of Budget Accounting and Statistics	None	164	4
Thailand	2010, 2015	National Statistics Office of Thailand	Orbis	180	5
United States	2010, 2019	U.S. Bureau of Economic Analysis	U.S. Bureau of Economic Analysis, Canada IOTs	71	5

IOT = input-output table, OECD = Organisation for Economic Co-operation and Development, SUT = supply and use table, US = United States

Source: Construction of the Digital Economy Measurement Framework study team.

References

Advisory Expert Group on National Accounts (AEG). 2019. *13th Meeting of the Advisory Expert Group on National Accounts: Framework for a Satellite Account on the Digital Economy*. Washington, D.C. https://unstats.un.org/unsd/nationalaccount/aeg/2019/M13.asp

M. Agrawal, S. Dutta, R. Kelly, and I. Millán. 2021. *COVID-19: An Inflection Point for Industry 4.0*. McKinsey & Company. 15 January. https://www.mckinsey.com/business-functions/operations/our-insights/covid-19-an-inflection-point-for-industry-40.

S. Ahmadi. 2019. *5G NR: Architecture, Technology, Implementation, and Operation of 3GPP New Radio Standards*. https://doi.org/10.1016/C2016-0-04944-6.

N. Ahmad and P. Schreyer. 2016. Measuring GDP in a Digitalised Economy. *OECD Statistics Working Papers*. No. 7.

N. Ahmad, J. Ribarsky and M. Reinsdorf. 2017. Can Potential Mismeasurement of the Digital Economy Explain the Post-Crisis Slowdown in GDP and Productivity Growth? *OECD Statistics Working Papers*. No. 85. https://doi.org/10.1787/18152031.

N. Ahmad and J. Ribarsky. 2018. *Towards a Framework for Measuring the Digital Economy*. 16th Conference of the International Association of Official Statisticians (IAOS). Paris: OECD.

N. Ahmad and P. van de Ven. 2018. *Recording and Measuring Data in the System of National Accounts*. Paris: OECD Publishing.

M. Al-Hashimi and A. Hamdan. 2021. *Artificial Intelligence and Coronavirus COVID-19: Applications, Impact and Future Implications*. https://dx.doi.org/10.1007%2F978-3-030-69221-6_64

J. Alvarez, G. Antonio, R. Consing III, P. Gonzales, J. Guinto, A. Juani, and M. Mariasingham. 2021. Forging Economic Resilience in the People's Republic of China Through Value Chain Upgrading and Economic Rebalancing. *ADB Briefs Series*. No. 178. https://dx.doi.org/10.22617/BRF210172-2.

Amazon. n.d. What Robots Do (and Don't Do) at Amazon Fulfilment Centres. https://www.aboutamazon.co.uk/amazon-fulfilment/what-robots-do-and-dont-do-at-amazon-fulfilment-centres

A. Amuno. 2021. The Five Types of Systems Software. *TurboFuture*. 12 January 2021. https://turbofuture.com/computers/The-Five-Types-of-System-Software (accessed February 2021).

J.T. Areddy. 2021. *China Creates Its Own Digital Currency, a First for Major Economy*. Wall Street Journal. 5 April. https://www.wsj.com/articles/china-creates-its-own-digital-currency-a-first-for-major-economy-11617634118

Asian Development Bank (ADB). 2020. *Key Indicators for Asia and the Pacific Database*. Regional Tables: Economy and Output, Gross Domestic Product. https://kidb.adb.org/kidb/regionalKI (accessed 4 June 2021).

ADB. 2021. *Asian Development Outlook 2021: Financing a Green and Inclusive Recovery*. Mandaluyong City, Philippines.

Autonomous Manufacturing. 2019. *Additive Manufacturing Around the World: What is the State of 3D Printing Adoption in North America and Europe?* https://amfg.ai/2019/11/07/additive-manufacturing-around-the-world-what-is-the-state-of-3d-printing-adoption-in-north-america-and-europe/

Autonomous Manufacturing. 2020. *40+ 3D Printing Industry Stats You Should Know*. https://amfg.ai/2020/01/14/40-3d-printing-industry-stats-you-should-know-2020-redirect/

Bain & Company, Google, and Temasek. 2020. *e-Conomy SEA 2020: At Full Velocity—Resilient and Racing Ahead*. https://www.thinkwithgoogle.com.

K. Barefoot, C. Dave, W. Jolliff, J. Nicholson, and R. Omohundro. 2018. *Defining and Measuring the Digital Economy*. United States Department of Commerce, Bureau of Economic Analysis.

C. Bean. 2016. Independent Review of UK Economic Statistics. Her Majesty's Treasury, Government of United Kingdom.

D.J. Bertulfo, E. Gentile, and G.D. Vries. 2019. The Employment Effects of Technological Innovation, Consumption, and Participation in Global Value Chains: Evidence from Developing Asia. *Asian Development Bank Economics Working Paper Series*. No. 572. Manila: Asian Development Bank.

Z. Bischof, R. Fontugne, and F. Bustamante. 2018. Untangling the World-Wide Mesh of Undersea Cables. *Proceedings of the 17th ACM Workshop on Hot Topics in Networks HotNets-XVII. IIJ Innovation Institute*.

I. Bosilkovski. 2020. *Stanford Grad Who Created the World's First 'Robot Lawyer' Raises $12 Million in Series A*. Forbes. 23 June. https://www.forbes.com/sites/igorbosilkovski/2020/06/23/stanford-grad-who-created-the-worlds-first-robot-lawyer-raises-12-million-in-series-a/?sh=177a0e5e3309.

C. Breisinger, M. Thomas, and J. Thurlow. 2010. *Social Accounting Matrices and Multiplier Analysis: An Introduction with Exercises*. Washington, D.C.: International Food Policy Research Institute.

British Broadcasting Corporation (BBC). 2007. Happy 20th Birthday to the CD. http://web.archive.org/web/20070219014205/http:/www.bbc.co.uk/skillswise/inthenews/numbers/0306.shtml.

British Telecom (BT). 2021. *About BT*. https://www.bt.com/about/bt.

S. Bryan, D. Fiocco, M. Issler, R.S. Mallya Perdur, and M. Taksyak. 2020. *Creating Value in Digital Farming Solutions*. McKinsey & Company. 20 October. https://www.mckinsey.com/industries/agriculture/our-insights/creating-value-in-digital-farming-solutions.

E. Brynjolfsson and K. Steffenson McElerhan. 2017. Data-Driven Decision Making in Action. *MIT IDE Research Brief*.

E. Brynjolfsson and A. Collis. 2019. November. How Should We Measure the Digital Economy? *Harvard Business Review*. November–December. https://hbr.org/2019/11/how-should-we-measure-the-digital-economy.

E. Brynjolfsson, A. Collis, W. E. Diewert, F. Eggers, and K. J. Fox. 2019. GDP-B: Accounting for the Value of New and Free Goods in the Digital Economy. *National Bureau of Economic Research Working Paper*. No. 25695. National Bureau of Economic Research.

E. Byrnjolfsson, A. Collis, and F. Eggers. 2019. Using Massive Online Choice Experiments to Measure Changes in Well-Being. *Proceedings of the National Academy of Sciences*. 116. pp. 7250–7255.

R. Bukht and R. Heeks. 2017. Defining, Conceptualising and Measuring the Digital Economy. Development Informatics Working Paper no. 68. Manchester, UK: Centre for Development Informatics. http://dx.doi.org/10.2139/ssrn.3431732.

Bureau van Dijk. 2018. *Orbis Database*. https://orbis.bvdinfo.com/.

D. Burkett. 2017. *Digitisation and Digitalisation: What Means What?* WorkingMouse. 19 December. https://workingmouse.com.au/innovation/digitisation-digitalisation-digital-transformation/.

D. Byrne, J. Fernald, and M. Reinsdorf. 2016. Does the United States have a Productivity Slowdown or a Measurement Problem? *Brookings Paper on Economic Activity.* Spring 2016. http://www.brookings.edu/about/projects/bpea/papers/2016/byrne-et-al-productivity-measurement.

W. Chai and I. Lazar. n.d. *Telecommunications.* https://searchnetworking.techtarget.com/definition/telecommunications-telecom

S. Chand. n.d. *Agriculture Development and ICTs in Fiji.* Government of Fiji, Ministry of Agriculture. https://www.itu.int/en/ITU-D/Regional-Presence/AsiaPacific/SiteAssets/Pages/Events/2016/Eagriculture/eagriculture/Session%202_Fiji_Sushma%20Chand.pdf.

China Academy of Information and Communication Technology. 2020. *Digital Economy Development in China.* http://www.caict.ac.cn/english/research/whitepapers/202007/P020200728343679920779.pdf.

S.P. Choudary. 2018. *How the Platform Economy Is Reshaping Global Trade.* INSEAD. 30 August. https://knowledge.insead.edu/blog/insead-blog/how-the-platform-economy-is-reshaping-global-trade-9991.

P. Christensson. 2015. *Internet Definition.* https://techterms.com.

Computer History Museum. n.d. *Timeline of Computer History.* https://www.computerhistory.org/timeline/computers/.

R. Consing III, M. Barsabal, J. Alvarez, and M. Mariasingham. 2020. The Wellness Economy, A Comprehensive System of National Accounts Approach. *Asian Development Bank Economics Working Paper Series.* No. 631. Manila: Asian Development Bank.

C. Corrado, J. Haskel, C. Jona-Lasinio, and M. Iommi. 2016. Intangible Investment in the EU and US Before and Since the Great Recession and its Contribution to Productivity Growth. *European Investment Bank Working Papers.* No. 8.

C. Date. n.d. *A.M Turing Award: Edgar F. ("Ted") Codd.* https://amturing.acm.org/award_winners/codd_1000892.cfm.

F. de Nicola, J. Timmis, and A. Akhlaque. 2020. *How is COVID-19 Transforming Global Value Chains? Lessons from Ethiopia and Vietnam*. World Bank Blogs. https://blogs.worldbank.org.

J. Defourny and E. Thorbecke. 1984. Structural Path Analysis and Multiplier Decomposition within a Social Accounting Framework. *The Economic Journal*. 94 (373). pp. 111–136.

Delivery Hero. 2021. Delivery Hero Finishes the Year with Strong Final Quarter – Orders Almost Doubling Again. Press release. February 10. https://www.deliveryhero.com/newsroom/delivery-hero-finishes-the-year-with-strong-final-quarter-orders-almost-doubling-again/ (accessed March 2021)

G. Dhillon, L. Sook Ling, M. Nandan, and J. Tze-Xi Nathan. 2021. Online Gambling in Malaysia: A Legal Analysis. Universiti Putra Malaysia Press. https://doi.org/10.47836/pjssh.29.1.12.

K. Dynan and L. Sheiner. 2018. GDP as a Measure of Economic Well-Being. *Hutchins Center Working Paper*. 43. https://www.brookings.edu/wp-content/uploads/2018/08/WP43-8.23.18.pdf.

C. Egeraat and D. Jacobson. 2004. The Rise and Demise of the Irish and Scottish Computer Hardware Industry. *European Planning Studies*. Vol. 12. 6.

European Union. 2020. *The Digital Economy and Society Index*. https://ec.europa.eu/digital-single-market/en/digital-economy-and-society-index-desi (accessed March 2021).

Eurostat. 2008. *The Eurostat Manual of Supply, Use and Input-Output Tables*. Luxembourg: Office for Official Publications of the European Communities.

Facebook. 2020. Facebook Reports Fourth Quarter and Full Year 2019 Results. Facebook Investor Relations. January 29. https://investor.fb.com/investor-news/press-release-details/2020/Facebook-Reports-Fourth-Quarter-and-Full-Year-2019-Results/default.aspx.

L. Feinier. 2021. Biden Signs Executive Order to Address Chip Shortage Through a Review to Strengthen Supply Chains. CNBC. 24 February. https://www.cnbc.com/2021/02/24/biden-signs-executive-order-to-address-chip-shortage-through-a-supply-chain-review.html.

Fiji Bureau of Statistics (FBS). 2014. *Economic Surveys: Information and Communication 2011*. https://www.statsfiji.gov.fj/.

FBS. 2018. *Economic Surveys: Information and Communication 2015*. https://www.statsfiji.gov.fj/.

Fortune Business Insights. 2021. *Industry 4.0 Market*. https://www.fortunebusinessinsights.com/industry-4-0-market-102375.

A. Franklin. 2019. *Software 101: A Complete Guide to Different Types of Software*. GoodCore. 28 August. https://www.goodcore.co.uk/blog/types-of-software/.

A. Fung. 2017. *A History of Cassette Tapes—Is that a Fossil?* Medium. 9 December. https://medium.com/@aaronnfung/a-history-of-cassette-tapes-is-that-a-fossil-760f40729333.

Z. Ghanem and L. Huang. 2014. *Value-Added Exports: Measurement Framework*. Statistics Canada, Industry Accounts Division.

Global Industry Analysts Inc. (GIA). 2021. Global Artificial Intelligence (AI) Market to Reach $228.3 Billion by 2026. Cision PR Newswire. 18 May. https://www.prnewswire.com/news-releases/global-artificial-intelligence-ai-market-to-reach-228-3-billion-by-2026--301293951.html.

G. Graetz and G. Michaels. 2018. Robots at Work. *Review of Economics and Statistics*. 100 (5). pp.

T. Haigh. n.d. *A.M. Turing Award: Charles William Bachman*. https://amturing.acm.org/award_winners/bachman_9385610.cfm.

S. Hanzawa. 2019. Geographical Dynamics of the Japanese Animation Industry. *Open Edition Journals*. 33-3/4. https://doi.org/10.4000/netcom.4546.

N. Heath. 2020. *What is AI? Everything You Need to Know About Artificial Intelligence*. ZDNet. 11 December. https://www.zdnet.com/article/what-is-ai-everything-you-need-to-know-about-artificial-intelligence/.

M. Hilbert and P. López. 2011. The World's Technological Capacity to Store, Communicate, and Compute Information. *Science*. 332 (6025). pp. 60–65. doi:10.1126/science.1200970

History. 2018. Automated Teller Machines. https://www.history.com/topics/inventions/automated-teller-machines.

Huawei and Oxford Economics. 2017. *Digital Spillover: Measuring the True Impact of the Digital Economy*. https://www.huawei.com/minisite/gci/en/digital-spillover/index.html.

Inter-American Development Bank (IDB). 2018. *Exponential Disruption in the Digital Economy*. https://publications.iadb.org/publications/english/document/ Exponential-Disruption-in-the-Digital-Economy.pdf.

Inter-Secretariat of Working Group on National Accounts (ISWGNA). 2020. *Recording and Measuring Data in the System of National Accounts*. 14th Meeting of the Advisory Expert Group on National Accounts.

International Business Machines (IBM). 1956. 650 RAMAC Announcement. Press Release. 14 September. https://www.ibm.com/ibm/history/exhibits/650/650_ pr2.html

IBM. 2021. *What is Facilities Management?* https://www.ibm.com/topics/facilities-management (accessed March 2021).

International Federation of Robotics (IFR). 2020a. *Executive Summary World Robotics 2020 Industrial Robots*. https://ifr.org/img/worldrobotics/Executive_Summary_ WR_2020_Industrial_Robots_1.pdf

IFR. 2020b. *IFR Press Conference*. https://ifr.org/downloads/press2018/Presentation_ WR_2020.pdf

IFR. 2020c. *Executive Summary World Robotics 2020 Service Robots*. https://ifr.org/ img/worldrobotics/Executive_Summary_WR_2020_Service_Robots.pdf

International Labour Organization (ILO). 2019. *Assessing the Effects of Trade on Employment: An Assessment Toolkit*. Geneva, Switzerland: International Labour Organization Office.

ILO. 2020. The future of Work in the Digital Economy. http://www.ilo.org/wcmsp5/ groups/public/---dgreports/---cabinet/documents/publication/wcms_771117. pdf.

International Monetary Fund (IMF). Exchange Rate Archives by Month. https://www.imf.org/external/np/fin/data/param_rms_mth.aspx.

IMF. 2018. *Measuring the Digital Economy*. Washington, D.C: International Monetary Fund.

IMF and Organisation for Economic Co-operation and Development. 2020. *The Recording of Crypto Assets*. 14th Meeting of the Advisory Expert Group on National Accounts. https://unstats.un.org/unsd/nationalaccount/aeg/2020/ M14_5_4_Crypto_Assets.pdf.

International Telecommunication Union (ITU). 2020. Economic Impact of COVID-19 on Digital Infrastructure: Report of an Economic Experts Roundtable organized by ITU. *GSR-20 Discussion Paper*. Geneva, Switzerland: International Telecommunications Union. https://www.itu.int/en/ITU-D/ Conferences/GSR/2020/Documents/GSR-20_Impact-COVID-19-on-digital-economy_DiscussionPaper.pdf.

ITU. 2021a. *Internet Users by Region and Country, 2010–2016*. https://www.itu.int/en/ITU-D/Statistics/Pages/stat/Treemap.aspx.

ITU. 2021b. *Measuring Digital Development: ICT Price Trends 2020*. Geneva: International Telecommunications Union. https://www.itu.int/en/ITU-D/ Statistics/Documents/publications/prices2020/ITU_ICTPriceTrends_2020.pdf.

L. Ioannou. 2020. *A Brewing U.S.-China Tech Cold War Rattles the Semiconductor Industry*. CNBC. 18 September. https://www.cnbc.com/2020/09/18/a-brewing-us-china-tech-cold-war-rattles-the-semiconductor-industry.html.

U. Kaufmann and H. Nakagawa. 2015. *Recent Developments and Changes in Demand for Tourism in Fiji*. https://www.taylorfrancis.com/chapters/ edit/10.4324/9781315773827-24/recent-developments-changes-demand-tourism-fiji-uwe-kaufmann-haruo-nakagawa.

A. Kharpal. 2021. *China has Given Away Millions in its Digital Yuan Trials: This is How it Works*. Consumer News and Business Channel (CNBC). 4 March. https://www.cnbc.com/2021/03/05/chinas-digital-yuan-what-is-it-and-how-does-it-work.html.

I. King, D. Wu, and D. Pogkas. 2021. *How a Chip Shortage Snarled Everything from Phones to Cars*. Bloomberg. 29 March. https://www.bloomberg.com/ graphics/2021-semiconductors-chips-shortage/?sref=ExbtjcSG.

W.J. Lee. 2020. Valuing Investments in Data Processing and Forecasting Systems. *World Meteorological Organization Bulletin*. 62 (1). https://public.wmo.int/en/ resources/bulletin/valuing-investments-data-processing-and-forecasting-systems

W. Leontief. 1936. Quantitative Input and Output Relations in the Economic System of the United States. *Review of Economics and Statistics*. 18.

LetsBuild. 2021. *How Digital Technology is Changing the Construction Industry*. https://www.letsbuild.com/blog/how-digital-technology-is-changing-the-construction-industry

K. Lueth. 2018. *State of the IoT 2018: Number of IoT Devices Now at 7B—Market Accelerating*. IOT Analytics. 8 August. https://iot-analytics.com/state-of-the-iot-update-q1-q2-2018-number-of-iot-devices-now-7b/.

K. Lueth. 2020. *State of the IoT 2020: 12 Billion IoT Connections, Surpassing Non-IoT for the First Time*. IOT Analytics. 19 November. https://iot-analytics.com/state-of-the-iot-2020-12-billion-iot-connections-surpassing-non-iot-for-the-first-time/.

W.C.Y. Li, M. Nirei, and K. Yamana. 2018. *Value of Data: There's No Such Thing as a Free Lunch in the Digital Economy*. Sixth IMF Statistical Forum. November 8. Washington, D.C.: International Monetary Fund.

S. Lund, J. Manyika, J. Woetzel, J. Bughin, M. Krishnan, J. Seong, and M. Muir. 2019. *Globalization in Transition: The Future of Trade and Value Chains*. McKinsey & Company. 16 January. https://www.mckinsey.com/featured-insights/innovation-and-growth/globalization-in-transition-the-future-of-trade-and-value-chains.

S. Lund, A. Madgavkar, J. Manyika, and S. Smit. 2020. *What's Next for Remote Work: An Analysis of 2,000 Tasks, 800 Jobs, and Nine Countries*. McKinsey & Company. 23 November. https://www.mckinsey.com/featured-insights/future-of-work/whats-next-for-remote-work-an-analysis-of-2000-tasks-800-jobs-and-nine-countries.

W. MacDougall. 2018. *The Digital Economy in Germany*. Berlin: Germany Trade and Invest. https://www.gtai.de/resource/blob/63904/c106af1ef8d5810a72e96e07ecdd81b4/fact-sheet-digital-en-data.pdf.

M. Mas, J. Fernández De Guevara Radoselovics, J. Robledo, M. Cardona, M. Lopez Cobo, R. Righi, and S. Samoili. 2018. *The 2018 PREDICT Key Facts Report. An Analysis of ICT and Research and Development in the EU and Beyond*. European Commission, 2018, JRC111954.

A. Mauldin. 2017. A Complete List of Content Providers› Submarine Cable Holdings. TeleGeography. 9 November. https://blog.telegeography.com/telegeographys-content-providers-submarine-cable-holdings-list.

McKinsey Global Institute. 2016. Digital Globalization: The New Era of Global Flows. https://www.mckinsey.com/~/media/McKinsey/Business%20Functions/McKinsey%20Digital/Our%20Insights/Digital%20globalization%20The%20new%20era%20of%20global%20flows/MGI-Digital-globalization-Full-report.ashx.

Michigan State University. 2020. *What is the Difference between CAD, CAE, and CAM?* April 2. https://online.egr.msu.edu/articles/cad-vs-cae-vs-cam-what-is-the-difference/.

R. Miller and P. Blair. 2009. *Input-Output Analysis: Foundations and Extensions*. Cambridge: Cambridge University Press.

B. Mitchell. 2019. *PSTN (Public Switched Telephone Network): The History and Current Relevance of Landline Phone Service*. Lifewire. 13 December. https://www.lifewire.com/pstn-public-switched-telephone-network-818168.

J. Mitchell. 2018. *A Proposed framework for Digital Supply-Use Tables*. OECD. https://www.oecd.org/officialdocuments/publicdisplaydocumentpdf/?cote=SDD/CSSP/WPNA(2018)3&docLanguage=En.

J. Mitchell. 2020. *Guidelines for Supply-Use tables for the Digital Economy*. OECD Informal Advisory Group on Measuring GDP in a Digitalised Economy.

M. Mueller and K. Grindal. 2018. *Is It "Trade?" Data Flows and the Digital Economy*. 46th Research Conference on Communication, Information and Internet Policy 2018. August 30. https://ssrn.com/abstract=3137819.

M. Mühleisen. 2018. The Long and Short of the Digital Revolution. *Finance & Development*. 55 (002).

J. Müller. 2020. *Enabling Technologies for Industry 5.0*. European Commission. https://www.4bt.us/wp-content/uploads/2021/04/INDUSTRY-5.0.pdf

P. Mullins. 2011. *Introduction to Computing for Liberal Arts*. Slippery Rock University. http://cs.sru.edu/~mullins/cpsc100book/IntroToCS.html.

L. Nakamura, J. Samuels, and R. Soloveichik. 2016. Valuing Free Media in GDP: An Experimental Approach. *BEA Working Papers*. 0133. Bureau of Economic Analysis. https://ideas.repec.org/p/bea/wpaper/0133.html.

National Research Council (United States). 2006. *Renewing U.S. Telecommunications Research*. Washington, DC: National Academic Press. https://doi.org/10.17226/11711.

D. Nguyen and M. Paczos. 2020. *Measuring the Economic Value of Data and Cross-Border Data Flows: A Business Perspective*. Paris: OECD Publishing.

North American Industry Classification System Association (NAICS). 2018. *NAICS Code Description*. https://www.naics.com/.

D. O'Boyle. 2020. *Danish i-Gaming Participation Rate Second-Highest in Europe*. i-Gaming Business (IGB). 27 October. https://igamingbusiness.com/danish-online-market-continues-to-grow-to-dkk5-2bn-in-2019/.

Organisation for Economic Co-operation and Development (OECD). 2011. *OECD Science, Technology and Industry Scoreboard 2011*. Paris: OECD Publishing. https://doi.org/10.1787/sti_scoreboard-2011-60-en.

OECD. 2014. *Defining the Relevant Market in Telecommunications*. https://www.oecd.org/daf/competition/Defining_Relevant_Market_in_Telecommunications_web.pdf.

OECD and Inter-American Development Bank. 2016. *Broadband Policies for Latin America and the Caribbean: A Digital Economy Toolkit*. Paris: OECD Publishing. https://doi.org/10.1787/9789264251823-en.

OECD. 2019. *Measuring the Digital Transformation: A Roadmap for the Future*. Paris: OECD Publishing. https://www.oecd.org/publications/measuring-the-digital-transformation-9789264311992-en.htm.

OECD. 2020. *ICT Access and Usage by Households and Individuals*. https://stats.oecd.org/Index.aspx?DataSetCode=ICT_HH2 (accessed April 2021).

OECD. 2021. *Creating Responsive Adult Learning Opportunities in Japan, Getting Skills Right*, OECD Publishing, Paris, https://doi.org/10.1787/cfe1ccd2-en.

M. Perry. 2016. *Technology has Advanced So Rapidly that a Laptop Computer Today is 96% Cheaper than a 1994 Model and 1,000X Better*. AEIdeas. 25 May. https://www.aei.org/carpe-diem/technology-has-advanced-so-rapidly-that-a-laptop-computer-today-is-96-cheaper-than-a-1994-model-and-1000x-better/

Preservation Metadata: Implementation Strategies (PREMIS). 2015. *Data Dictionary for Preservation Metadata version 3.0*. https://www.loc.gov/standards/premis/v3/premis-3-0-final.pdf.

G. Press. 2016. *A Very Short History of Digitization*. Forbes. 27 December. https://www.forbes.com/sites/gilpress/2015/12/27/a-very-short-history-of-digitization/?sh=664d11d649ac.

C. Ravets. 2016. *The Internet Economy*. Presented at the 10th Meeting of the Advisory Expert Group on National Accounts. https://unstats.un.org/unsd/nationalaccount/aeg/2016/4_Internet_Economy.pdf.

R. Regan. 2018. *Data Processing*. https://www.encyclopedia.com/science-and-technology/computers-and-electrical-engineering/computers-and-computing/data-processing.

L. Reijnders and G. de Vries. 2018. Trade, Technology and the Rise of Non-Routine Jobs. *Journal of Development Economics*. 135. pp. 412–32.

M. Reinsdorf. 2020. *Status Report on the Work of the Subgroup on the Treatment of Free Products*. United Nations Economic Commission for Europe. October 5. https://unece.org/statistics/events/webinars-group-experts-national-accounts

U. Rinne and K. F. Zimmermann. 2012. Another Economic Miracle? The German Labor Market and the Great Recession. *IZA Journal of Labor Policy*. 1 (3). https://doi.org/10.1186/2193-9004-1-3

J. Round. 2003. *Social Accounting Matrices and SAM-based Multiplier Analysis*. The Impact of Economic Policies on Poverty and Income Distribution: Evaluation Techniques and Tools. 261 (276).

A. Scupola. 2019. *Digital Transformation of Public Administration Services in Denmark: A Process Tracing Case Study*. https://www.riverpublishers.com/journal/journal_articles/RP_Journal_1902-097X_2018114.pdf

J. Shalf. 2020. *The Future of Computing Beyond Moore's Law*. The Royal Society Publishing. 20 January. https://doi.org/10.1098/rsta.2019.0061.

R. Shannon. 2012. *Internet File Formats*. HTML Source. 21 August. https://www.yourhtmlsource.com/starthere/fileformats.html.

D. Shapardson and K. Freifield. 2019. *Trump Administration Hits China's Huawei with One-Two Punch*. Reuters. 16 May. https://www.reuters.com/article/us-usa-china-trump-telecommunications/trump-administration-hits-chinas-huawei-with-one-two-punch-idUSKCN1SL2QX.

D. Sher. 2020. *This is How Much Additive Manufacturing is Worth in the Top Global AM Markets*. 3D Printing Media Network. 15 January. https://www.3dprintingmedia.network/the-top-20-global-am-markets/

T. Simatupang, S. Rustiadi, and D. B. M. Situmorang. 2012. Enhancing the Competitiveness of the Creative Services Sectors in Indonesia. In T.S. Tullao and H. H. Lim (eds.), *Developing ASEAN Economic Community (AEC) into A Global Services Hub*. Economic Research Institute for ASEAN and East Asia, Research Project Report 2011-1. pp. 173–270. Jakarta: Economic Research Institute for ASEAN and East Asia.

J. Spataro. 2020. *Microsoft Teams Reaches 115 Million DAU*. Microsoft 365 Blog. 28 October. https://www.microsoft.com/en-us/microsoft-365/blog/2020/10/28/ microsoft-teams-reaches-115-million-dau-plus-a-new-daily-collaboration-minutes-metric-for-microsoft-365/.

A. Sraders. 2020. *What Is Fintech? Uses and Examples in 2020*. TheStreet. 8 March. https://www.thestreet.com/technology/what-is-fintech-14885154.

Statista. 2018. *Enterprise Artificial Intelligence Market Revenue Worldwide 2016–2025*. https://blogs-images.forbes.com/louiscolumbus/files/2018/01/AI-for-enterprise-Apps.jpg.

Statista. 2020. *Leading Countries in the Electronics Industry in 2016, Based on Market Size*. https://www.statista.com/statistics/268398/market-size-of-the-global-electronics-industry-by-country/ (accessed 22 May 2021).

Statistics Canada. 2019. *The Value of Data in Canada: Experimental Estimates*. 22 April. https://www150.statcan.gc.ca/n1/pub/13-605-x/2019001/article/00009-eng.htm

Statistics Canada. 2021. *Digital Supply and Use Tables, 2017 to 2019*. https://www150.statcan.gc.ca/n1/daily-quotidien/210420/dq210420a-eng.htm.

I. Süßmann. 2015. *German Book Market 2014: Nonfiction Up, Overall Sales Down*. Publishing Perspectives. 16 June. https://publishingperspectives.com/2015/06/ german-book-market-2014-nonfiction-up-overall-sales-down/.

C. Sui. 2013. *BBC Future*, Technology and Innovation. 18 September.

D. Tapscott. 1996. *The Digital Economy: Promise and Peril in the Age of Networked Intelligence*. New York: McGraw-Hill.

T. ten Raa. 2006. *The Economics of Input-Output Analysis*. Cambridge: Cambridge University Press. doi:10.1017/CBO9780511610783.

Thales. 2021. *5G and IoT in 2021*. https://www.thalesgroup.com/en/markets/digital-identity-and-security/iot/resources/innovation-technology/5G-iot.

The Economist. 2015. The Great Chain of Being Sure About Things. 31 October. https://www.economist.com/briefing/2015/10/31/the-great-chain-of-being-sure-about-things.

The Economist. 2019a. Amazon and Alibaba Are Pacesetters of the Next Supply-Chain Revolution. 13 July. https://www.economist.com/special-report/2019/07/11/ amazon-and-alibaba-are-pacesetters-of-the-next-supply-chain-revolution.

The Economist. 2019b. Slowbalisation: The Steam Has Gone Out of Globalization. 24 January. https://www.economist.com/leaders/2019/01/24/the-steam-has-gone-out-of-globalisation.

The Economist. 2021a. The Digital Currencies that Matter. May 8. https://www.economist.com/leaders/2021/05/08/the-digital-currencies-that-matter.

The Economist. 2021b. Intel Should Beware of Becoming a National Champion. March 31. https://www.economist.com/business/2021/03/31/intel-should-beware-of-becoming-a-national-champion.

M. Timmer, editor, A. A. Erumban, R. Gouma, B. Los, U. Temurshoev, G. de Vries, I. Arto, V. A. A. Genty, F. Neuwahl, J. M. Rueda-Cantuche, A. Villanueva, J. Francois, O. Pindyuk, J. Pöschl, and R. Stehrer. 2012. *The World Input-Output Database (WIOD): Contents, Sources and Methods.* World Input Output Database. http://www.wiod.org/publications/source_docs/WIOD_sources.pdf.

M. Timmer, R. Stehrer, B. Los, E. Dietzenbacher, and G. de Vries. 2015. An Illustrated User Guide to the World Input–Output Database: The Case of Global Automotive Production. *Review of International Economics.* 23. pp. 575-605.

Transforma Insights. 2020. *Global IoT Market to Grow to 24.1 Billion Devices in 2030, Generating $1.5 Trillion Annual Revenue.* May 19. https://transformainsights.com/news/iot-market-24-billion-usd15-trillion-revenue-2030.

United Nations (UN). 2008. *Central Product Classification: Version 2.* New York: United Nations.

UN. 2008. *International Standard Industrial Classification of All Economic Activities (ISIC), Rev. 4.* New York: United Nations. https://unstats.un.org/unsd/publication/seriesm/seriesm_4rev4e.pdf.

UN, European Commission, IMF, OECD, and World Bank. 2009. System of National Accounts 2008. New York: United Nations.

UN. 2017. *UN Comtrade Database.* http://comtrade.un.org/ (accessed December 2020).

UN. 2018. *Handbook on Supply and Use Tables and Input Output-Tables with Extensions and Applications.* Department of Economic and Social Affairs Statistics Division. New York: United Nations.

United Nations Conference on Trade and Development (UNCTAD). 2008. Developing World Now Leads in Production, Export of Information and Communication Goods. Press Release. 6 February. https://unctad.org/press-material/developing-world-now-leads-production-export-information-and-communication-goods.

UNCTAD. 2013. *World Investment Report, Global Value Chains: Investment and Trade for Development.* https://unctad.org/system/files/official-document/wir2013_en.pdf.

UNCTAD. 2019a. *Structural Transformation, Industry 4.0 and Inequality: Science, Technology and Innovation Policy Challenges.* Geneva, Switzerland: United Nations.

UNCTAD. 2019b. *Digital Economy Report 2019: Value Creation and Capture— Implications for Developing Countries.* https://unctad.org/system/files/official-document/der2019_en.pdf.

UNCTAD. 2019c. *Trade War Leaves Both US and China Worse Off.* 6 November. https://unctad.org/news/trade-war-leaves-both-us-and-china-worse.

UNCTAD. 2021. *COVID-19 and e-Commerce: A Global Review.* https://unctad.org/webflyer/covid-19-and-e-commerce-global-review.

United States Bureau of Labor Statistics (USBLS). *Producer Price Index by Commodity: Machinery and Equipment: Portable Computers, Laptops, Tablets and Other Single User Computers.* https://fred.stlouisfed.org/series/WPU11510115 (accessed 22 May 2021).

M. Vollmer. 2018. *What is Industry 5.0?* Medium. 12 September. https://medium.com/@marcellvollmer/what-is-industry-5-0-a363041a6f0a.

Z. Wang, S.J. Wei, X. Yu, and K. Zhu. 2017. Measures of Participation in Global Value Chains and Global Business Cycles. *National Bureau of Economic Research Working Paper.* No. 23222. Cambridge, MA: National Bureau of Economic Research.

J. Wertz. 2020. *From Malls to Marketplaces: How the Virtual Shift is Unfolding for E-Commerce at Scale.* Forbes. 15 October. https://www.forbes.com/sites/jiawertz/2020/10/15/from-malls-to-marketplaces-how-the-virtual-shift-is-unfolding-for-e-commerce-at-scale/?sh=3d064787fa57.

Wohlers Associates, Inc. 2021. New Wohlers Report 2021 Finds 7.5% Growth in Additive Manufacturing Industry Despite Pandemic. Press Release. 16 March. http://wohlersassociates.com/press83.html

World Bank. 2020. *World Development Indicators*. https://databank.worldbank.org/source/world-development-indicators (accessed March 2021)

World Economic Forum (WEF). 2019. *Travel and Tourism Competitiveness Report 2019*. http://reports.weforum.org/travel-and-tourism-competitiveness-report-2019/wp-content/blogs.dir/144/mp/files/pages/files/ap3.pdf

WEF. 2020. *The Future of Jobs Report 2020*. Switzerland: World Economic Forum. http://www3.weforum.org/docs/WEF_Future_of_Jobs_2020.pdf

World Trade Organization (WTO). 2017. *20 Years of the Information Technology Agreement: Boosting trade, innovation and digital connectivity*. Geneva: World Trade Organization

N. Yashiro. 2011. Why labour market flexibility in Japan is so difficult. East Asia Forum. https://www.eastasiaforum.org/2011/04/06/why-labour-market-flexibility-in-japan-is-so-difficult/. Accessed on 23 July 2021.

Zoom Video Communications, Inc. 2021. Zoom Video Communications Reports Fourth Quarter and Fiscal Year 2021 Financial Results. Press release, March 1, 2021. https://investors.zoom.us/news-releases/news-release-details/zoom-video-communications-reports-fourth-quarter-and-fiscal-0

J. Zweig. 2020. *A Simple Investing Playbook for the "Great Cessation."* Wall Street Journal. 24 March. https://www.wsj.com/articles/a-simple-investing-playbook-for-the-great-cessation-11585047600.